Student Resource Manual
to Accompany

MATHEMATICS
for Elementary Teachers

AN INTERACTIVE APPROACH

Thomas A. Sonnabend

SALLY C. MAYBERRY
St. Thomas University

JOHN B. BATH
Florida International University

SAUNDERS COLLEGE PUBLISHING
Harcourt Brace College Publishers

Fort Worth Philadelphia San Diego New York Orlando San Antonio
Toronto Montreal London Sydney Tokyo

Printed in the United States of America.

Mayberry/Bath: Student Resource Manual to accompany MATHEMATICS FOR ELEMENTARY TEACHERS, by Thomas Sonnabend

ISBN 0-03-020713-4

345 021 987654321

Mathematics for Elementary Teachers
An Interactive Approach

Preface

About this Resource Manual

Mathematics for Elementary Teachers: An Interactive Approach – Student Resource Manual presents a problem-solving, hands-on/minds-on approach to the teaching and learning of elementary school mathematics. The activities in this manual correspond to the chapter titles in *Mathematics for Elementary Teachers.: An Interactive Approach* by Thomas Sonnabend (Saunders College Publishing, 1993). This manual is designed to supplement the textbook or to be used on its own merit for preservice/inservice courses with elementary teachers.

Chapter Sections

We have made this manual distinctive by including the chapter sections that follow.

▼ Problem Challenge

The National Council of Teachers of Mathematics in the*Curriculum and Evaluation Standards for School Mathematics* (NCTM, 1989) has designated problem solving as the number one area of emphasis for elementary school mathematics. In support of this theme, each chapter of this resource manual begins with a *Problem Challenge*. The problems are of varying levels of difficulty requiring higher levels of thinking. There is often more than one way of solving each problem. We hope to encourage critical thinking with each *Problem Challenge* and, in turn, to encourage you to challenge your present and future students.

✳ Key Ideas

At the beginning of each chapter section, *Key Ideas* will provide a brief explanation of that section. *Key Ideas* identifies the main ideas of the section.

☞ Activities

The purpose of the hands-on/minds-on activities is to teach students how mathematical concepts are developed and why each concept is useful. The activities are varied and usually incorporate the use of the *Activity Cards* at the end of the manual. Each activity has a stated objective and list of materials which are necessary to complete the activity. Research shows that teachers teach in the same manner in which they are taught. Therefore, it is important that preservice and inservice elementary teachers experience these activities as if they were students themselves.

✎ Journal

When students record in writing their thoughts and ideas on mathematics, they practice making a connection between mathematics and language arts. Ideas for journal writing appear throughout each chapter. We encourage you to write in the journal sections or in your own journal on a regular basis. Journal writing should be a pleasant activity, modeled by the teacher, and accepted in an informal format. After trust is developed, the mathematics journal quickly becomes a communication vehicle between the student and the teacher. Teachers should provide positive responses to the student journals. Corrections, however, are not recommended.

✈ Extensions ✈

In *Extensions* you may revisit some of the concepts and activities presented in each chapter. Sections include: Mental Computation, Calculators, Critical Thinking, Alternative Assessment, and Mathematics for the 21st Century.

✈ Mental Computation

This section provides an opportunity for students to enhance their abilities in *Mental Computation* and to increase flexible thinking. Mental computation practice enables students to think quickly without the aid of paper and pencil.

✈ Calculators

Calculators play a vital role in the elementary school mathematics classroom. We have provided activities that require the use of a calculator in many chapters. We encourage you to use the calculator extensively in these activities as well as for any mathematical activity at all grade levels.

✈ Critical Thinking

We provide questions under the heading of *Critical Thinking* to encourage higher levels of thinking. Students are asked to compare, contrast, evaluate, and defend their solutions to these problems. We hope you will practice effective questioning skills and that questioning to promote critical and creative thinking will be a natural part of each mathematics lesson.

✈ Alternative Assessment

Evaluation is an integral part of each mathematics lesson. Alternative assessment provides numerous ways in which the teacher can add new evaluation techniques to traditional paper and pencil tests. This section includes definitions and ways to implement alternative assessment into daily mathematics lessons. Sections include: Journals, Portfolios, Performance Assessment, Open-ended Questions, Observations, Interviews, Student Self-assessments, Conferences, Classroom Management, Implementing Assessment Models, Checklists, and Parent Newsletters.

✈ Mathematics for the 21st Century

To prepare students for the 21st century, our elementary mathematics curriculum must reflect current research recommendations. Sections here include ideas for the ways and the means to keep your mathematics classroom updated and to better prepare students to be citizens of the 21st century. According to the recommendations in the NCTM *Curriculum and Evaluation Standards for School Mathematics*, we have included the following sections: the *Standards*, Mathematics as Problem Solving, Manipulatives, Cooperative Learning, Mathematics as Communication, Questioning Techniques, Developmentally Appropriate Practices, Alternative Assessment, Mathematical Connections, Implementing Technology, Estimation and Mental Computation, Dealing with Equity and Diversity, Attitudes, and Parent Involvement.

❖ Appendices ❖

❖ Appendix A—Solutions

Solutions are provided for selected odd-numbered activities. Students are encouraged to work through each activity before referring to this section.

❖ Appendix B—Resources for Mathematics Materials

A list of suppliers of mathematics manipulatives for the elementary classroom teacher is provided. In addition, outstanding books and references on mathematics manipulatives may also be obtained from these companies.

❖ Appendix C—Resources for Computer Software

Included here are suppliers of mathematics computer software for the elementary classroom. Free catalogs are available upon request.

❖ Appendix D—Selected Readings

Resources are provided from *The Arithmetic Teacher* to further enhance your understanding of the concepts and activities presented in this manual. Other suggested references appear at the end of the section.

❖ Appendix E—Activity Cards

Activity Cards to accompany the chapter activities appear at the end of this manual. Each activity card is numbered by the chapter and activity in which it first appears. For example, *Activity Card 3.8* refers to chapter 3, activity 8. Each activity card is perforated. An asterisk on the *Activity Card List* denotes color activity cards that are out of numerical sequence and are placed at the back of this manual. We encourage you to use these activity cards.

In Appreciation

We express our appreciation to the following people for their assistance in the preparation of the resource manual:

Sally's husband, Bill, and John's wife, Tracie, for their encouragement and patience;

Bob Stern and Beth Sweet of Saunders College Publishing for their support of our ideas and their expert advice;

Nick Murray, our Developmental Editor, for his thoughtful review of materials and suggestions for revision;

Diane Cole for her assistance in the typing of parts of the manuscript;

Peggy Garner, Clemson University; Donna Erickson, Central Michigan University; James Trudnowski, Carroll College; Arlene Brett, University of Miami; and Jane Shielack, Texas A&M University; who reviewed this manual and provided recommendations for revision; and

Our elementary education students and faculty who have lent their suggestions and support.

We hope you will find this resource manual both meaningful and useful. We wish you every joy and success as you promote outstanding mathematical teaching using a hands-on problem-solving approach in the elementary school.

Sally C. Mayberry
John B. Bath

Brief Contents

Contents

1

Problem Solving

UNDERSTANDING PROBLEM SOLVING

1. Problem Solving
2. Problem Solving Strategies

▼ PROBLEM CHALLENGE: A Puzzle of Coins

How can you place these 9 coins
(4 dimes, 3 quarters, and 2 nickels) in
the 3 by 3 array below to ensure that each
row and each column contain a different
total amount of money?

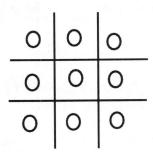

HANDS-ON MATHEMATICS ACTIVITIES

The following activities are provided to enhance your understanding of
mathematical reasoning and problem solving.

Problem Solving

 Key Ideas: According to the *Curriculum and Evaluation Standards for School Mathematics* (NCTM, 1989), The focus of every elementary mathematic classroom should be problem solving. Elementary students need many opportunities to experience problem solving. Students should understand the use of problem-solving strategies and share their thoughts and thought processes with fellow students and teachers. Problems in the elementary mathematics classroom should be varied, of high interest, promote high-order thinkingskills, implement estimation skills, and pertain to the real world of the students. Children learn by doing; thus, manipulatives and cooperative learning should be incorporated into the daily problem-solving lessons. Students should be engaged in worthwhile tasks of a problem-solving nature and learn the problem-solving process rather than the product. Opportunities should be provided for students to create their own problem situations and to provide multiple solutions. Communication and reasoning should be emphasized to empower elementary students with the ability to recognize a sensible answer and to experience the joy of becoming successful problem solvers.

Problem solvingis represented here by three different problem types:
1. One-step translation problems;
2. multi-step translation problems; and
3. puzzle problems

One-step problems are simple word problems that entail the use of one single computation. Multi-step problems are typical textbook problems that involve more than one step and one or more types of computation. Puzzle problems are those non-routine problems for which there is no obvious answer. Puzzle problems develop high-order flexible thinking skills andare those practiced in this chapter.

☞ **Activity 1: The License Plate**

Purpose: To engage students in the problem-solving process.
Materials: Activity Card 1.1—The License Plate

❑   The license plate on Mireya's new red sports car consists of 5 different digits. The car salesman was in a hurry and put the license on upside down, but it still shows a 5 digit number. The new license number (upside down) is 63,783 more than the original tag. What was the number on the original tag?

Questions to stress the problem-solving process:
   a. How did you decide where to begin?
   b. What strategy did you use?
   c. Did you make any wrong turns?
   d. How did the wrong turns prove beneficial?

☞ **Activity 2: Toothpick Puzzles**

Purpose: To solve problems that develop high-level thinking skills.
Materials: Activity Card 1.2—Toothpick Puzzle
        Toothpicks (optional)

❑   a.

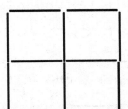

1. Remove 2 toothpicks, leaving 2 squares.
2. Move 2 toothpicks to make 7 squares.
3. Move 3 toothpicks to make 3 squares.

❑   b.

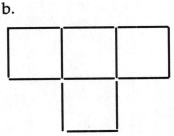

Remove 1 toothpick,
leaving 3 squares.

❑   c.

Move 3 toothpicks
to make 5 triangles
instead of three.

❑   d.

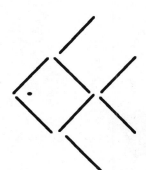

Make the fish swim in the
opposite direction by
moving 3 toothpicks.

Questions to stress the problem-solving process:

a. What strategy did you use?
b. How does making a wrong move provide useful information?

☞ **Activity 3: The Dart Board**

Purpose: To engage students in the problem-solving process.
Materials: Activity Card 1.3—Dart Board

❑   Two students were engaged in a game of darts. The winner's score was 35. What was the least number of darts that could have been thrown by the winner? Estimate the number of darts necessary to total 35.

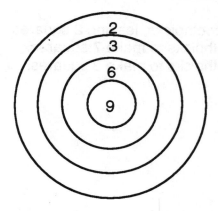

    a. Which number should you select first?
    b. Why?

☞ **Activity 4: The Hidden Cube**

Purpose: To engage students in the problem-solving process.
Materials: Activity Card 1.4—The Hidden Cube

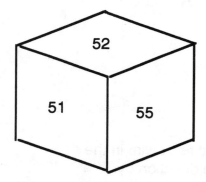

❑   All faces of the pictured cube have consecutive numbers. Three of the numbers are illustrated. What is the sum of the numbers on all of the faces of the cube?

    a. Is there more than one possible solution?
    b. What reasoning did you apply in the problem-solving process?

☞ **Activity 5: The Magic Box**

Purpose: To engage students in the problem-solving process.
Materials: Activity Card 1.5—Magic Box

❑   Fill in the following figure using the digits 1 through 8 so that no consecutive numbers touch at any side or corner.

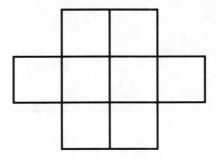

a.   Write a paragraph to a friend explaining the tactics you used to solve the Magic Box.
b.   Are there any special tactics that you would consider using in another problem-solving situation? Why?

 ## Journal

1.   Write how you feel about problem solving.

2.   How can you use problem solving in your daily activities?

3.   Why do you think problem solving emphasizes the process rather than the product?

Problem-Solving Strategies

 Key Ideas: In order to promote growth in problem-solving skills, students need to learn and apply a variety of problem-solving strategies. A poster in the classroom listing the strategies allows students to use visual aids to strengthen problem-solving skills. Some favorite problem-solving strategies follow:

1. guess and check
2. make a table
3. draw a picture
4. solve a simpler problem
5. use inductive reasoning
6. use deductive reasoning
7. find a pattern
8. try again

1.   Guess and Check

 Key Ideas: In order to use the *Guess and Check Strategy*, students do what the name suggests: they guess. After taking a guess at the solution, the students check to see if their guess is correct. If the guess is incorrect, the guess is refined using the information gained from the first try. Repeat the guess and check procedure. Students continue in this manner until a solution is reached.

☛ **Activity 6: Guess and Check Strategy**

Purpose: To improve problem-solving skills.
Materials: Activity Card 1.6 — Guess and Check Strategy

❑   Cathy and Jennifer are enthusiastic collectors of troll dolls. Cathy had 8 more trolls than Jennifer. When the girls counted all of their trolls, they found a total of 24. How many trolls did Jennifer have?

a. What is your first estimate? Why?

b. How should you check to determine if your guess is correct?

c. Write each of your guesses and show how you checked your work.

☞ **Activity 7: Homework**

Purpose: To use the Guess and Check Strategy.
Materials: Activity Card 1.7—Homework

❑   In an attempt to motivate his daughter, Bibiana, to complete her mathematics homework correctly, her father offered to pay her 8 cents for each correct solution, but would deduct 5 cents for each incorrect solution. After 26 problems, father and daughter were even—neither one owed the other any money. How many problems did Bibiana complete correctly?

   a. Create a table using each of your estimates.
   b. What combinations of 26 will you try first?
   c. Show how you checked your answer.

---

2.   Make a Table

> ✳ **Key Ideas:**   The *Make a Table Strategy* is useful in finding solutions and in organizing the data which one uses when applying other strategies. It is also useful when one is trying to learn about a group of numbers generated by a specific rule.

☞ **Activity 8: Make a Table Strategy**

Purpose: To use the Make a Table Strategy to promote the use of problem-solving skills.
Materials: Activity Card 1.8— Court Jester's Coins
                Coins

❑   The court jester presented the king with a new problem-solving situation. The jester placed three pennies in the boxes on the right and 3 nickels in the boxes on the left. The center square is unoccupied. He explained that the goal of the problem is to switch the coins so that the pennies are on the left and the nickels are on the right, the reverse order. Can you help the king solve the puzzle? The jester says that the coins may be moved forward either by a direct move of one space or by jumping another coin. No backward moves are allowed. How many moves will it take?

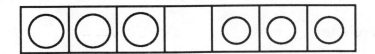

   a. Estimate the number of moves it will take to solve the puzzle.
   b. Plan your first move.
   c. What process will you use to reach your goal?

☛ **Activity 9: Make a Table Strategy**

Purpose: To apply the Make a Table Strategy to problem solving.
Materials: Activity Card 1.9 — Blue Eyes

❑   Will read an interesting article about people with blue eyes. The article said that 2 out of 5 people have blue eyes. He decided to use this new information to predict how many people in his fourth-grade classroom of 35 students would have blue eyes. How many did he predict would have blue eyes?
  a. What is your estimate?
  b. How will you complete the procedure?
  c. Remember to look for a pattern.

---

3.   Draw a Picture

✳ **Key Ideas: Sometimes problems involve situations that can be clarified by drawing a picture. This enables the problem solver to visualize a plan to solve the problem.**

☛ **Activity 10:   Draw a Picture**

Purpose: To use the Draw a Picture Strategy for problem-solving.
Materials: Activity Card 1.10a — The Elevator Problem
               Activity Card 1.10b — The Fish Problem

❑   **1. The Elevator Problem**

   Absent-minded Felipe got on the elevator and went down 6 floors. He then went up 8 floors and down 5 floors. When the elevator finally stopped, he was on the third floor. Felipe, however, discovered that he left his hat on the floor on which he entered the elevator. The problem is that Felipe has forgotten where he entered the elevator. Can you help him? In order for Felipe to find his hat, which elevator button should he push?
     a. Sketch a diagram of the movement of the elevator.
     b. Must he start on the ground floor? Why or why not?

❑   **2. The Fish Problem**

   The head of a fish is one-third as long as its body. The tail of the fish is as long as its head and its body together. The entire length of the fish is 48 centimeters. How long is each part of the fish? Use the picture on Activity Card 1.10b to solve the problem.

4. Solve a Simpler Problem

Key Ideas: The *Solve a Simpler Problem Strategy* is useful when the problem contains large numbers, decimals, fractions, or complicated computations. Changing the numbers to smaller ones makes the solution easier to find. After solving the simpler problem, the same solution process may be used to solve the more difficult problem.

☞ **Activity 11: Solve a Simpler Problem**

Purpose: To use the Solve a Simpler Problem Strategy.
Materials: Activity Card 1.11a — The Handshake Problem
Activity Card 1.11b — The Birthday Party Problem

❑ **1. The Handshake Problem**

Eight elementary mathematics teachers met at a picnic. Each teacher shook hands with every other teacher exactly one time. And, yes, each used only one hand. How many handshakes took place at the picnic?
a. In order to simplify the problem, try it with 2, 3 and 4 teachers.
b. What is the pattern?

❑ **2. The Birthday Party**

Caroline's mother is planning a birthday party for her. The headwaiter at the restaurant has told her that she may use 20 tables pushed together to make one long table for the party. Each table will seat one person on each side. How many people can Caroline invite to her party?
a. Try using fewer tables.
b. What is the pattern?

Journal

1. What problem solving strategy do you find most useful?

2. If new students join the class, how will you explain problem-solving strategies to them?

5.   Inductive Reasoning

> ✳ **Key Ideas:**   Inductive Reasoning (specific to general) involves the examination of several specific situations to look for patterns, test conjectures, and then create a generalization that applies to each specific situation. These generalizations can then be used to solve other problems. Induction, making guesses from observations, is not totally reliable because an event which occurs several times might not continue to occur following the same pattern. Inductive reasoning is the theorem which is developed.
>
> **Example:** To formulate a rule that states that the sum of any consecutive three whole numbers can be divided by 3. In order to create this theorem, one should use several specific examples to be certain that it will work.
>
> $$4 + 5 + 6 = 15 \text{ (divisible by 3?, yes) OK}$$
> $$7 + 8 + 9 = 24 \text{ (divisible by 3?, yes) OK}$$
> $$22 + 23 + 24 = 69 \text{ (divisible by 3?, yes) OK}$$
>
> Therefore, using inductive reasoning, we theorize that the sum of any consecutive three whole numbers is divisible by 3.

☞   **Activity 12:   What Comes Next?**

Purpose: To practice the use of Inductive Reasoning.
Materials: Activity Card 1.12 — Base Ten Pieces

Patterns are arranged in sections using the Base Ten Pieces. For example, in *a*, the first section contains 5 *ones*, the second section contains 6 *ones*, next 8 *ones*, followed by 11. The base ten blocks allow students to easily visualize the specific pattern.

❑   Complete each pattern and explain why you got your answer. (Each pattern can have more than one answer.)

a.   5, 6, 8, 11, ___, ___, ___, ___
b.   1, 4, 1, 9, 1, 14, ___, ___, ___, ___
c.   1, 2, 4, ___, ___, ___
d.   Explain inductive reasoning and create your own problem here.

6.   Deductive Reasoning

✳ **Key Ideas:**   Deductive Reasoning (general to specific) is the process of examining a rule or set of rules and applying those rules to specific situations. Just as inductive reasoning is the theorem, deductive reasoning is the proof.

Example: Apply the rule that states the product of two negative numbers is always positive to specific situations.

$$(-5) \times (-7) = +35$$
$$(-20) \times (-3) = +60$$

☛ **Activity 13:   Mustard - Ketchup - Relish (A Game)**

Purpose: To use Deductive Reasoning in a game.
Materials: Activity Card 1.13 — Game Board

❑   This game is a numerical version of the game *Mastermind*. The leader selects a three-digit number in which no two digits are the same. Students then try to guess the correct number. When a number is guessed, the following response clues will be given:

Mustard: One digit is correct, but in the wrong place.
Ketchup: One digit is correct, and in the right place.
Relish: No number in the guess is correct.
   The three response clues might be placed on the overhead or the blackboard for easy reference by students.

Sample Game: Number selected is 427.

Guess #1:	538	Reply:	Relish
Guess #2:	149	Reply:	Mustard
Guess #3:	194	Reply:	Mustard
Guess #4:	419	Reply:	Ketchup
Guess #5:	429	Reply:	Ketchup, Ketchup,
Guess #6:	427	Reply:	Ketchup, Ketchup, Ketchup,

The game is concluded when someone receives three replies of Ketchup.

Problem-Solving Hints:
   • On your first try, what answer would be most beneficial to you?
   • How could you win the game in the least number of tries?
   • If the reply is "Mustard," what is your best strategy?
   • If the reply is "Ketchup," what is your best strategy?
   • What different strategy would you use for the next game?

☞   **Activity 14:   Logic Puzzle**

Purpose: Using logical reasoning to organize data and solve a problem.
Materials: Activity Card 1.14 — Logic Puzzle

Angelica, Bob, Carlos, and Damaris all have different tastes in music:
country, rock and roll, jazz, and classical. Angelica has never been
interested in jazz music. One of Angelica's friends likes jazz the best.
Carlos and Damaris do not like classical. Bob's favorite music is country.
Damaris did like rock and roll, but her taste in music has changed.

❑   a. What is Damaris's favorite type of music now?

        b. Who likes classical best?

        c. Complete the activity card to discover the solution.

✎ **Journal**_____

        How would you use deductive reasoning when buying a new car?

        How would you use inductive reasoning for purchasing a new stereo?

7.   Find a Pattern

✳ **Key Ideas:**   Finding a pattern helps children develop their problem-solving skills. It is an essential skill in elementary mathematics. Students need a variety of experiences with recognition of patterns as well as with the rule for the pattern. When looking for a pattern, the student lists several parts of the problem and then steps back to a look for an emerging pattern. The *Find a Pattern Strategy* may be beneficial when a sequence of numbers is provided, a list of data is given, one is asked to make a prediction, or the information given can be expressed in an organized table or chart.

☞ **Activity 15:   Dogsitting for Aunt Augusta**

Purpose: Use the Find a Pattern Strategy to assist with problem solving.
Materials: Activity Card 1.15 — Dogsitting Dilemma

❑   A rich, but eccentric aunt gave Elizabeth two choices of pay for dogsitting with her Irish setter, Shannon, for 12 days. She could receive $36 at the end of the 12 days; or, be paid 1 cent the first day, 2 cents the second day, 4 cents the third day, 8 cents the fourth day. The amount would continue to be doubled for each of the 12 days. Elizabeth is in a quandary as to which she should choose. Can you help her make the best decision?

a. Use estimation to determine the decision Elizabeth might make.

b. Look for a pattern.

☞ **Activity 16:   The Calculator Club**

Purpose: To provide practice in looking for a pattern.
Materials: Activity Card 1.16 — Counters

❑   Addison is starting a calculator games club, of which he is the only current member. His plan is to ask each new member joining to invite 2 other new members each month. Addison selected 2 members the first month. How many club members will there be in exactly 12 months?

a. Estimate your answer.

b. Determine how many members there would be at 3, 4, and 5 months.

8.   Try Again

 Key Ideas: Remember, if you are puzzled by the process of problem-solving, sometimes it is best to put the problem away, take a brief break, come back, and try again. A fresh start will be beneficial. Now you are ready to enjoy the process of problem-solving once again.

Successful problem solvers have certain characteristics in common. These students
- take time to explore and think the problem through.
- look at the problem in different ways.
- run through the list of strategies to see which is best.
- organize their work.
- ask lots of questions.
- are not afraid to change the strategy if the first does not work.
- work lots of problems.
- reread or rewrite the problem to see if it is understood.
- accept the challenge of solving a good problem.

Journal

Write about patterns that you have seen in your daily adventures. Give two specific examples of patterns you saw or used this past week.

What problem-solving strategies did you find beneficial when solving the problems in this chapter? Why?

✈ EXTENSIONS ✈

 Key Ideas: In Extensions, you may revisit some of the concepts and activities presented in this chapter. The following activities allow you to explore some ideas a little further. Sections include Mental Computation, Calculators, Critical Thinking, Alternative Assessment, and Mathematics for the 21st Century.

✈ Mental Computation ✈

Problems can generally be solved in three ways: mental computation, paper and pencil, or a calculator. In order to distinguish between the three and use the most efficient approach, students need a great deal of practice.

To help students develop their skills in determining whether an answer makes sense, include the use of mental computation as a regular part of the daily mathematics activities.

In order to become proficient, mental computation should be an active part of each elementary mathematics class. Try introducing a five-minute warm-up time in mental computation skills each day. Students will quickly ascertain how rapidly they can develop their abilities in mental computation to become mental gymnasts.

☞ **Activity 17: In Your Head**

Purpose: To complete computations mentally.

❑ Compute the following in your head without the aid of calculator or paper/pencil:

a. $16 + 16 + 5 - (11 \times 3) + 7 =$

b. $25 + 14 - 10 + (1 \times 2) - 7 =$

c. $40 + 20 + 2 - (30 \times 2) \times 0 =$

d. $100 - 50 + (10 \times 2) - 25 + 5 =$

e. Without using your calculator or pencil/paper, select the best answer.

A 3-line advertisement runs in a local newspaper for 7 days. The cost for the advertisement is $4.56 per day. What is the total cost of the ad?

• less than $28   • more than $35   • between $28 and $35

✈ Calculators ✈

The calculator is a powerful computational device and instructional tool. Its importance in the elementary mathematics classroom can only be realized when students have routine access to it. The major roles of the calculator are to assist in the development of concepts, to help reinforce computation skills, to promote higher level thinking, and to enhance problem-solving instruction. Students who are led to use the calculator intelligently can develop a sound number sense and become powerful problem solvers and mental mathematicians.

☞ **Activity 18:   What Is My Range?**

Purpose: To develop calculator skills.
Materials: Calculator

These activities help to promote the understanding of number sense, estimation, computation, and mathematical reasoning.

❑   Enter the number 36 in the calculator. Choose a second number which when added to 36 provides a sum in the range from 70 to 80.

1. What is the smallest number that you can choose?

2. What is the largest number you can choose?

3. Create a range problem of your own. How can you make the problem more difficult? Try it with a classmate.

❑   Enter the number 65 in the calculator. Choose a second factor which when multiplied by 65 provides a product in the range from 600 to 700.

1. What is the smallest number that you can choose?

2. What is the largest number you can choose?

3. Create a range problem of your own. How can you make the problem more difficult? Try it with a classmate.

4. Create a range problem that involves decimal or rational numbers.

✦ Critical Thinking ✦

The acquisition of basic facts is an important component of a child's learning. In addition, however, children need skills to enable them to make important personal decisions and to analyze their surroundings. Instead of teaching simply the facts, the focus of classroom questioning should be on the relationship between various facts on the conceptual level. Students may be given opportunities to use the information and concepts which they have acquired to solve actual problems or to interpret given situations. Beyond this level, students may relate their knowledge and learning to their own beliefs, feelings, and behaviors. These questioning techniques should begin early in the primary years in order to ensure success in the higher grades.

Questions can be used to stimulate student thinking or to give assistance in the area of problem solving. Questions may also assist students in evaluating their own thinking and attitudes toward mathematical problem solving.

The following are some questions to ask:

- Can you describe the problem in your own words?

- Does this problem remind you of others you have previously solved?

- Which strategy did you apply first?

- How did you determine which data was essential to solve the problem?

- How did you determine what your first step would be?

- Why did you choose that particular procedure?

- Can you describe any blind alleys you followed?

- How do you know that your strategy was successful?

- What different approach would you take next time?

- How certain are you that your solution is correct?

- Do you think that there might be another way to solve this problem?

- How do you feel about implementing problem-solving procedures?

✈ Alternative Assessment ✈

Journals

In journal writing, it is important that trust be developed between student and teacher. Students must feel assured that they may openly express their ideas without any fear of criticism. Journal writing should take place daily. Students may add to their journals at any time and in any place.

Should teachers comment in student journals? Most experts agree that, yes, teachers should comment, but they should not correct student journals. Often teachers who have students write daily ask them to select one journal entry per week to be reviewed by the teacher.

Student journals may take many forms. Some writing might center on the current topic of instruction, a general review of daily events in the classroom, or an open-ended question.

Journal writing allows the teacher to stay in touch with the progress of each student on a regular basis. It can also reveal the student's feelings about his/her own work, classroom problems, and misconceptions which might occur.

Some ideas for journal starters include the following:
- Today in class I learned that...
- Today I discovered...
- When you said the word "fractions", I...
- I understand the homework better now that...
- I like working in groups because...
- My favorite mathematics manipulative is...
- Solving a puzzle problem is...
- Write an autobiography of your early mathematics experiences.
- Write a letter to a classmate who has the chicken pox explaining what you did in mathematics class today.
- Describe a time when you were "stuck" on a problem, and explain how you figured out the problem.
- What I like most about mathematics class is...
- What I like least about mathematics class is...
- A question I have about mathematics is...
- Design a bumper sticker for mathematics.

For further information on alternative assessment see Stenmark, J.K. (1991). *Mathematics Assessment: Myths, Models, Good Questions, and Practical Suggestions.* Reston (VA): NCTM.

✈ Mathematics for the 21st Century ✈

The Standards

Curriculum and Evaluation Standards for School Mathematics, Reston, VA: NCTM, 1989.

The Curriculum and Evaluation Standards for School Mathematics is usually referred to as the *Standards.* Published in 1989 by the National Council of Teachers of Mathematics, the *Standards* clearly reflect the need for reform in the teaching and learning of mathematics (*A Nation At Risk,* 1983). The central theme is that all students have a need to learn more, as well as different, mathematics and that school instruction in mathematics must change significantly. The *Standards* were written to guide the revision of the school mathematics curriculum and evaluation. The educational goals for individual students need to reflect the importance of being literate in mathematics.

Five general goals for students were formulated. Students should:
1. learn to value mathematics;
2. develop mathematical confidence;
3. become mathematical problem solvers;
4. learn to communicate mathematically; and
5. learn to reason mathematically.

These goals will enable individual students to develop self-confidence and achieve mathematical power. Three features of mathematics are ingrained in the *Standards.* The first is that "knowing" mathematics is the same as "doing" mathematics. This emphasizes the learning of mathematics as an active process and that instruction should stress "doing" rather than merely "knowing". Second, the mathematics curriculum should provide opportunities for all students to develop an understanding of mathematical structures and simulations that can be applied to other disciplines. Third, technology has changed the face of mathematics learning. Because of this, it has been stated that calculators should be available for all students at all times. A computer should also be available in each classroom for demonstration. Each student should have access to a computer for both individual and group activities. Students should learn to use the computer as a word processor and to investigate problem solving.

The *Standards* stress the fact that the number one goal for all elementary school mathematics is problem solving, and that students need to experience real-world problems on a regular basis.

The Curriculum Standards

Grades K–4 are as follows:

Standard 1:   Mathematics as Problem Solving

Standard 2:   Mathematics as Communication

Standard 3:   Mathematics as Reasoning

Standard 4:   Mathematical Connections

Standard 5:   Estimation

Standard 6:   Number Systems and Numeration

Standard 7:   Concepts of Whole Number Operations

Standard 8:   Whole Number Computation

Standard 9:   Geometry and Spatial Sense

Standard 10: Measurement

Standard 11: Statistics and Probability

Standard 12: Fractions and Decimals

Standard 13: Patterns and Relationships

Major Methodology Changes and Considerations:

1. Use manipulative materials.
2. Use cooperative learning groups.
3. Stress problem solving.
4. Teach the language of mathematics.
5. Stress integration of content and writing.
6. Use calculators and computers.

National Council of Teachers of Mathematics, *Curriculum and Evaluations Standards for School Mathematics*, 1989. Used with permission.

The Curriculum Standards

Grades 5–8 are as follows:

Standard 1: Mathematics as Problem Solving

Standard 2: Mathematics as Communication

Standard 3: Mathematics as Reasoning

Standard 4: Mathematical Connections

Standard 5: Number and Number Relationships

Standard 6: Number Systems and Number Theory

Standard 7: Computation and Estimation

Standard 8: Patterns and Functions

Standard 9: Algebra

Standard 10: Statistics

Standard 11: Probability

Standard 12: Geometry

Standard 13: Measurement

Major Methodology Changes and Considerations for Grades 5–8:

1. Use cooperative learning groups to explore, conjecture, analyze and apply mathematics.
2. Use calculators and computers.
3. Use concrete materials (manipulatives).
4. Stress the use of estimation in problem-solving.
5. Teach mathematics in a real world context.

These practices promote a problem-solving atmosphere in each elementary mathematics classroom. The long-standing preoccupation with computation is put aside to encourage children to see mathematics as a sense-making experience. With the incorporation of the *Standards* into elementary mathematics classrooms, students will become active participants in the creation mathematical knowledge.

2
Sets

UNDERSTANDING SETS

1. Sets
2. Set Operations

▼ PROBLEM CHALLENGE: Attribute Magic Square

Use Attribute Pieces (Activity Card 2.1) to fill in the boxes of the square so that each row, column, and diagonal contains the four different shapes (triangle, square, circle, and rectangle) and four different colors (red, blue, yellow, and green). Use the large pieces only. One diagonal has been completed for you.

HANDS-ON MATHEMATICS ACTIVITIES

The following activities are provided to enhance your understanding of sets.

Sets

✳ **Key Ideas:** Sets are an integral part of every area of mathematics. These activities introduce some basic ideas that help clarify set theory.

☞ **Activity 1:   Beginning with Sets**

Purpose: To gain an understanding of sets.
Materials: Activity Card 2.1—Attribute Pieces

Recall that a set is a collection of objects and the objects are called *members* or *elements* of the set.

❑   A set is a collection of objects.
    Example: The set of circle attribute pieces = {red, blue, yellow, and
                green circles}. See circle below and at the left.

1. Determine another set and draw it in the circle on the right.

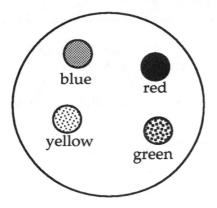   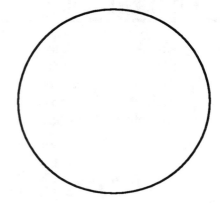

❑   Sets can have subsets.
    Example: Red circles are a subset of red attribute pieces.

2. Use the two sets you created earlier in this activity. What are some subsets of the sets you created? Place them in the sets below.

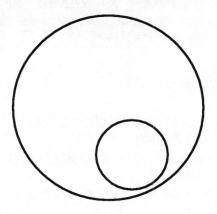   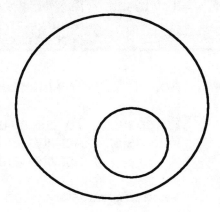

❑   Sets can be empty.
   Example: In the set of attribute pieces there are no octagons.

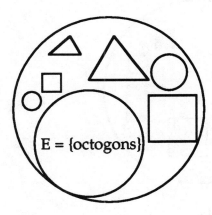

E = {octogons}

3. Place an empty set in the two sets you created earlier in this activity.

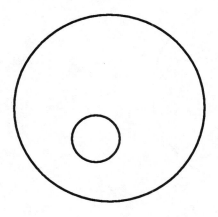   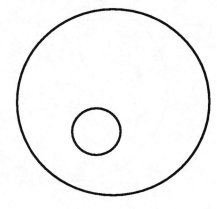

Set Operations

✳   **Key Ideas:**   Recall that a set operation is something you do to two sets that results in another set. The following activities look at this binary operation applied twice to incorporate three sets.

☛   **Activity 2:**   **The Intersection of Two Sets**

Purpose: To gain an understanding of the intersection of two sets.
Materials: Activity Card 2.1—Attribute Pieces
Activity Card 2.2—Venn Diagram (two-circle)

Venn diagrams are a convenient way of showing the operation of intersecting sets.

❑   The intersection of two sets contains elements in both sets.
Example: The set of red blocks and the set of squares.

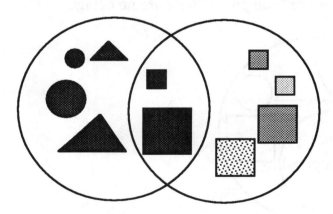

1.   Create two intersecting sets.

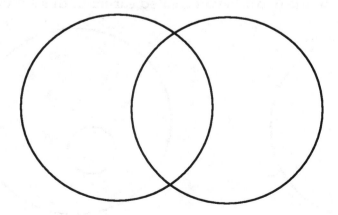

❑   Sometimes the intersection of two sets indicates there are no elements
      in common.
      Example: The set of red squares and the set of yellow squares.

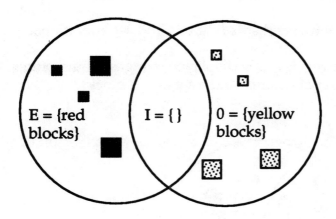

2. Create two sets with no elements in common.

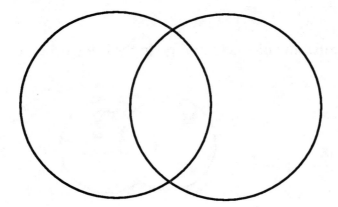

☛   **Activity 3:   Set Problems**

Purpose: To gain an understanding of sets and their intersections.
Materials: Activity Card 2.1 — Attribute Pieces
                 Activity Card 2.2 — Venn Diagram (2-circle)

Attribute pieces are useful for displaying sets and set operations.

❏   The interaction of two sets is easily displayed using attribute pieces.
    Example: Consider a set of squares and a set of red blocks.

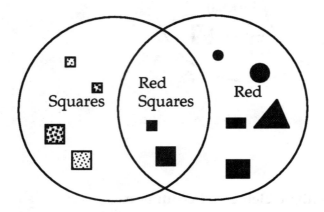

❏   1. Determine which attribute pieces would go in the intersection of each
        pair of sets..

a.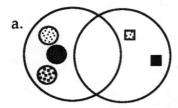

b.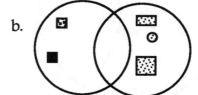

c.

d.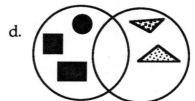

❑   The intersection of two sets is easily displayed using attribute pieces.
Example: Consider a set of squares and an intersection of red squares. The
second set of objects must be red to create the correct intersection.

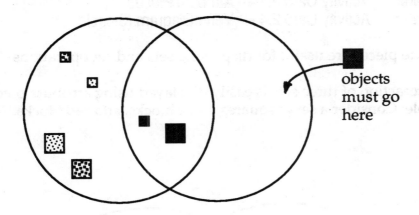

objects
must go
here

❑   2. Determine the attribute pieces that go in the second set of each pair.

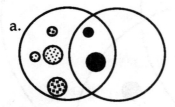

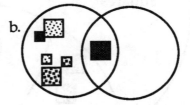

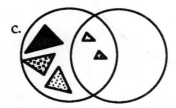

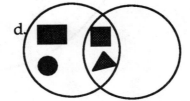

☞   **Activity 4:   Set Problems**

Purpose: To gain an understanding of sets and their intersection.
Materials: Activity Card 2.1 — Attribute Pieces
                 Activity Card 2.4 — Venn Diagram (3-circle)

Attribute pieces are useful for displaying sets and set operations.

❏   The interaction of three sets is easily displayed using attribute pieces.
     Example: Consider a set of squares, large blocks, and red blocks.

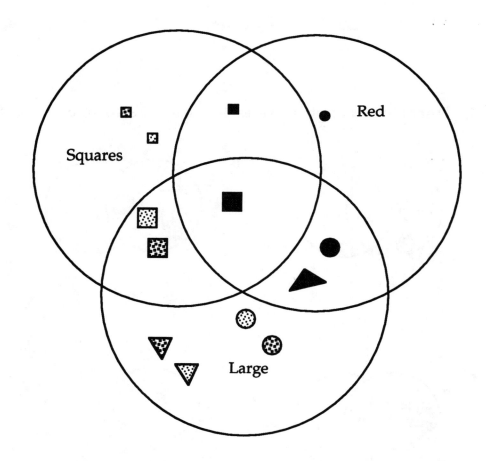

❑   How do you define the intersections of two or more sets?

❑   Determine the intersections of these sets.

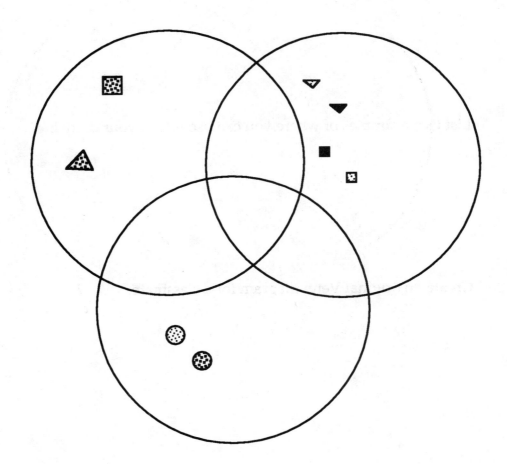

Journal

Create a problem which involves the use of sets.

Write a description of a set. Share your description with a friend.

List two examples of where you can use sets in your daily life.

Create an original Venn diagram for a classmate.

✈ EXTENSIONS ✈

> ✳ **Key Ideas:**   In Extensions, you may revisit some of the concepts and activities presented in this chapter. The following activities allow you to explore some ideas a little further. Topics in the Extensions section of the chapter include Mental Computation, Calculators, Critical Thinking, Alternative Assessment, and Mathematics for the 21st Century.

✈ Mental Computation ✈

As each new unit is introduced, mental computation should play a vital part in the mathematics classroom. A five-minute warm-up session or a problem challenge can start the day by enhancing the students' skills in this area. After a few weeks of mental computation practice, students can begin to create the exercises for the class. Be certain to encourage students to create accurate problems and to check the solution before presenting it to the class as a whole.

☛ **Activity 5:   What Is the Sum?**

Purpose: To mentally determine a sum

Here is a problem that can be used for a paper-and-pencil problem, but is even more impressive when used as a mental computation exercise.

❑   Using mental computation (with no paper and pencil), determine the sum of the 6th row of the following triangle. What is the sum of the 8th row?

$$0$$
$$1 + 2$$
$$3 + 4 + 5$$
$$6 + 7 + 8 + 9$$
$$10 + 11 + 12 + 13 + 14$$
$$? + ? + ? + ? + ? + ?$$

1. What problem solving strategy would be useful? Why?

2. Share the steps in your problem-solving process.

✈ Calculators ✈

The National Council of Teachers of Mathematics recommends that all elementary school programs fully implement the use of calculators in mathematics. It is recommended that pupils be provided continuous access to calculators and that calculator use be integrated into the curriculum on a regular basis. The calculator is a powerful computational device, but its power does not become obvious until students have routine access to it. Calculators can be used to enhance the objectives of most mathematics lessons. Calculators can, however, be placed out of view when routine paper-and-pencil tasks are to be accomplished. Calculators can assist in the development of concepts, reinforce skills, promote high-level thinking, and encourage the use of problem-solving strategies.

☞ **Activity 6: My Dear Aunt Sally**

Purpose: To gain an understanding of the order of operations.

The phrase, MY DEAR AUNT SALLY, is a mnemonic device for the following rule: Multiplication and Division are performed BEFORE Addition and Subtraction. When using the calculator, it is necessary to carefully note that the order of calculation makes sense.

For example: $14 + 12 \times 3$

Order of calculation: $12 \times 3 = 36; 14 + 36 =$

Correct result: 50   (An incorrect computation is 78).

❑   **Use your calculator to complete the following computations:**

Computation	Order of Performance on Calculator
$75 + 3 \times 10 = 105$	
$15 \times 10 + 84 \times 10 = 990$	
$84 - 35 + 235 \times 2 = 519$	

✈ Critical Thinking ✈

The *Curriculum and Evaluation Standards for School Mathematics* emphasizes that the classroom climate should place critical thinking at the very center of all mathematics instruction. Students need to understand that being able to explain and to justify their thinking is an important part of the problem-solving process. The way in which a problem is solved is as important as the answer to the problem. After set theory is introduced and discussed, it is wise to ask questions that emphasize higher-order thinking skills and not rote memorization. Sample questions might include the following:

1. How can you determine whether or not a set is infinite?
2. How can the intersection of two sets be determined?

Besides the implementation of higher-order questioning techniques, students (in cooperative groups) can be given the task of creating a question that can be answered using a Venn diagram. Poster paper and magic markers will enable each group to illustrate their idea for use with the whole group.

Some ideas to start the thinking process might include the following:

1. I am wearing blue today.
    I am wearing red today.
    (I am wearing red and blue today.)

2. I am comfortable using calculators in my classroom.
    I am comfortable using computers in my classroom.
    (I am comfortable using calculators and computers in my classroom.)

3. Mathematics is one of my favorite subjects.
    Science is one of my favorite subjects.
    (Mathematics and Science are two of my favorite subjects.)

☞ **Activity 7:**   **Critical Thinking Puzzle**

Purpose: To use critical thinking for problem solving.

❑   Each can illustrated below is labeled incorrectly. The labels themselves are correct, but misplaced. One can contains two dimes, another, two nickels, and the last one, one nickel and one dime. How can you determine the correct labels for all three cans if you can look at only one coin?

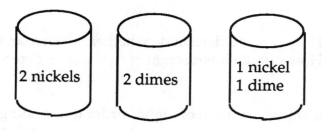

1. How many tries did it take?

2. What strategy did you use?

3. Were you successful?

✦ Alternative Assessment ✦

Portfolios

A portfolio is a collection of student work, a showcase of the student's accomplishments in the field of mathematics. A portfolio may include writing, projects, reports, journals, self assessments, open-ended problems, a mathematical autobiography, an interview, photographs of the student using mathematics manipulatives (a classroom Polaroid camera is handy for this), art work, group work, and any other examples of classroom participation and assessment. The student portfolio illustrates student progress and understanding in mathematics.

Discuss portfolios with the entire class. Since this form of assessment may be new to the majority of the class, several discussion sessions are recommended. If possible, a sample portfolio, perhaps one belonging to a teacher or a previous student, will clarify the subject for the class.

Students are led to understand that the contents of the portfolio are to be self-selected. The teacher may recommend that an exceptional paper or project be included in the portfolio, but the ultimate decision rests with the student.

A student mathematics portfolio reveals more than a Friday afternoon quiz. Portfolios allow students to demonstrate their learning and creative ideas, far exceeding mere factual knowledge revealed on classroom tests.

The teacher can discuss the portfolio contents, what mathematics means to the student, and what progress is being made in understanding concepts. There are no minimum or maximum requirements for the portfolio. Items selected for placement in the portfolio can illustrate the student's ability to gather and analyze data, recognize patterns, prepare logical arguments, implement problem-solving skills, and communicate mathematically.

Portfolios may be taken home to show improvement over time and can be useful discussion starters for a parent-child-teacher conference. They can be a real turning point in alleviating math anxiety in both students and parents. Student likes and dislikes, areas of improvement, and areas of excellence can be discussed using the portfolio.

Portfolios help students learn to value mathematics as a lifelong skill. They are a powerful assessment tool and one which empowers students to demonstrate the best possible representation of themselves as student mathematicians to their peers, parents, teachers, and the school system.

✈ Mathematics for the 21st Century ✈

Mathematics as Problem Solving

The National Council of Teachers of Mathematics in their *Curriculum and Evaluation Standards for School Mathematics* (1989), recommends that problem solving be the central focus of the entire K-12 mathematics curriculum. Problem solving and decision making are two of the most important abilities which students need to develop for use in their daily activities. National studies, however, such as the National Assessment of Educational Progress (NAEP), indicate that students continue to reflect low performance levels in the area of mathematical problem solving on standardized tests. Numerous elementary teachers respond that they feel inadequate in the area of teaching problem solving and problem-solving strategies and therefore avoid making the investment of time required to implement a quality problem-solving curriculum.

Problem solving, instead of being identified as time spent on a Friday afternoon solving one lone textbook story problem, should permeate the entire mathematics curriculum to be an integral part of each and every unit studied. This shift demands a total change from the current elementary mathematics curriculum that is computation-driven, to one in which every mathematics class is problem-solving based.

How is true problem solving defined? Often problem solving is equated with the story problems found in elementary mathematics textbooks. Such traditional story problems are a part of problem solving, but a minor part. Problem solving is more accurately defined as the process used to overcome barriers when a problem solution is not immediately obvious to the problem solver. A true non-traditional problem requires intense analysis and insight before a valid solution can be reached.

While it is commonly acknowledged that problem solving is a critical part of each elementary student's mathematical education, more emphasis must be placed on the development of problem-solving strategies and their integration across the curriculum. Present teaching styles appear to be inadequate. We must reexamine the way in which problem solving is taught if we are to nurture critical and creative problem solving in the classroom.

George Polya, considered the father of problem solving, in his book *How to Solve It* (1959) recommended a four-step process for empowering students to become successful problem solvers.

Four Steps to Problem Solving:

Step 1: <u>Understand the problem</u>. Ensure that each student discusses and understands what the problem is asking.

Step 2: <u>Create a plan.</u> Using problem-solving strategies, design a plan to solve the problem.

Step 3: <u>Implement the plan.</u> Carry out the ideas which you suggested in Step 2.

Step 4: <u>Look back and check.</u> Check the solution for accuracy. Ask if the answer makes sense.

Promoting Problem-Solving Skill Development

There are three immediate ways in which teachers can promote problem-solving skill development in students:

1. <u>Concepts</u>. Empower students by assisting them in the mastery of mathematical concepts and skills which ensure success within a problem-solving curriculum.

2. <u>Strategies.</u> Create a classroom climate, using manipulatives and cooperative learning, enabling students to develop multiple problem-solving strategies.

3. <u>Quality Time and Quality Problems.</u> Provide students with multiple opportunities to implement problem-solving strategies in quality situations.

In the process, teachers need to allot time to the understanding and development of problem-solving techniques. Realistic problem situations which require estimation and provide a challenge are recommended. The use of multiple solutions is the rule rather than the exception.

Problem-Solving Strategies to Implement (see Chapter 1)

1. Guess and check
2. Make a table or list
3. Draw a picture
4. Solve a simpler problem
5. Inductive reasoning
6. Deductive reasoning
7. Find a pattern
8. Try again

Group situations can promote the use of problem-solving skills. In cooperative learning groups, students can discuss and plan solutions together. This enables group members to visualize the problem-solving process and refine their reasoning and communication skills. In order for students to develop successful problem-solving techniques, instruction must begin early and be continually nurtured as they pass through each K-12 level.

3

Whole Numbers

UNDERSTANDING WHOLE NUMBERS

1. Numeration Systems
2. Addition and Subtraction
3. Multiplication and Division
4. Properties
5. Estimation and Mental Computation
6. Place Value, Renaming, and Expanded Notation

▼ PROBLEM CHALLENGE: Cycle Parade

Solve this problem more than one way:

Children ride their bicycles and tricycles in a holiday parade. In a group of cyclists, John counted seven cycles pass him. Sally said she counted 17 wheels. How many bicycles and how many tricycles passed John and Sally?

HANDS-ON MATHEMATICS ACTIVITIES

The following activities are provided to enhance your understanding of whole numbers.

Numeration Systems

 Key Ideas: Civilizations have used various systems of numeration. Efficient numeration systems have certain characteristics in common. Some of these characteristics include the use of a base, place value, additive and multiplicative properties, and a symbol for zero.

☞ **Activity 1: Roman Numerals**

Purpose: To gain an understanding of the Roman numeration system.

Recall that basic Roman numerals have the following values:

Roman numeral
(Hindu-Arabic numeral)

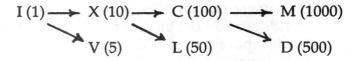

Determine the value of the Roman numeral by adding the value of each symbol to the symbol on the right of equal or greater value. Subtract the value of I, X, or C when they occur to the left of a symbol of greater value. Arrows indicate symbols that you may subtract and the symbol you subtracted from. I, for example, is subtracted when located to the left of V and X.

❑   Roman numerals are additive.
Example: XXVI = 10 + 10 + 5 + 1 = 26

1. Determine the Hindu-Arabic equivalent for each Roman numeral.

a.   XXXVII   b.   LXIII   c.   MDCLVI   d.   MMDCL

❑   Some Roman numerals can be subtracted (see rules above).
Example: CMXLIV = (1000 – 100) + (50 – 10) + (5 – 1) = 994

2. Determine the Hindu-Arabic equivalent for each Roman numeral.

a.   XXIV   b.   XLIV   c.   XCIV   d.   CMXXXIV

❑   The Roman numeral symbols I, X, C, and M can be repeated three times.
      Example: MMMCCCXXXIII = 3333

   3. Determine the Hindu-Arabic equivalent for each Roman numeral.

   a.   XXIII   b.   LXXXVII   c.   DCCCXIII   d.   MMCCCXXII

   4. Determine the Roman equivalent for each Hindu-Arabic numeral.

   a.   99   b.   276   c.   444   d.   2944

☛   **Activity 2: Base Five Numerals**

Purpose: To gain an understanding of base five numeration.
Materials: Activity Card 3.2a—Place Value Mat
                Activity Card 3.2b—Base Five Coins

Base five place values begin with the *ones* place on the far right. To the left
of the *ones* is 5^1 (five to the first power) or 5. To the left of the *fives* is 5^2
(five to the second power) or 25. The 1¢, 5¢, and 25¢ coins may help you
gain further understanding of base five numeration.

Twenty-fives	Fives	Ones
5^2	5^1	5^0
25¢	5¢	1¢

❑   We can write base five numerals by thinking of 1¢, 5¢, and 25¢ coins.
      Example: 333_{five} = 3 quarters, 3 nickels and 3 pennies = 93¢ (base ten)

   1. Use the coins and place value mat to determine the Hindu-Arabic
       equivalents for each base five numeral.

   a. 202_{five} b. 321_{five} c. 10_{five} d. 101_{five}

❑   Base five numerals are multiplicative. The value of a digit varies
      according to its position in the numeral.
      Example: 111_{five} = (1 x 25) + (1 x 5) + (1 x 1) = 31 (base ten)

   2. Use the coins and place value mat to determine the Hindu-Arabic
       equivalents for each base five numeral.

   a. 202_{five} b. 321_{five} c. 10_{five} d. 101_{five}

❑   Base five numerals are additive.
       Example: $123_{five} = (1 \times 25) + (2 \times 5) + (3 \times 1) = 25 + 5 + 1 = 36$ (base ten)

   3. Use the coins and place value mat to write each base five numeral in
       expanded notation and determine the Hindu-Arabic equivalent.

   a. 214_{five} b. 444_{five} c. 204_{five} d. 320_{five}

❑   Hindu-Arabic numerals can be written as base five numerals if you use
       the base five coins.
       Example: $62_{ten} = (2 \times 25) + (2 \times 5) + (2 \times 1) = 222_{five}$

   4. Use the coins and place value mat to determine the base five
       equivalents for each Hindu-Arabic numeral.

   a.   5   b.   24   c.   57   d.   103

☞   **Activity 3: Mayan Numerals**

Purpose: To gain an understanding of the Mayan numeration system.

The Mayans used a numeration system based on 20. The bottom place
represents ones and the second place represents twenties. The third place
is not consistent. It represents 20 x 18. The system is consistent base 20
from there. The fourth place represents 20 x 18 x 20 and so on. Some
Mayan numerals appear below, using beads with a value of 1 and rods
having a value of 5. The Mayans used θ for the symbol 0.

1	2	3	4	5	6	7	8	9	10
•	••	•••	••••	____	•	••	•••	••••	____ ____

11	12	13	14	15	16	17	18	19	20
•	••	•••	••••	____	•	••	•••	••••	• θ

Here are some additional Mayan numerals with their Hindu-Arabic equivalents. The value of each symbol is given below the Mayan numeral.

21	22	29	38	40	41	42	60	80	100
•	•	•	•	••	••	••	•••	••••	——
•	••	••••	•••	0	•	••	0	0	0
1 x 20	1 x 20	1 x 20	1 x 20	2 x 20	2 x 20	2 x 20	3 x 20	4 x 20	5 x 20
1	2	9	18	0	1	2	0	0	0

❑   Mayan Numerals are multiplicative.
    Example: •••• =   (9 x 20) = 160

                       • • =   (12 x 1) = 12   160 + 12 = 172

Write each Mayan numeral in expanded form and determine the Hindu-Arabic equivalent.

a. •••   b. ••••   c. •••   d. ••••

    ••••   ••   •••   ••••

Journal

Roman numerals do not use place value. Mayan numerals depend upon place value. The Romans did not have a symbol for zero, while the Mayans did. Must a system have a zero to be a place value system? Why?

Look at some elementary school arithmetic textbooks. How does the author introduce students to the Roman numeral system? Why do we continue to teach Roman numerals? What other numeration systems should we teach? Why?

Addition and Subtraction

> ✳ **Key Ideas:** We add and subtract almost without thought. We have performed these processes so often it is automatic. These activities may help you understand the computational process.

☞ **Activity 4: Addition and Subtraction**

Purpose: To gain an understanding of addition and subtraction.
Materials: Activity Card 3.4—Centimeter Strips

One definition of addition and of subtraction is easily shown with centimeter strips. Addition is the process of finding the sum given two addends. Subtraction is the process of finding the missing addend given the sum and a known addend.

❑   Addition is the process of finding the sum given two addends. Centimeter strips show this concept.
Example: $6 + 2 = 8$

This addend represents 6	This is 2

This strip represents the sum of 8

1. Determine the sums using centimeter strips. Label the addends and sum in each equation.

a. $7 + 3 =$ b. $3 + 4 =$ c. $5 + 2 =$ d. $6 + 3 =$

❑   Subtraction is the process of finding the missing addend given a sum and a known addend. Centimeter strips illustrate this concept.
Example: $8 - 2 = 6$

This strip represents the sum of 8

This is 2	The missing addend is 6

2. Determine the missing addends using centimeter strips. Label the addends and sum in each equation.

a. $7 - 3 =$ b. $9 - 4 =$ c. $5 - 2 =$ d. $8 - 5 =$

☛   **Activity 5: Addition**

Purpose: To gain an understanding of one addition algorithm.
Materials: Activity Card 1.16 — Counters
            Activity Card 3.2a — Place Value Mat

❑   Use a place value mat and counters to show the traditional addition
      algorithm for adding two 2-digit numbers with renaming .

      The four steps of the addition algorithm are shown below.
      Example $17 + 14 = 31$
             1. Place the counters on the place value mat. Use 1 red and 7
                 blacks for 17 and 1 red and 4 blacks for 14.
             2. Add the black counters (ones).
             3. If there are ten or more black counters, rename.
             4. Add the red counters (tens).

Step 1 Set up	Step 2 Add the ones	Step 3 Trade	Step 4 Add the tens

17 • ooooo
     oo
+ 14 • oooo
	ooooo
	ooooo
	         o
	17 •
	+ 14 • _____
		1 •
		17 •
		+ 14 • _____
		      1 o
			17
			+ 14 _____
			31 ••• o

❑   Complete the four-step algorithm using counters and a place value mat
      for each computation.

      a. $15 + 19 =$ b. $24 + 17 =$ c. $38 + 7 =$ d. $49 + 13 =$

Step 1 Set up	Step 2 Add the ones	Step 3 Trade	Step 4 Add the tens

☞   **Activity 6: Subtraction**

Purpose: To gain an understanding of one subtraction algorithm.
Materials: Activity Card 1.16 — Counters
              Activity Card 3.2a — Place Value Mat

A place value mat and counters show the traditional subtraction algorithm for two 2-digit numbers with renaming. Remember, subtraction is the process of finding the missing addend given the sum and known addend. Both addends are in the sum.

❑   The four steps of the algorithm are shown below.
    Example: 31 – 17 = 14
        1. Place counters representing 31 (3 reds and 1 black) on the mat.
        2. There are not enough black counters. Rename.
        3. Subtract the black counters (ones).
        4. Subtract the red counters (tens).

Step 1 Set up	Step 2 Trade	Step 3 Subtract the ones	Step 4 Subtract the tens

31 •••   o
 	
$\underline{-17}$ _____
	31 •• ooooo
	         ooooo
	            o
	
	$\underline{-17}$ _____
		2
		З 1 ••
		
		        ooooo
		$\underline{-17}$ oo
		   4 oooo
			2
			З 1
			
			        ooooo
			$\underline{-17}$ • oo
			  1 4 • oooo

Complete the four-step algorithm using counters and a place value mat for each computation.

a.   32 – 16 =   b.   45 – 18 =   c.   37 + 19 =   d.   23 + 18 =

Step 1 Set up	Step 2 Trade	Step 3 Subtract the ones	Step 4 Subtract the tens

☞ **Activity 7: Addition**

Purpose: To use a low-stress algorithm for addition.

Hutching's low-stress algorithm is another procedure for adding a column of numbers. Some people find it a useful replacement for the traditional addition algorithm.

❑   Hutching's low-stress algorithm is shown below.

```
7                                    7
1                                 1 8 5        7 + 8 = 15, write as shown
9                                 1 9 4        5 + 9 = 14, write as shown
6                                 1 6 0        4 + 6 = 10, write as shown
6          The tens digit is the    6 6        0 + 6 = 6, write as shown
+ 8        number of "1"s         1 8 4        6 + 8 = 14, write as shown
           written to the left of  4 4
           each addend            The ones digit is from the 4 in the 14
```

1.   Add using Hutching's low-stress algorithm. When you add the "1"s, bring that total to the top of the tens column.

```
a.    2 3        b.    4 5        c.    6 8        d.    9 3
      8 7              9 5              4 4              3 7
      6 7              3 5              4 7              3 8
      6 1              5 9              4 8              7 3
      9 3              3 8              9 4              6 3
      8 2              1 4              2 5              2 8
    + 8 5            + 9 7              7 3              9 5
```

❑   Hutching's low-stress algorithm has both positive and negative properties.

2.   Use the centimeter strips to add one of the columns of numbers. Try to duplicate Hutching's low-stress algorithm with the centimeter strips. Write comments about Hutching's low-stress algorithm .

☞ **Activity 8: Subtraction**

Purpose: To use the modified algorithm for subtraction.

The modified algorithm is another procedure for subtracting numbers. Some people find it a useful replacement for the traditional algorithm.

❑ The modified algorithm is shown below.

Step 1 Set up	Step 2 Rename	Step 3 Subtract from 10 and add ones	Step 4 Subtract tens
3 4 – 1 8	2 3 4 10 – 1 8	$10 - 8 + 4 = 6$ 2 3 4 10 – 1 8 6	2 3 4 10 – 1 8 1 6

Use the centimeter strips to illustrate 34 – 18 = 16. Remember to place 3 *tens* strips and 4 *ones* strips to represent the sum. The sum contains both addends, the known addend of 18, and the missing addend.

1. Subtract using the modified algorithm.

   a.   4 3   b.   7 5   c.   6 2   d.   9 3

       – 2 7   – 3 8   – 4 7   – 3 7

2. Write comments about the modified algorithm.

3. How can you continue using the modified algorithm for subtracting
    3- or 4-digit numbers?

a.   4 3 2   b.   7 5 7   c.   6 2 3

     -1 6 7 -3 8 5 -4 7 6

 ## Journal

Add the following numbers as many different ways as you can:

              6
              3
              8
              4
              2
          $+$ 7

What are the advantages of each way?

What are the disadvantages?

Should we show elementary students more than one way to add? Why?

Multiplication and Division

✳ **Key Ideas:**   Multiplication is defined as repeated addition of sets. Five sets of four is twenty, for example: $4 + 4 + 4 + 4 + 4 = 20$. Another definition for multiplication is the row-by-column set model. This defines the first factor as the number of sets (of groups) and the second factor as the number of elements in each set. Many teachers consider division the most difficult algorithm to master. To correctly use division, students must have a thorough understanding of place value, estimation, and mental computation along with subtraction and multiplication skills. Students should consider two concepts for division; partitioning and repeated subtraction.

☞ **Activity 9: Multiplication Defined**

Purpose: To define multiplication using the repeated addition model.
Materials: Activity Card 3.9 — Color Pieces
Yarn or String

Color pieces and yarn show the repeated addition model of multiplication. Use the color pieces to form sets and the yarn to define each set.

❏   Use color pieces to form 5 sets with 4 pieces in each set. Use 5 circles of yarn to define each set.

1.   What is the total number of color pieces used?

2.   Use color pieces and yarn to create sets that illustrate the following computations and record your illustrations.

a. $3 \times 9 =$ b. $6 \times 7 =$ c. $8 \times 2 =$ d. $4 \times 8 =$

3.   Select 36 color pieces. Create three different ways to illustrate multiplication facts with a product of 36, and record your illustrations.

Base Ten Blocks

☞ **Activity 10:   Multiplication Arrays**

Purpose: To understand array (row-by-column) models for multiplication.
Materials: Activity Card 3.9 — Color Pieces

❑   Color pieces are helpful to show arrays. Create an array of color pieces
    containing 4 rows and 6 columns.

                            6 Columns

                            X X X X X X
            4 Rows   X X X X X X
                            X X X X X X
                            X X X X X X

    1. How many color pieces did you use in the array?

    2. What multiplication fact does the array illustrate?

    3. Use color pieces to create arrays illustrating the following
        computations and record your illustrations.

    a.   3 x 9 =   b.   6 x 7 =   c.   8 x 2 =   d.   4 x 8 =

    4. Select 24 color pieces. Create three different arrays to illustrate
        multiplication facts with a product of 24. Record your illustrations.

☞ **Activity 11:   Lattice Multiplication**

Purpose: To understand the concept of lattice multiplication.

❑   Lattice multiplication

The lattice multiplication algorithm involves The following:
1. Select a problem such as 25 x 48 =
2. Construct an appropriate lattice. Place one factor on the top of the lattice and the second factor on the right of the lattice.
3. Fill each box with the appropriate multiplication facts.
4. Add diagonally, beginning in the lower right corner and moving to the top left corner.
5. Read the product from the top left around the corner to the bottom right.

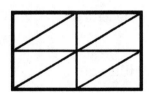

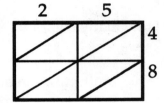

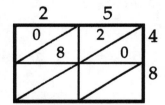

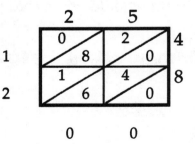

Study the sample lattice multiplication.

Notice the addition along each diagonal.

Notice the renaming that occurs from the tens to hundreds.

The product of 25 x 48 is 1200.

❑   Create your own lattice to illustrate each of the following computations:

a. 13 x 29 =   b. 46 x 67 =   c. 38 x 12 =   d. 74 x 38 =

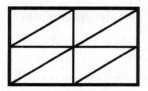   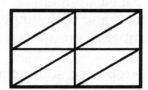

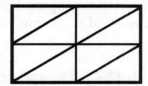   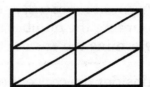

☛   **Activity 12:   Partition Division**

Purpose: To understand partition division.
Materials: Activity Card 3.9 — Color Pieces
                   Six Pieces of Yarn or String

In partition division, the total number of objects and number of groups is given. We must determine the number of objects in each group.

❑   The partition division model

Example: There are 25 objects in 5 groups. How many objects are in each group?

We could distribute or partition the 25 objects, one at a time, to the five groups. Counting the number of objects in each group would result in an answer of 5. We could determine the answer by dividing: 25 ÷ 5 = 5.

Consider the concept of partitioning with 42 ÷ 6. Place pieces of yarn to form 6 circles on your desk along with 42 color pieces. Distribute the color pieces among the 6 circles of yarn. How many pieces are in each circle?

☞ **Activity 13:   Division as Repeated Subtraction (Measurement)**

Purpose: To understand repeated subtraction.
Materials: Activity Card 3.9 — Color Pieces

In a measurement or repeated subtraction problem, the total number of objects and the number of objects included in each group is given. The number of groups needed is to be determined.

❏   The repeated subtraction model

Example: Place 32 objects in groups with 4 objects per group. How many groups are needed?

We could repeatedly subtract 4 from 32 until there are no objects left. Counting the number of groups results in an answer of 8. We could determine the answer by dividing: 32 ÷ 4 = 8.

Consider the concept of repeated subtraction with 42 ÷ 6. Place 42 color pieces on your desk. Repeatedly subtract 6 cubes. How many groups of 6 were formed?

☞ **Activity 14:   Repeated Subtraction and Partition Division**

Purpose: To identify repeated subtraction and partition activities.
Materials: Activity Card 3.9 — Color Pieces

❏   Identify the problems as repeated subtraction or partition division.

_____ 1.   Forty-five dinosaur erasers come in a bag. Each student will receive 9 dinosaur erasers. How many students can receive dinosaur erasers?

_____ 2.   There are 36 comic books in a collection. Two boys divide the books evenly. How many comic books does each boy get?

_____ 3.   There are 48 students planning a trip by car. Each car can carry 4 students. How many cars are needed to take the students on the trip?

Journal

Two algorithms for multiplying 12 x 47 are illustrated below. Study each to understand the mechanics of each step.

```
      4 7            4 7
    x 1 2          x 1 2
      1 4            9 4
      8 0          4 7 0
      7 0          5 6 4
    4 0 0
    5 6 4
```

Why should we introduce elementary students to each of these multiplication algorithms?

When should teachers introduce elementary students to the traditional multiplication algorithm, dropping the use of "0"s in each of the partial products?

Properties

 Key Ideas: Certain number patterns are very useful, and we should understand and commit them to memory. These include the commutative, associative, distributive, and identity properties.

☛ **Activity 15: Commutative Property**

Purpose: Discover the commutative property of whole numbers.
Materials: Activity Card 3.4 — Centimeter Strips

❑   1. Illustrate each computation using centimeter strips.

    a. $7 + 3 =$ b. $3 + 4 =$ c. $5 + 2 =$ d. $6 + 3 =$

        $3 + 7 =$ $4 + 3 =$ $2 + 5 =$ $3 + 6 =$

❑   2. Illustrate each computation using centimeter strips.

    a. $4 \times 2 =$ b. $3 \times 4 =$ c. $5 \times 2 =$ d. $6 \times 3 =$

        $2 \times 4 =$ $4 \times 3 =$ $2 \times 5 =$ $3 \times 6 =$

Write a general statement, in your own words, explaining the commutative property.

☞ **Activity 16:   Associative Property**

Purpose: Discover the associative property of whole numbers.
Materials: Activity Card 3.4 — Centimeter Strips

❑   1. Illustrate each computation using centimeter strips. Be sure to add
       the numbers in parenthesis first.

   a. $7 + (3 + 5) =$ b. $3 + (4 + 2) =$ c. $5 + (2 + 7) =$

        $(7 + 3) + 5 =$ $(3 + 4) + 2 =$ $(5 + 2) + 7 =$

❑   2. Illustrate each computation using centimeter strips. Be sure to
       multiply the numbers in parenthesis first.

   a. $2 \times (2 \times 3) =$ b. $3 \times (4 \times 2) =$ c. $5 \times (2 \times 2) =$

        $(2 \times 2) \times 3 =$ $(3 \times 4) \times 2 =$ $(5 \times 2) \times 2 =$

Write a general statement explaining the associative property.

☞ **Activity 17:   Identity Property**

Purpose: Discover the identity property of whole numbers.
Materials: Activity Card 3.4 — Centimeter Strips

❑   1. Illustrate each computation using centimeter strips.

   a. $7 + 0 =$ b. $3 + 0 =$ c. $5 + 0 =$

❑   2. Illustrate each computation using centimeter strips.

   a. $7 \times 1 =$ b. $9 \times 1 =$ c. $1 \times 5 =$

Write a general statement explaining the identity property in your own
words.

☞ **Activity 18:   Distributive Property**

Purpose: Discover the distributive property of whole numbers.
Materials: Activity Card 3.4 — Centimeter Strips

❑   Illustrate each computation using centimeter strips. Be sure to add the
     numbers in parentheses first.

   a.   2 x (3 + 4) =   b.   4 x (5 + 3) =

           (2 x 2) + (2 x 4) =   (4 x 5) + (4 x 3) =

Write a general statement explaining the distributive property of
whole-number multiplication over addition.

❑   Illustrate each computation using centimeter strips. Be sure to
     multiply the numbers in parentheses first.

   a.   2 x (3 − 4) =   b.   4 x (5 − 3) =

           (2 x 2) − (2 x 4) =   (4 x 5) − (4 x 3) =

Write a general statement, in your own words, explaining the distributive
property of whole-number multiplication over subtraction.

Journal

Illustrate each of the mathematical properties by giving an example and drawing a picture.

Commutative Property

Associative Property

Identity Property

Distributive Property

Estimation and Mental Computation

> ✳ **Key Ideas:**   Estimation and mental computation are closely linked. Estimation is the process of discovering an answer that is close enough to the true answer to allow a decision to be made. Mental computation, on the other hand, is defined as the process of discovering the specific answer involving computation without the use of any external aids such as paper and pencil or a calculator.

☞ **Activity 19:   Rounding**

Purpose: To discover the rounding strategy.

The rounding strategy is useful with any computational operation. It involves rounding given numbers to the nearest ten and computing.

❏   Round numbers to the nearest ten and compute the sum or product. Example: To estimate the product of 38 x 73, round and multiply to obtain 40 x 70 = 280.

Use the rounding strategy to find estimates for each computation.

a.   29 + 75 =   b.   51 + 36 =   c.   89 x 21 =   d.   77 x 19 =

☞ **Activity 20:   Compatible Numbers**

Purpose: To explore the compatible-numbers strategy.

The compatible-numbers strategy encourages the student to search for numbers that total a "neat" sum like 10 or 100.

❏   Combine numbers whose sum is 10 and add.
Example: 1 + 2 + 3 + 4 + 5 + 6 + 7 + 8 + 9 = ___.
(1 + 9) + (2 + 8) + (3 + 7) + (4 + 6) = 40.
40 plus the remaining 5 = 45.
Some prefer other number combinations such as
(1 + 2 + 3 + 4 + 5) + (6 + 9) + (7 + 8) = 45.

Use groups of 10 or 100 to determine the sums.

a.   5 + 4 + 2 + 9 + 5 + 1 + 6 + 7 =
b.   7 + 2 + 9 + 3 + 1 + 3 + 8 + 6 + 2 =
c.   21 + 38 + 79 + 62 =
d.   34 + 56 + 69 + 82 + 45 + 19 + 89 =

☛ **Activity 21:   Front-end Strategy**

Purpose: To practice the front-end strategy.

The front-end strategy involves two steps.

1) Perform the computation using the digits at the front of each number (add only the tens place digits, ignoring the ones).
2) Adjust the estimate by performing the computation with the remaining digits.

❑   Use the front-end strategy to determine the sums.

Example: 154 + 323 + 417 = ___.
• Add the hundreds digits. 1 + 3 + 4 = 8 or 800.
• To adjust, round the remaining digits and add. 50 + 20 + 20 = 90.
• 800 + 90 = 890. The estimate is 890.

Use the front-end strategy to determine the sums.

a.	145 + 216 + 221 + 319 =	b.	251 + 695 + 122 + 345 =
c.	98 + 45 + 23 + 78 + 56 =	d.	391 + 542 + 289 + 458 =

 Journal _____

How can the skill of estimation help elementary students in mathematics?

Explain the front-end strategy in two or three sentences and state when it would be beneficial to use.

Place Value, Renaming, and Expanded Notation

Key Ideas: A solid foundation in the understanding of place value and renaming is critical to understanding computation and computation algorithms. Expanded notation is useful for understanding number concepts.

☞   **Activity 22:   Places of Value**

Purpose: To understand place value.
Materials: Activity Card 3.22 — Number Cubes
                Activity Card 3.2a — Place Value Mat

Digits are worth differing values according to their position within the numeral.

❑   **The Places of Value Game**

Each player rolls the number cube seven times. The object of the game is to add the seven numbers to obtain a sum closest to 100 without going over. Write the digit that is obtained during a roll in either the tens or ones column of the Place Value Mat. Use the digit "0" to fill in the blanks. Add the numbers to obtain a sum. The player closest to 100 without going over wins.

Example:

		Places of Value				**Places of Value**	
Player 1		Tens	Ones	Player 2		Tens	Ones
1.	rolls a 5	0	5		rolls a 6	0	6
2.	rolls a 1	1	0		rolls a 7	7	0
3.	rolls a 6	0	6		rolls a 1	1	0
4.	rolls a 3	3	0		rolls a 4	0	4
5.	rolls a 4	4	0		rolls a 2	0	2
6.	rolls a 4	0	4		rolls a 1	0	1
7.	rolls a 6	0	6		rolls a 6	0	6
	Total	1 0	1		Total	9	9

Player one loses, since 101 is over 100 and 99 is closest to 100.

☛   **Activity 23:   Trading-Up**

Purpose: To understand renaming.
Materials: Activity Card 3.22 — Number Cubes
                 Activity Card 1.16 — Counters

Renaming is a difficult concept for children. This is a useful game to explore the concept of renaming and promote understanding.

❑   **The Trading-Up Game**

Two to four participants can play the game. Each participant rolls a number cube and picks up white counters equivalent to the number rolled. White counters are worth 1. Three white counters must be traded for one black counter, three black counters must be traded for one red counter, and three red counters must be traded for one green counter. Each participant rolls the number cube in turn and always collects white counters from the bank. Trades for blue counters must be made before the next player rolls the number cube. Blue and red counters are traded when appropriate. The first player to obtain a green counter wins the game.

1.   What is the value of each counter?   White?   Blue?   Red?   Green?

2.   In what base is the game played?

3.   What advantages are there in playing in base three?

☛   **Activity 24:   Trading-Down**

Purpose: To understand renaming.
Materials: Activity Card 3.22 — Number Cubes
                 Activity Card 1.16 — Counters

Renaming in subtraction is an especially difficult concept for children. This is a useful game for exploring the concept of renaming.

❑   **The Trading-Down Game**

This game is similar to the Trading-Up Game. Each player starts with a green counter and rolls a number cube. White counters equivalent to the number rolled must be given back to the bank. Each green counter is worth three reds, one red counter is worth three blues, and one blue is worth three white. The first player to give up all counters wins the game.

☛   **Activity 25:   Expanded Notation**

Purpose: To understand expanded notation.
Materials: Activity Card 1.12 — Base Ten Pieces

Writing numbers in expanded notation format can help students visualize place value and renaming.

❏   Write numbers in expanded notation and compute.

Example: Consider subtracting two 2-digit numbers with no renaming.

$$
\begin{array}{rcl}
5\ 4 &=& 50\ +\ 4 \\
-4\ 2 &=& \underline{40\ +\ 2} \\
1\ 2 &=& 10\ +\ 2
\end{array}
$$

Example: Consider subtracting two 2-digit numbers with renaming.

$$
\begin{array}{rclcl}
3\ 4 &=& 30\ +\ 4 &=& 20\ +\ 14 \\
-1\ 7 &=& \underline{10\ +\ 7} &=& \underline{10\ +\ 7} \\
 & & &=& 10\ +\ 7\ =\ 17
\end{array}
$$

❏   Use base ten pieces to illustrate each computation.

a. $45 + 67 = 112$ b. $45 - 28 = 17$

c. $3 \times 27 = 81$ d. $44 \div 3 = 14, r\ 2$

Journal

Describe one new concept that you have learned in this chapter.

What questions would you like to ask about whole-number concepts?

How do manipulatives enhance the understanding of whole numbers?

Draw a picture telling how you feel about whole-number concepts.

✈ EXTENSIONS ✈

✳ **Key Ideas:**   In Extensions, you may revisit some of the concepts and activities presented in this chapter. The following activities allow you to explore some ideas a little further. Sections include Mental Computation, Calculators, Critical Thinking, Alternative Assessment, and Mathematics for the 21st Century.

✈ Mental Computation ✈

☞ **Activity 26:   The Zero Rule**

Purpose: To explore multiplication by numbers ending in zero.
Materials: Calculator

❑   1.   Use a calculator to multiply the following numbers. Look for a pattern.

a.   23 x 10 =   b.   23 x 100 =   c.   230 x 10 =   d.   230 x 100 =

What is a shortcut method for multiplying by a number that ends in zero or zeros? Write your rule here.

2.   Use your rule to complete the following computations. Check your work using a calculator.

a.   2.3 x 10 =   b.   2.3 x 100 =   c.   2.30 x 10 =   d.   2.30 x 100 =

Did your written rule work?

If not, rewrite the rule.

✈ Calculators ✈

☞ **Activity 27:   Further Understanding of Place Value**

Purpose: To explore number relationships using a calculator.
Materials: Calculator

Use the digits 2, 3, 4, 5 and 6 (use each once) to create a 2-digit and 3-digit number. Use a calculator to determine the product. Rearrange the digits of these numbers to form new 2-digit and 3-digit numbers, and determine the product. What arrangement of digits results in the largest product?

Example: 23 x 456 = 10,488

❏   Use the results of the two largest products. Write the partial products for each computation. Critique the results and create a rule that will give you the largest product when multiplying 2- and 3-digit numbers.

☞ **Activity 28:   Understanding Place Value**

Purpose: To explore number relationships using a calculator.
Materials: Calculator

Use the digits 6, 7, 8, and 9 to write two 2-digit numbers that when multiplied together result in the largest product.

❏   Determine a pattern for the numbers that gave you the largest product. Write a rule here. Repeat the problem using the numbers 1, 2, 3, and 4.

☞ **Activity 29:   Addition with a Calculator**

Purpose: To examine an elementary level activity.
Materials: Calculator

❏   Each letter of the alphabet is worth a different numerical value. *A* is worth 1, *B* is worth 2, *C* is worth 3,…, and *Z* is worth 26. Create words and determine their value by adding the letter amounts. For instance the word *bad* is worth 2 + 1 + 4 = 7.
　　　　1. What is the value of your name?
　　　　2. Find a word with the value of $1.00.
　　　　3. What state name has the most value?
　　　　4. What holiday has the most value?

➜ Critical Thinking ➜

☞   **Activity 30:   Higher-Order Questions**

Purpose: To encourage higher-order thinking and questions.

1. Why is a symbol for *zero* important in a numeration system?

2. What is the advantage of a place-value numeration system?

3. How can studying other numeration systems help children understand the Hindu-Arabic numeration system?

4. Compare our Hindu-Arabic system with the Roman numeral system.

✈ Alternative Assessment ✈

Performance Assessment

Part 1

There are numerous ways to incorporate alternative assessment in your elementary mathematics classroom, including performance assessment, journals, portfolios, observations, and interviews. In this chapter, we will deal with performance assessment.

Performance assessment in elementary mathematics involves providing elementary students with a mathematical task or investigation. The teacher observes, interviews, or evaluates the student production in order to determine what students know and what they can do. This type of assessment can be used with groups as well as individuals.

The advantages for students are the following:

1. Students can display numerous mathematical abilities, not simply those of speed and computational accuracy;

2. Students understand that mathematics is a process related to real life and not only a set of rules to be memorized;

3. Problems are more creative and encourage the development of higher-order thinking skills.

Tasks for Performance Assessment

1. **Place Value**—Ask each pair of students to explain how they would teach a primary student the meaning of *ones* and *tens* on a place value chart. Encourage the students to illustrate the explanation with a story to be presented on poster board.

2. **Division**—Delete the traditional division test of 25 computations. Instead, assign each group of students a different division problem. The task assigned for each group is to create a poster explaining how they solved their individual problem. The poster should clearly explain the procedure to ensure that beginning division students will grasp the idea. Color markers may be used to find each step of the illustration.

✈ Mathematics for the 21st Century ✈

Manipulatives

Using mathematics manipulatives in elementary mathematics activities is emphasized by the *Curriculum and Evaluation Standards for School Mathematics* (NCTM, 1989). The value of having manipulatives continuously available in the elementary classroom is that the promotion of understanding is the key area of focus.

George Polya (1887-1985), considered to be the father of mathematical problem solving, related four steps to the problem-solving process. They are:

1. Understand the task.
2. Create a plan.
3. Carry out the plan to complete the task.
4. Look back and check the outcome to see if it makes sense.

Manipulatives are used in all four steps. Using manipulatives in the elementary school mathematics classroom promotes understanding of the task at hand. This is an arena that has too often been neglected. Children need concrete experiences before being introduced to the abstract.

Manipulatives provide a concrete *hands-on* way to promote the understanding of mathematical concepts that previously may have appeared too abstract. Students can now see and touch materials that promote understanding of the abstract concept. Manipulatives allow mathematics to make sense and to become fun. Mathematical ideas become easier to comprehend when the students "own" and "understand" the concept. Often problems that appeared unsolvable become solvable.

Using manipulatives to create a hands-on plan for solving a specific problem provides both fun and team spirit. Students working together in pairs or groups of four can easily visualize whether their particular solutions will work or not.

After creating a plan using manipulatives, the students can carry out the plan and practice using it with another set of partners. Thus, problem solving that involves manipulatives is no longer threatening nor fearful, but an exciting experience that is shared with friends.

Finally, students are able to look back at the way they solved the problem to see if the answer was a reasonable one. At this time, they may envision multiple ways to solve the problem. Students may even visualize an extension to the problem that they would like to explore.

Thinking and reasoning skills are enhanced when mathematics manipulatives are available in the classroom. Using manipulatives, students, as well as teachers, become more aware of their own questions and thought processes. In place of rote memorization, one can hear the question "why" being asked over and over again.

When a manipulative is first introduced, it is imperative that the students be given time for free exploration. Students should be encouraged to become familiar with the various manipulative pieces and to discover how they relate to one another. As students freely explore the manipulatives, the teacher moves around the room observing and expressing interest in the results of the explorations.

Next, begin a guided exploration activity that the class can do as a whole while the teacher demonstrates using the overhead projector and overhead manipulatives. Last, divide the class into cooperative groups to complete the manipulative activity. This routine can be adapted to suit the needs of individual classrooms.

Manipulatives are often used in elementary school mathematics are
  1. base 10 blocks
  2. counters (one-color and two-color, various shapes)
  3. attribute shapes
  4. geoboards
  5. color pieces
  6. centimeter strips
  7. snap cubes
  8. color cubes
  9. tangrams
  10. fraction pieces
  11. decimal pieces
  12. unifix cubes
  13. linkits
  14. attrilinks
  15. calculators

Using manipulatives in the elementary classroom produces curiosity. Students become aware of their thought processes and of multiple answers instead of the first available solution. With practice, higher order-thinking skills begin to guide the manipulative activities.

When used correctly, manipulatives provide the students with mathematical power. Manipulatives can be used to clarify problem statements, generate questions for investigation, formulate concepts, promote discovery of mathematical facts, and challenge students to become totally involved in mathematics.

4

Number Theory

UNDERSTANDING NUMBER THEORY

1. Factors
2. Divisibility
3. Primes and Composites
4. Common Factors and Multiples

▼ PROBLEM CHALLENGE: Life on the Farm

Solve this problem in more than one way:

A farmer has chickens and pigs. One day he counts 120 legs and 40 heads. How many pigs and how many chickens does the farmer have?

HANDS-ON MATHEMATICS ACTIVITIES

The following activities are provided to enhance your understanding of number theory.

Factors

✳ **Key Ideas:**   The term *factor* is used to describe the two parts of a multiplication computation such as 3 x 6 = 18. The 3 and the 6 are called *factors*, while the 18 is called the *product*.

☞ **Activity 1: Factors**

Purpose: To gain an understanding of factors.
Materials: Activity Card 1.16 — Counters

In the previous chapter we used counters to make array models for multiplication. The number of rows represented one factor, and the number of columns represented the second factor. The product was the total number of counters in the array. Some products can be represented with many different arrays, indicating that the number has many factors.

❑   Example: What are the factors of 24?

Place 24 counters in front of you. Make as many different arrays as you can.

xxxxxxxxxxxxxxxxxxxxxxxx

1 x 24 = 24

xxxxxxxxxxxx   xxxxxxx   xxxxx
xxxxxxxxxxxx   xxxxxxx   xxxxx
                       xxxxxxx   xxxxx
                                          xxxxx

2 x 12 = 24   3 x 8 = 24   4 x 6 = 24

The numbers 2, 3, 4, 6, 8, and 12 are factors of 24.

❑   Use counters to make as many rectangular arrays as you can for each number:

a. 18   b. 28   c. 36   d. 48

☞ **Activity 2: Odd and Even Numbers**

Purpose: To gain an understanding of odd and even numbers.
Materials: Activity Card 1.16 — Counters

❑   Use the counters to make rectangular arrays, each consisting of two rows, to represent each of the following numbers: 3, 4, 5, 6, 7, and 8.

1.   What patterns do you find?
2.   Which numbers are even?
3.   Define even and odd numbers using counters.
4.   Define even and odd numbers using the term *factor*.

☞ **Activity 3: Square Numbers**

Purpose: To gain an understanding of square numbers.
Materials: Activity Card 1.16 — Counters

❑   Use counters to make as many rectangular arrays as you can for each number: 1, 4, 9, 25, 36, 49, and 64.

1.   How many factors does each number have?
2.   What do the rectangular arrays have in common?
3.   Why are these numbers called square numbers?

✎ Journal

What did you find most challenging about factors, odd and even numbers, and square numbers?

How would you describe square numbers to your younger brother or a friend?

Divisibility

Key Ideas: There are many useful patterns to sets of numbers. The following patterns are helpful for determining whether or not a number is divisible by a smaller number.

☛ **Activity 4: Numbers Divisible by 2**

Purpose: To gain an understanding of the divisibility rule for 2.
Materials: Activity Card 4.4 — Multiplication Tables

Observe the multiplication card for the "two times" table.

$$2 \times 0 = 0$$
$$2 \times 1 = 2$$
$$2 \times 2 = 4$$
$$2 \times 3 = 6$$
$$2 \times 4 = 8$$
$$2 \times 5 = 10$$
$$2 \times 6 = 12$$
$$2 \times 7 = 14$$
$$2 \times 8 = 16$$
$$2 \times 9 = 18$$

❑ 1. List all the patterns that you can.

2. What kind of number is each product?

3. What number always occurs in the ones place?

4. How can you determine if a number is divisible by 2?

☛ **Activity 5: Numbers Divisible by 5**

Purpose: To gain an understanding of the divisibility rule for 5.
Materials: Activity Card 4.4 — Multiplication Tables

Observe the multiplication card for the "five times" table.

5 x 0 = 0	5 x 5 = 25
5 x 1 = 5	5 x 6 = 30
5 x 2 = 10	5 x 7 = 35
5 x 3 = 15	5 x 8 = 40
5 x 4 = 20	5 x 9 = 45

❏ 1. List all the patterns that you can.

2. What numbers always occur in the ones place?

3. How can you determine if a number is divisible by 5?

☛ **Activity 6: Numbers Divisible by 10**

Purpose: To gain an understanding of the divisibility rule for 10.
Materials: Activity Card 4.4 — Multiplication Tables

Observe the multiplication card for the "ten times" table.

10 x 0 = 0	10 x 5 = 50
10 x 1 = 10	10 x 6 = 60
10 x 2 = 20	10 x 7 = 70
10 x 3 = 30	10 x 8 = 80
10 x 4 = 40	10 x 9 = 90

❏ 1. List all the patterns that you can.

2. What number always occurs in the ones place?

3. How can you determine if a number is divisible by 10?

4. Why do the 2 and 5 divisibility rules also work for the multiples of 10?

☞ **Activity 7: Numbers Divisible by 9**

Purpose: To gain an understanding of the divisibility rule for 9.
Materials: Activity Card 4.4 — Multiplication Tables

Observe the multiplication card for the "nine times" table.

$9 \times 0 = 0$ $9 \times 5 = 45$
$9 \times 1 = 9$ $9 \times 6 = 54$
$9 \times 2 = 18$ $9 \times 7 = 63$
$9 \times 3 = 27$ $9 \times 8 = 72$
$9 \times 4 = 36$ $9 \times 9 = 81$

The patterns for the multiples of 9 are a little more difficult than the patterns for the multiples of 2, 5, and 10. Try adding the digits of each factor.

❑   1.   List all the patterns that you can.

2.   What is the sum of the digits of each product?

3.   How can you determine if a number is divisible by 9?

☞ **Activity 8: Numbers Divisible by 3**

Purpose: To gain an understanding of the divisibility rule for 3.
Materials: Activity Card 4.4 — Multiplication Tables

Observe the multiplication card for the "three times" table.

$3 \times 0 = 0$ $3 \times 5 = 15$
$3 \times 1 = 3$ $3 \times 6 = 18$
$3 \times 2 = 6$ $3 \times 7 = 21$
$3 \times 3 = 9$ $3 \times 8 = 24$
$3 \times 4 = 12$ $3 \times 9 = 27$

❑   1.   List all the patterns that you can.

2.   What is the sum of the digits of each product?

3.   How can you determine if a number is divisible by 3?

☛   **Activity 9: Numbers Divisible by 6**

Purpose: To gain an understanding of the divisibility rule for 6.
Materials: Activity Card 4.4 — Multiplication Tables

Observe the multiplication card for the "six times" table.

6 x 0 = 0	6 x 5 = 30
6 x 1 = 6	6 x 6 = 36
6 x 2 = 12	6 x 7 = 42
6 x 3 = 18	6 x 8 = 48
6 x 4 = 24	6 x 9 = 54

❑   1. List all the patterns that you can.

2. What is the sum of the digits of each product?

3. How can you determine if a number is divisible by 6? (What two previous divisibility rules apply?)

✎ **Journal**

Write a riddle about the divisibility rules.

Create a divisibility rule for 12.

Primes and Composites

✳ Key Ideas: Whole numbers greater than 1 can be divided into two subsets, primes and composites. Understanding primes and composites will be useful in our continued study of mathematics.

☞ **Activity 10:   Sieve of Eratosthenes**

Purpose: To gain an understanding of odd and even numbers.
Materials: Activity Card 4.10 — Hundreds Chart

You may have seen the Sieve of Eratosthenes in a text. Follow the directions below to find all prime numbers less than or equal to 100.

   a.   Use the 100's chart.
   b.   Cross out 1.
   c.   Circle 2. Use the divisibility rule for 2 to cross out all numbers divisible by 2.
   d.   Circle 3. Use the divisibility rule for 3 to cross out all numbers divisible by 3.
   e.   Circle 5. Use the divisibility rule for 5 to cross out all numbers divisible by 5.
   f.   Circle the smallest number not yet crossed out. Count by that number and cross out all numbers not already crossed out.
   g.   Repeat *step f* until there are no more numbers to cross out.

   The circled numbers are prime.

☐   1.   As you may know, the numbers 2, 3, 5, and 7 are prime. How can you use the prime number test to know that you should stop at *step f* above?

   2.   At first glance, 51 may look like a prime number. What divisibility rule lets you know that 51 is not prime?

☛   **Activity 11:   Factor Trees**

Purpose: To understand the fundamental theorem of arithmetic.

The fundamental theorem of arithmetic states that every composite number has exactly one prime factorization. The factor-tree method is one way to demonstrate this theorem. In the factor-tree method we begin with a number and find any 2 factors. Then we continue finding prime factors until all factors are prime.

Factor Trees

Example: Find the prime factorization of 24.

Start with 24 and find any 2 factors. Then continue finding prime factors for these factors until all factors are prime.

1st way	2nd way	3rd way
24	24	24
2 x 12	3 x 8	4 x 6
2 x 2 x 6	3 x 2 x 4	2 x 2 x 6
2 x 2 x 2 x 3	3 x 2 x 2 x 2	2 x 2 x 2 x 3

The result $24 = 2^3 \times 3$ (2 x 2 x 2 x 3) is the prime factorization of 24.

There are usually several ways of forming the factor tree, but the end result will always be the same prime factors.

❑   Find the prime factorization of the following numbers using the factor tree method:
        a. 36   b. 54   c. 81   d. 100

 # Journal

How do you think factor trees received their name?

If you could suggest another name for factor trees, what would it be?

Common Factors and Multiples

> ✳ **Key Ideas:** Some of the concepts in this chapter on number theory are useful for our further study of mathematics. Activities involving greatest common factor and least common multiple are useful for developing readiness concepts for fractions. The methods used in activities 12 and 13 are relatively less abstract and easy to understand. They are the first methods presented to elementary school students and work well with small numbers. The methods are useful for elementary school fractions, which usually involve small numbers.

☞ **Activity 12:   Greatest Common Factor**

Purpose: To gain an understanding of the greatest common factor.

The greatest common factor of two numbers is useful when simplifying fractions.

Example: Simplify the following fraction: $\dfrac{12}{18}$

Use the divisibility rules to determine a factor list of each number (the numerator and denominator) in the fraction.

Factors of 12	Factors of 18
1, 2, 3, **6**, 12	1, 2, 3, **6**, 9, 18

First, list the common factors. Determine the greatest common factor (6). The fraction can be simplified by dividing both the numerator and denominator by 6.

$$\frac{12}{18} = \frac{2}{3}$$

❑   Use factor lists to find the greatest common factor of the following pairs of numbers:

a. (14, 42)   b. (18, 81)   c. (18, 24)   d. (15, 27)

☞ **Activity 13:   Least Common Multiple**

Purpose: To gain an understanding of least common multiple.
Materials: Activity Card 3.4 — Centimeter Strips
                        Activity Card 4.13 — Centimeter Ruler

The least common multiple of two numbers is useful when finding a common denominator in order to add or subtract two fractions.

Example: What is the least common multiple of 4 and 6?

Use the centimeter strips and centimeter rule. Lay five or six 4-centimeter strips in a train alongside the centimeter ruler. Note the multiples of 4 along the centimeter ruler (4, 8, 12, 16, 20, etc.) at the end of each 4-centimeter strip.

Now lay four 6-centimeter strips alongside the 4-centimeter strips already down. Note the multiples of 6 along the centimeter ruler (6, 12, 18, 24, 30, etc.) at the end of each 6-centimeter strip.

The common multiples are 12 and 24. The least common multiple, the number where a 4-centimeter strip and a 6-centimeter strip end, is 12.

4	8	12	16	20	24
6		12		18	24

❑   Use centimeter strips to find the common multiples for the following sets of numbers and then determine the least common multiple.

        a. 3, 7   b. 2, 5   c. 5, 6   d. 6, 8

 Journal _____

How would explain the difference between the greatest common factor and the least common multiple?

If you were teaching these two concepts to a new class member, which would be easier to explain? Why?

✈ EXESIONS ✈

✳ **Key Ideas:** In Extensions, you may revisit some of the concepts and activities presented in this chapter. The following activities allow you to explore some ideas a little further. Sections include Mental Computation, Calculators, Critical Thinking, Alternative Assessment, and Mathematics for the 21st Century.

✈ Mental Computation ✈

☛ **Activity 14: Simplifying Fractions**

Purpose: To practice using divisibility rules.

❏ Simplify each fraction using the divisibility rules:

a. $\dfrac{20}{30} =$ b. $\dfrac{15}{35} =$ c. $\dfrac{18}{33} =$ d. $\dfrac{18}{42} =$ e. $\dfrac{27}{72} =$

☛ **Activity 15: Finding Patterns**

Purpose: To find a simple way to multiply by 5.

❏ Observe the following multiplication sentences:

$$
\begin{array}{ll}
5 \times 4 \ \ = 20 & 5 \times \ 44 = 220 \\
5 \times 6 \ \ = 30 & 5 \times \ 64 = 320 \\
5 \times 8 \ \ = 40 & 5 \times \ 86 = 430 \\
5 \times 10 = 50 & 5 \times \ 98 = 490 \\
5 \times 12 = 60 & 5 \times 124 = 620
\end{array}
$$

❏ 1. List all the patterns you see.
   2. What kind of number is each product?
   3. What number is always in the ones place of the product?
   4. How are the digits to the left of the 0 in the product related to the factor being multiplied by 5?
   5. How can you mentally multiply an even number by 5?
   6. Extend your rule for odd numbers.

✈ Calculators ✈

☞ **Activity 16:   Factors and Prime Numbers**

Purpose: To explore factors using a calculator.
Materials: Calculator

❑   1. Use your calculator, the divisibility rules, and the prime factor rule to determine all the factors of the following numbers:

   a. 360   b. 720   c. 1500   d. 2000   e. 2500

   2. Use your calculator and divisibility rules to determine which of the following numbers are prime:

   a. 41   b. 51   c. 71   d. 741   e. 799

   f. 979   g. 997   h. 1001   i. 1003   j. 1007

✈ Critical Thinking ✈

☞ **Activity 17:   More Patterns**

Purpose: To find patterns useful for multiplying by 9.

   Observe the multiplication card for the "nine times" table.

9 x 0 = 0	9 x 5 = 45
9 x 1 = 9	9 x 6 = 54
9 x 2 = 18	9 x 7 = 63
9 x 3 = 27	9 x 8 = 72
9 x 4 = 36	9 x 9 = 81

❑   1. What is the relationship between the digit in the ones place of the product and the factor being multiplied by 9?

   2. What is the sum of the digits in the product?

   3. Use these two patterns to ascertain how children might determine the multiplication facts for nines.

☞   **Activity 18:   Still More Patterns**

Purpose: To find patterns useful for multiplying by 11.

❑   Observe the multiplication card for the "eleven times" table.

$$11 \times 0 = \ 0 \qquad\qquad 11 \times 5 = 55$$
$$11 \times 1 = 11 \qquad\qquad 11 \times 6 = 66$$
$$11 \times 2 = 22 \qquad\qquad 11 \times 7 = 77$$
$$11 \times 3 = 33 \qquad\qquad 11 \times 8 = 88$$
$$11 \times 4 = 44 \qquad\qquad 11 \times 9 = 99$$

1. What is the pattern for multiplying a single digit by 11?
2. How can you mentally multiply a single digit by 11?

❑   Observe the multiplication card for the "eleven times" table.

$$11 \times 12 = 132 \qquad\qquad 11 \times 65 = 715$$
$$11 \times 18 = 198 \qquad\qquad 11 \times 76 = 836$$
$$11 \times 25 = 275 \qquad\qquad 11 \times 88 = 968$$
$$11 \times 36 = 396 \qquad\qquad 11 \times 47 = 517$$
$$11 \times 45 = 495 \qquad\qquad 11 \times 94 = 1014$$

1. What is the pattern for the first and last digits of the product and the factor being multiplied by 11?

2. What is the pattern for the number in the tens place of the product and the numbers in the hundreds and ones places?

3. How can you mentally multiply a 2-digit number by 11?

❑   Observe the multiplication card for the "eleven times" table.

$$11 \times 19 = 209 \qquad\qquad 11 \times 46 = 506$$
$$11 \times 28 = 308 \qquad\qquad 11 \times 55 = 605$$
$$11 \times 37 = 407 \qquad\qquad 11 \times 64 = 704$$

1. What is the pattern for multiplying these 2-digit numbers by 11?

2. Write a divisibility rule or rules for determining if a number is divisible by 11.

✦ Alternative Assessment ✦

Performance Assessment

Part II

In working on Performance Assessment, it is best to begin by assessing one single important idea. On a clipboard containing self-stick labels, observations can be recorded stating how students are implementing the idea to be assessed.

When observing groups of students solving the chickens and pigs problem (see the Problem Challenge at the beginning of this chapter), some questions might be:

Is the student...

1. exhibiting creativity?

2. participating actively as a group member?

3. thorough in the work produced?

4. cooperative?

5. flexible?

6. willing to listen to new ideas?

7. able to explain the strategies used?

8. able to collect and organize the necessary data?

9. able to understand, define, and clarify the problem?

10. able to formulate a logical conclusion?

Each question would be the focus of one day's observations and assessment. A performance assessment record may be kept on individuals or on the group as a whole.

✈ Mathematics for the 21st Century ✈

Cooperative Grouping

Cooperative grouping occurs when students work in groups or teams of two to four on an activity, game, or project assigned by the teacher for a designated period of time. Cooperative grouping is the step in between individualization and total class teaching. Students, as well as teachers, usually find that they like learning better when they participate in a small group.

Begin by first selecting an activity or series of activities which coordinate with the current mathematics unit. Each chapter has cooperative activities which you may implement. Next, decide on a time frame. It is recommended that cooperative grouping be tried in pairs first for a fifteen to thirty minute period three days per week. Time and frequency may be increased gradually. Later, two pairs of students may be combined to make a group of four.

It is best to practice the cooperative grouping activity yourself before introducing it to the class. On the first day, select one group of four students to model the cooperative grouping rules and procedures for the forthcoming activity. Be certain to allow time for questions. You may want to have the one group repeat the procedure a second time before starting the entire class on the same activity. This is an excellent opportunity for students to practice their problem-solving strategies.

For the initial introduction and first set of activities, it is best for the teacher to select the groups. Activities often progress favorably when students begin working in pairs and progress to groups of four after a few trial sessions. You select the groups of four before you begin. Each group could be composed of one strong student, two average students , and one struggling student. In creating groups, notify the children that the groups will change every three weeks. After the first three weeks, use random order to select groups and explain the procedure to the students. The procedure begins with your passing each student one 3 by 5 card which is taken from a lunch bag. The bag contains four cards of each represented color. For 32 students, you will need four cards of eight different colors in the bag. The color of the card selected designates the group. Later, students can be grouped by drawing numbers out of a hat, by birthdays, alphabetical order, or by using geometric shapes.

Classroom rules for cooperative grouping should be clearly discussed and understood before groups begin to work together actively. Rules might include the following:

1. Each student is responsible for his/her own behavior;
2. Each group member is unique and will be expected to use his/her own unique qualities and abilities for the benefit of the group;
3. When the group has a question for the teacher, all members of the group must agree on the question and all hands are to be raised.

First, review the rules for cooperative grouping. Then proceed with modeling the activity, followed by a discussion about an acceptable noise level. In order to establish an "acceptable noise level", ask each group member to speak together with his/her group quietly. Listen for a few minutes and then say, "That sounds acceptable to me. However, if it gets louder, I will turn the lights off. (Turn the lights off, then on again.) If the lights are turned off a second time (turn the lights off and on again), this activity will cease immediately." Following through on the "approved noise level" is critical for the success of cooperative grouping. As time passes, students may become insensitive to the use of the signal for "It is too noisy." Signals may be changed each month or each grading period. Begin with the lights out, then clap your hands, ring a bell, blow a whistle, or play the harmonica to signal unacceptable noise levels.

When you are enthusiastic about the activity and you follow the previous suggestions presented, the students stay "on task." Once you and the class have practiced the procedure three or four times, the students, as a general rule, are eager to begin the cooperative activity and to continue once they have started. Setting the ground rules, being enthusiastic, and moving the activity at an appropriate pace are guidelines that lead to success.

In order to reestablish control after a cooperative grouping activity, it is best to give a two-minute warning immediately prior to cleanup time. This allows students to prepare for the completion of the activity period. Again, use the timer for the two-minute cleanup and then have a specific way for them to show they are ready for the next subject. This can be sitting quietly with folded hands, or with the right hand raised, or with a book open to a certain page. The signal may be changed monthly or you may keep it the same throughout. When students know the expectations for an activity and have had an opportunity to practice the proper procedures, cooperative grouping becomes a positive activity.

Integers

▼ PROBLEM CHALLENGE: Integer Magic Square

A magic square is a square array of numbers in which the sums of all rows and columns (horizontal, vertical, and diagonal) are always identical. Using the numbers below, turn the grid into a magic square. There may be more than one possible solution.

–10, –8, –6, –4, 0, 2, 4, 6

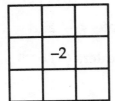

HANDS-ON MATHEMATICS ACTIVITIES

The following activities are provided to enhance your understanding of positive and negative numbers.

Addition and Subtraction of Integers

> ✳ **Key Ideas:** Integers are defined as the set of positive and negative whole numbers: {... ⁻5, ⁻4, ⁻3, ⁻2, ⁻1, 0, +1, +2, +3, +4, +5 ...}. Integers are seen as an extension of whole numbers to include their negative values. An integer involves both magnitude and direction (positive or negative). Mathematics involving integers is more abstract than whole-number mathematics because of the inclusion of negative numbers. Elementary students need experiences involving integers. They encounter integers to record negative temperatures, football players lose yards in an attempt to pass, and building elevators go several floors below ground.

☛ **Activity 1: Integer Models**

Purpose: To build models of positive and negative integers.
Materials: Activity Card 1.16 — Counters

The following sets represent ⁺4 and ⁻5. Blue counters represent positive integers, and red counters represent negative integers. If there are 4 blue and 5 red counters, the four of each color cancel each other leaving 1 red. The equation to represent this illustration is ⁺4 + ⁻5 = ⁻1

            Black   Red

Counters can also be modeled in different ways to show ⁻5.

⊙ ⊙ ∅ ✦   7 red counters (–) and

⊙ ⊙ ⊙ ∅ ✦   2 blue counters (+) = ⁻5

❑   Cancel the appropriate counters.

● ● ● ● ⊙ ⊙   9 red counters (–) and

⊙ ⊙ ⊙ ⊙ ⊙ ⊙   4 blue counters (+) = ⁻5

❑   Using counters, make at least two different models for each given integer:

        a. ⁻3   b. ⁺7   c. ⁻6   d. ⁻9

☞ ### Activity 2: Addition of Integers

Purpose: To provide practice in visualizing the addition of integers.

The number-line model is useful for integer addition. The arrow is drawn to the right to indicate a positive integer and drawn to the left to indicate a negative integer.

$^+3$ + $^-4$ is illustrated by drawing an arrow 3 spaces to the right and then drawing one 4 spaces to the left. The result is $^-1$.

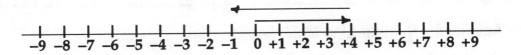

❑   Draw a number line indicating $^+3$ + $^+5$ and $^+7$ + $^-9$.

☞ ### Activity 3: Models for Subtraction

Purpose: To encourage the student to visualize the subtraction of integers.

The number-line model continues to be useful for integer subtraction. For subtraction, the arrow starts at 0 and is drawn to the right for positive integers. The subtraction sign indicates an arrow drawn to the left for positive integers, but drawn to the right when when subtracting negative integers. Observe the illustrations below.

$7 - 2 = 5$

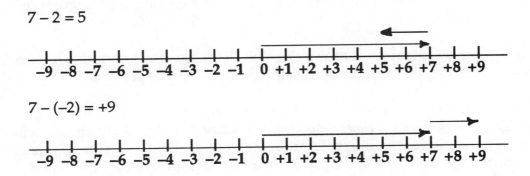

$7 - (-2) = +9$

❑   Draw a number line indicating $^-3 - (^-4)$ and $6 - (^-3)$.

Multiplication of Integers

Key Ideas: The familiar rule for the multiplication of integers, *a negative number times a negative number is positive*, can be illustrated by using a vertical number line. A vertical number line can help clarify the concept of multiplication of integers and help to illustrate the products of positive and negative integers.

Rules of signs for multiplication:

1. Positive times negative equals negative.
2. Negative times positive equals negative.
3. Negative times negative equals positive.

☛ **Activity 4: Number-Line Multiplication**

Purpose: To visually illustrate multiplication of integers.
Materials: Activity Card 5.4 — Thermometer and Vertical Number Line

The number-line model for multiplication of integers is similar to the addition model (multiplication is repeated addition). The example $3 \times -2 = -6$ is illustrated below. The 3 indicates the number of moves and the -2 indicates the length of each arrow drawn to the left.

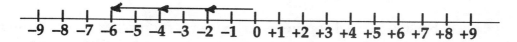

Compute the following temperatures using the vertical number line.

1. The temperature in Maine is now 0 degrees. What will the temperature be 3 hours from now if the temperature is decreasing 3 degrees per hour?

2. The temperature is now 0 degrees. What was the temperature 5 hours ago if it has been dropping steadily at 2 degrees per hour?

The rule, *a negative times a negative is positive*, is more easily shown with a pattern. Notice the first column in the example below. As the first factor decreases from 3 to 0, the products increase from -6 to 0. The second column continues the pattern.

$$3 \times -2 = -6 \qquad\qquad -1 \times -2 = +2$$
$$2 \times -2 = -4 \qquad\qquad -2 \times -2 = +4$$
$$1 \times -2 = -2 \qquad\qquad -3 \times -2 = +6$$
$$0 \times -2 = 0$$

DIVISION OF INTEGERS

✳ **Key Ideas:** Blue and red counters are used to illustrate the concept of division for negative and positive integers. To show (⁻10) divided by (⁻2), we begin with 10 red counters and subtract or measure off as many groups of 2 red counters as possible. The conclusion is 5 groups of 2, therefore (⁻10) ÷ (⁻2) = 5. This illustrates the measurement or repeated subtraction concept of division.

```
1 | 2 | 3 | 4 | 5
0 | 0 | 0 | 0 | 0
0 | 0 | 0 | 0 | 0
```

Real-life interpretation: If the cost of office doughnuts is $10, it can be shared among 5 people, with each person paying $2.

Rules of signs for division:

1. Positive divided by negative equals negative.
2. Negative divided by positive equals negative.
3. Negative divided by negative equals positive.

☞ **Activity 5: Division of Integers**

Purpose: To illustrate the concept of division of integers.

The rule, *negative divided by negative equals positive*, is more easily shown with a pattern. Notice the left-hand examples below. As the first column decreases from 6 to 0 the solutions increase from –3 to 0. The right-hand examples continue the pattern.

$$6 \div -2 = -3 \qquad\qquad -2 \div -2 = +1$$
$$4 \div -2 = -2 \qquad\qquad -4 \div -2 = +2$$
$$2 \div -2 = -1 \qquad\qquad -6 \div -2 = +3$$
$$0 \div -2 = 0$$

Illustrate each computation using a pattern.

a) (⁻10) divided by (⁻5) =

b) (⁻9) divided by 3 =

Properties of Integer Operations

 Key Ideas: Integer operations contain the same properties as whole numbers (see chapter 3). Commutative, associative, distributive, and identity properties remain the same in integer operations as in whole-number operations.

Properties of Integer Operations:

1. *Closure property for addition and multiplication:* Any two integers added or multiplied together equal an integer.

2. *Commutative property or addition and multiplication:* For any two integers, the order of addition or multiplication does not affect the sum or the product.

3. *Associative property for addition and multiplication:* For any integers a, b, and c, (a + b) + c = a + (b + c) and (ab)c = a(bc).

4. *Identity property for addition and multiplication:* For integers, the addition identity is 0 and the multiplication identity is 1. For any integer a: a + 0 = 0 + a = a; and a x 1 = 1 x a = a.

5. *Distributive property:* Integer multiplication is distributive over addition and subtraction. For any integers a, b, and c: a(b + c) = ab + ac and a (b - c) = ab − ac.

The set of integer operations has two properties, in addition to those above, which are <u>not</u> shared with whole numbers.

6. *Additive inverse property:* For every integer, there is an additive inverse. For example: the (⁺3) + (⁻3) = 0; therefore, the additive inverse of ⁺ 3 is ⁻3 and vice versa. Another way to phrase this is that ⁺3 and ⁻3 are additive inverses because ⁻3 and ⁺3 = 0.

7. *Closure property for integer subtraction:* For any two integers a and b, a − b is a unique integer. Integer subtraction is closed.

☞ **Activity 6: Integer Concentration**

Purpose: To provide an understanding of positive and negative integers.
Materials: Two identical sets of 3 by 5 cards on which are written the negative and positive integers ranging from –10 to 10.

❑   The goal of the game is to finish with the largest number of matching cards in front of you. The game is appropriate for two players.

Directions:
The cards are shuffled and placed face down on the floor or table. The first player selects two cards and reads their values aloud. If the two cards match, the player may place them in a pile. If the two cards do not match, the player returns the cards to their respective places and tries to remember their exact location for future plays. Play continues until all cards are placed in front of one player or the other. The cards are counted, and the player with the most cards wins.

☞ **Activity 7: Number-Line Game**

Purpose: To provide an understanding of positive and negative integers.
Materials: Activity Card 3.22 — Number Cubes
               Activity Card 5.4 — Vertical Number Line
               Two Game Markers

❑   The goal of this game is to be the first player to reach 10 or –10. Note: the blue number cube represents positive integers and the red number cube represents negative integers. The game is suitable for two players.

Directions:
Each player starts off with her marker resting on the zero of the number line. The players roll the number cube to see who will be the first player, with the higher number going first. The first player rolls the number cubes and adds the positive integer on the blue number cube to the negative number which is shown on the red number cube. This sum indicates the type of move to be made on the number line. If the sum is negative, the player moves to the bottom of the vertical line. If positive, the move is made to the top of the vertical line. If by chance the sum is zero, the player loses her turn and does not move. The first player to reach +10 or –10 is the winner.

Journal

Why are the properties of integers useful to understand?

How do you feel about using integers now?

What is important about the use of integers?

How can this be applied in your life?

Summarize and demonstrate with counters the sum of a negative and positive number.

Summarize and demonstrate with counters the difference of a negative and positive number.

✈ EXTENSIONS ✈

Key Ideas: In Extensions, you may revisit some of the concepts and activities presented in this chapter. The following activities allow you to explore some ideas a little further. Sections include Mental Computation, Calculators, Critical Thinking, Alternative Assessment, and Mathematics for the 21st Century.

✈ Mental Computation ✈

☞ **Activity 8: Integer Computations**

Purpose: To provide an understanding of computing with integers.

The acquisition of number sense is critical in elementary school mathematics. Mental computation skills are extended from whole numbers to include integers as well. Mental mathematics can encourage students to understand and use the properties of integers and to discover, on their own, the computational shortcuts that are available to them.

❑   Try these computations in your head:

a. $40 + (^-24) + (^-60) =$ b. $(^-4) \times 20 \times (^-3) =$

There are numerous solutions to these problems. One solution for each problem is illustrated below:

a. $40 + (^-24) + (^-60) =$ $^+40 + (^-60) = ^-20$
                                 $^-20 + (^-24) = ^-44$

b. $(^-4) \times 20 \times (^-3) =$ $^-4 \times (^-3) = 12$
                                        $12 \times 20 = 240$

❑   Complete the following computation mentally using a substitution that makes sense to you.

c. $^-6 \times 18 =$

One possible solution:

c. $^-6 \times 18 = ^-6 \times (20 + ^-2)$ and with the distributive property this equals

$^-120 + 12 = ^-108.$

✈ Calculators ✈

☞ **Activity 9: Integers and the Calculator**

Purpose: To provide an understanding of computing with integers.
Materials: Calculator

The calculator change-of-sign key (+/−) is useful when subtracting negative integers.

If you want to compute (⁻356) – (⁻104), for example, you would use the following steps:

Step	Procedure	Display
1	press 356 and +/− Key	−356
2	press −Key	−356
3	press 104 and +/−Key	−104
4	press =	−252

❑   Now try these:

a)   (⁻789) – (298) =

Step 1:

Step 2:

Step 3:

Step 4:

b)   (⁻598) + (⁻345) =

Step 1:

Step 2:

Step 3:

Step 4:

✈ Critical Thinking ✈

☞ **Activity 10:   Critical Thinking with Integers**

Purpose: To provide an understanding of positive and negative integers.

A satisfactory understanding of the concept of integers is an important component of elementary school mathematics. As students practice with the concept and application of integers, their critical-thinking skills will be enhanced.

Quality questioning techniques strongly promote the learning of this concept. Some questions you might ask are the following:

- What is meant by the term *integer*?

- How are integers different from whole numbers?

- Why do we study integers?

- When will you be able to use integers in your everyday lives?

- Was there any confusion about solving problems with integers?

- How did you deal with this confusion?

- What additional questions would you like to ask about integers?

✈ Alternative Assessment ✈

Open-Ended Questions

Open-ended questions are those in which the students are presented with a situation and are asked to write out (or communicate) their solution to that situation. Open-ended questions may be as simple as asking a student to explain his or her work to the teacher. Open-ended questions are a valid technique for assessment in the elementary mathematics classroom.

One example of an open-ended question would be to present the student with a copy of a graph and ask what interpretation can be reached while reading the graph. Heuristic problems, those for which there is no obvious solution, are excellent examples for implementing open-ended questions.

The advantages of open-ended questions are numerous. The teacher who uses this strategy for assessment has multiple opportunities to observe and evaluate students. Students quickly learn that there are many possible ways to reach an appropriate response and that their thinking is stretched. The teacher can also quickly learn whether the students involved are able to following:

- understand the critical points of the situation;

- interpret the information;

- organize the information;

- express their ideas clearly on paper;

- draw accurate conclusions.

A sample open-ended question:
Jim is aware that half of the students in his fifth grade-class are on the Honor Roll. He also knows that half of the class is active in the Student Council. Jim concludes that this adds up to 100%; therefore every student in his class is either on the Honor Roll or active in Student Council. Can you explain (using pictures and writing) why Jim's idea is incorrect?

Illustration:

Comments:

✈ Mathematics for the 21st Century ✈

Mathematics as Communication

Throughout history, elementary mathematics classrooms have focused on whether or not students could reach the correct answer or conclusion. How well they communicated their thought processes and ideas was not a consideration. Yet, the way in which a student presents his/her own work is an essential part of communication to the teacher and to peers. Oral and written communication should play a vital part in the elementary mathematics classroom and not be limited to language arts activities.

Mathematics is a language and students become powerful in their ability to communicate mathematical concepts as their facility with the language of mathematics increases.

First, it is recommended that elementary mathematics programs include opportunities for students to become familiar with mathematical terminology, be able to use that terminology, and improve their communication skills. Elementary mathematics classes should provide students with the opportunity to increase their proficiency with the use of mathematical vocabulary, notations, and symbols to describe and clearly explain their mathematical ideas and solutions.

Second, in addition to mathematical vocabulary development, students need to be able to communicate information to their peers and teachers by way of graphs, charts, tables, and models. This type of visual presentation can be a powerful conveyor of information to the audience. Students should be able to understand, construct, and present this type of information in a problem-solving situation frequently and with ease.

Third, students should be able to present reports and projects, whether group or individual, with a clarity of purpose that enables the audience to easily understand the mathematical concepts. Thoughts should be organized, coherent, and provide enough detailed information for the audience to clearly follow the train of thought of the presenter or presenters.

These three communication skills are interwoven and interrelated. The elementary mathematics teacher should look for ways to creatively assess the development of all three skills in the students.

When the elementary mathematics student is communicating with ease, one realizes that the issue at hand is not "What is the answer?" but "What does it mean, how did we get there, and does it make sense?"

6

Rational Numbers

UNDERSTANDING RATIONAL NUMBERS

1. Rational Numbers
2. Addition and Subtraction of Rational Numbers
3. Multiplication and Division of Rational Numbers
4. Properties of Rational Numbers

▼ PROBLEM CHALLENGE: Four 4's

Using four 4's and any of the four operations (addition, subtraction, multiplication, and division), create at least one equation to equal each number from 1 to 20.

Example: Here are several equations equal to 1.

$$1 = 4 - 4 + 4 \div 4, \text{ or } 4 - 4 + \frac{4}{4}$$

$$1 = 44 \div 44, \text{ or } \frac{44}{44}$$

$$1 = (4 + 4) \div (4 + 4), \text{ or } \frac{4 + 4}{4 + 4}$$

$$4\frac{4}{4} - 4$$

HANDS-ON MATHEMATICS ACTIVITIES

The following activities are provided to enhance your understanding of rational numbers.

Rational Numbers

❋ **Key Ideas:**   Rational numbers, or fractions, are numbers such as $\frac{p}{q}$,
in which p and q are both whole numbers, and q is not equal to zero.
In the fraction $\frac{p}{q}$, p is the numerator, and q is the denominator. The
numerator indicates the total number of pieces that you have. The
denominator indicates the total number of pieces in the whole.
When the numerator is larger than the denominator, the fraction is
called an *improper fraction.*

☛ **Activity 1: Equivalent Fraction Strips**

Purpose: To promote the understanding of equivalent fractions.
Materials: Construction Paper
                       Scissors
                       Envelopes

Fractions can be seen as a whole divided into a given number of equal
pieces. To promote understanding of the concept of fractions, each student
will create a set of fraction strips. Five different colors of construction
paper (12 by 18) are used: red, blue, yellow, green, and purple. Cut each
color into 3 by 16 inch strips. Each person has five strips, one of each
color. Using the construction paper, let one long red piece represent one
whole. Write "one whole" in the center of the strip.

Now, fold the blue strip in half and cut. Label each piece "1/2" and place
the first and last initials of the student on each. The yellow piece is folded
in half and in half again to form four fourths. Label each piece with initials
and "1/4". Now fold the green piece to form eighths, label, and initial.
This is followed by the purple being cut into sixteenths, labeled and
initialed. At the conclusion, all pieces are placed in an envelope bearing
the name of the student.

❑   An introductory activity involving the fraction pieces can be used for a
       total classroom activity. Holding up the half, ask students to display on
       their desks how many eighths are equal to one half. Other sample
       questions follow:

              1. How many fourths are equal to one whole?
              2. How many sixteenths are equal to two-eighths?
              3. How many halves are equal to one whole?
              4. How many fourths are equal to one-half?

☞   **Activity 2. The Equivalent Concentration Game**

Purpose: To promote the understanding of equivalent fractions.
Materials: Forty 3 by 5 cards

The game is for two players. Write the following values on two sets of cards: $\frac{0}{0}, \frac{1}{2}, \frac{1}{4}, \frac{2}{4}, \frac{3}{4}, \frac{1}{8}, \frac{2}{8}, \frac{3}{8}, \frac{4}{8}, \frac{5}{8}, \frac{6}{8}, \frac{7}{8}, \frac{1}{16}, \frac{2}{16}, \frac{3}{16}, \frac{4}{16}, \frac{5}{16}, \frac{6}{16}, \frac{7}{16}, \frac{8}{16}$.
Shuffle the cards and place them face down on the table. One at a time, players pick up two cards, reading the cards aloud, and setting any matches aside. If the two cards selected do not match, they are replaced in the original position. The goal of the game is to have the larger number of matching pairs when all cards are claimed. A variation of the game can be played with a change of rules. Matching pairs may be either exactly alike or may be equivalent fractions, in which case the student reads the cards aloud, "four-eighths equals one-half."

☞   **Activity 3: Fraction Puzzles**

Purpose: To understand the concept of equivalent fractions.
Materials: Activity Card 3.9 — Color Pieces
               Activity Card 6.3 — One-inch Graph Paper

Each pair of students needs 40 color pieces, ten of each color, and a piece of one-inch graph paper. Ask students (working in partners) to build a rectangle that is $\frac{1}{2}$ blue and $\frac{1}{2}$ red.

a. Record the number of pieces used.
b. What pattern do you observe?

❑   Form each rectangle and record on the graph paper.

     a. $\frac{1}{2}$ yellow, $\frac{1}{4}$ green, $\frac{1}{4}$ blue

     b. $\frac{1}{2}$ yellow, $\frac{1}{4}$ green, $\frac{1}{8}$ blue, $\frac{1}{8}$ red

     c. $\frac{1}{8}$ yellow, $\frac{3}{8}$ green, $\frac{1}{2}$ blue

While students are attempting to solve the puzzles, the teacher may want to circulate and observe the use of strategies. Students can be asked to explain how they reached a particular conclusion. An extension of this game is to find a different solution for each problem.

Addition and Subtraction of Rational Numbers

✳   **Key Ideas:**   Elementary students first learn to add and subtract rational numbers with like denominators. When fractions do not have a common denominator, one must be found. When both fractions are written in terms of the same denominator, they may then be added or subtracted.

☞   **Activity 4: Fraction Add**

Purpose: To provide understanding of addition of fractions.
Material: Activity Card 6.4a — Fraction Pieces (or Fraction Strips)
Activity Card 6.4b — Fraction Cubes

❑   The game is designed for two players. The goal is to cover up the fraction piece representing the whole with other fraction pieces. Each player rolls a fraction cube and places the fraction piece of that value on the whole that is placed on the desk. Each player uses a separate whole and the first to cover it up with fraction pieces is declared the winner. If either player goes over, the other player is declared the winner.

Activity 5: Fraction Subtract

Purpose: To promote understanding of subtraction of fractions.
Materials: Activity Card 6.4a — Fraction Pieces
Activity Card 6.4b — Fraction Cubes

❑   This game is a variation of the game Fraction Add. Instead of throwing the fraction cube and adding fraction pieces until you get a total of one, players subtract the number indicated on the fraction cube from one whole. The goal of the game is to go from one whole down to zero.

✎ **Journal**

Explaining the logic of the answer is critical to the promotion of understanding. Write a brief explanation telling **why** each example is correct or incorrect.

a. $\dfrac{1}{2} + \dfrac{3}{6} = \dfrac{4}{8}$ b. $\dfrac{3}{4} + \dfrac{6}{8} = \dfrac{9}{12}$

c. $\dfrac{1}{6} + \dfrac{1}{2} = \dfrac{2}{8}$ d. $\dfrac{1}{3} + \dfrac{1}{3} = \dfrac{2}{3}$

Multiplication and Division of Rational Numbers

 Key Ideas: Students should first be able to understand the multiplication of a fraction and a whole number such as : $\frac{1}{2}$ x 6 = 3. After understanding this concept, students may progress to computations such as $\frac{1}{2}$ x $\frac{1}{4}$.

☞ **Activity 6: Fold and Multiply**

Purpose: To provide practice in the concept of multiplication of fractions.
Materials: Eight-inch Square Paper

Each student receives one piece of square paper. First, fold the paper in half and in half again. The paper is now divided into fourths. Without unfolding the fourths, fold the paper in the other direction, into thirds. You now have twelve twelfths.

The drawing illustrates $\frac{1}{3}$ x $\frac{1}{4}$ = $\frac{1}{12}$ by using the paper-folding method.

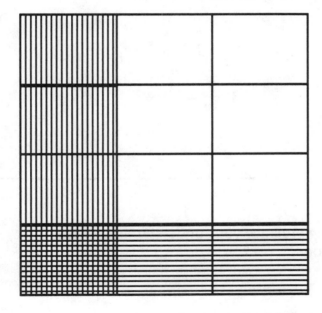

❑   Open up the paper and illustrate the following:

a. $\frac{1}{3}$ x $\frac{1}{4}$ = $\frac{1}{12}$ b. $\frac{1}{2}$ x $\frac{1}{3}$ = $\frac{1}{6}$

c. $\frac{1}{2}$ x $\frac{2}{3}$ = $\frac{2}{6}$ = $\frac{1}{3}$ d. $\frac{2}{3}$ x $\frac{3}{4}$ = $\frac{6}{12}$ = $\frac{1}{2}$

☞ **Activity 7: Manipulative Divide**

Purpose: To understand the concept of division of rational numbers.
Materials: Activity Card 6.7—Fraction Circles
                Activity Card 6.4a — Fraction Pieces

Using the fraction circles, illustrate $\frac{1}{2} \div \frac{1}{8}$.

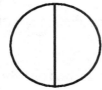 

Use the eighths as an overlay on top of the one-half to determine the solution for: $\frac{1}{2} \div \frac{1}{8} = 4$.

   Determine the following using the fraction pieces:

   a. $1 \div \frac{1}{2} =$ b. $\frac{1}{4} \div \frac{1}{8} =$

   c. $\frac{1}{2} \div \frac{1}{6} =$ d. $\frac{3}{16} \div \frac{1}{16} =$

✎ **Journal**

How does paper folding enhance your understanding of the multiplication of fractions?

Write a general statement for dividing fractions.

Read and explain your statement to a classmate.

Properties of Rational Numbers

✳ **Key Ideas: Properties of Rational Numbers**
Rational-number operations retain the same commutative, associative, identity, inverse, closure, and distributive properties as integer operations.
1. Addition, subtraction, and multiplication of rational numbers are all closed.
2. Both addition and multiplication are commutative.
3. Addition and multiplication are also associative.
4. The additive identity number is 0, and the multiplicative identity number is 1.
5. The additive inverse is: $(\frac{w}{x}) + (-\frac{w}{x}) = (-\frac{w}{x}) + (\frac{w}{x})$.
6. Multiplication is distributive over addition and distributive over subtraction with rational numbers.

☞ **Activity 8:   Additive Inverses**

Purpose: To understand the concept of additive inverses.
Materials: Activity Card 3.9 — Color Pieces

❑   Use the color pieces (blue for positive and red for negative) to illustrate the following additive inverses:

$$a. \quad \frac{1}{2} + \frac{-1}{2} = 0$$

$$b. \quad \frac{3}{4} + \frac{-3}{4} = 0$$

$$c. \quad \frac{3}{5} + \frac{-3}{5} = 0$$

☞ **Activity 9:   Multiplicative Inverses**

Purpose: To understand the concept of multiplicative inverses.
Materials: Activity Card 3.9—Color Pieces

❑   Using the color pieces illustrate the following:

$$a. \quad \frac{1}{2} \times \frac{2}{1} = 1 \qquad\qquad b. \quad \frac{3}{4} \times \frac{4}{3} = 1$$

$$c. \quad \frac{6}{8} \times \frac{8}{6} = 1 \qquad\qquad d. \quad \frac{4}{5} \times \frac{5}{4} = 1$$

✈ EXTENSIONS ✈

✳ **Key Ideas:**   In Extensions, you may revisit some of the concepts and activities presented in this chapter. The following activities allow you to explore some ideas a little further. Sections include Mental Computation, Calculators, Critical Thinking, Alternative Assessment, and Mathematics for the 21st Century.

✈ Mental Computation ✈

  Activity 10:   Fraction Computations

Purpose: To understand mental computation with fractions.

In providing practice in mental computation, students can be given oral problems to solve without the aid of paper and pencil. The teacher can begin with simple fractions and gradually progress to more difficult ones. After several weeks of practice, mental computation activities may be provided in a team format instead of an individual format.

❑   Some sample mental computations might include the following:

a. $\dfrac{1}{2} + \dfrac{1}{2} + \dfrac{1}{2} =$ b. $\dfrac{2}{3} + \dfrac{2}{3} + \dfrac{2}{3} =$

c. $\dfrac{1}{2} + \dfrac{1}{3} =$ d. $\dfrac{1}{2} + \dfrac{2}{4} + \dfrac{1}{2} =$

e. $\dfrac{4}{5} + \dfrac{2}{5} + \dfrac{1}{5} =$ f. $1\dfrac{1}{2} + 2 + 4\dfrac{1}{2}$

g. $\dfrac{1}{8} + \dfrac{1}{4} + \dfrac{1}{2} =$ g. $2 + 3 + 1\dfrac{4}{5} + 1 =$

How are you learning to become more adept at mental computation?

How can you use mental computation in your everyday life?

☛ **Activity 11: Fractions and the Calculator**

Purpose: To understand how calculators can compute fractions.
Material: Calculator

Calculators can play a vital part in the elementary mathematics classroom when a unit on fractions is introduced. Students need to understand the relationship between decimals, fractions, and percentage. In looking for books at a book sale, for example, students need to recognize that books marked "$\frac{1}{2}$ price" are the same as those marked "50% off." To provide students with practice, call a list of fractions to the class, and ask them to find the correct percentage or decimal.

Find the decimal and percent equivalent for the fractions below:

Example: $\frac{1}{2}$ = 0.50 = 50%

a. $\frac{1}{3}$ = ____ = ____   b. $\frac{4}{5}$ = ____ = ____

c. $\frac{9}{10}$ = ____ = ____   d. $\frac{3}{4}$ = ____ = ____

e. $\frac{2}{5}$ = ____ = ____   f. $\frac{7}{8}$ = ____ = ____

✎ **Journal**

What patterns can you discover when finding the equivalent decimal (or percent) for each fraction?

What part does the use of percent play in your life?

✈ Critical Thinking ✈

☞ **Activity 12:   Comparing Fractions**

Purpose: To compare two fractions to determine the larger.
Materials: Activity Card 6.4a — Fraction Pieces

In teaching a unit on fractions, questions that lead to high-order thinking responses are recommended. To promote understanding of rational numbers, students can be asked to determine which fraction is the larger of the two provided, using fraction pieces or strips.

❑   **Which is larger?**

     a. $\frac{1}{2}$ or $\frac{2}{4}$?   b. $\frac{1}{2}$ or $\frac{1}{3}$?

     c. $\frac{1}{2}$ or $\frac{1}{4}$?   d. $\frac{2}{3}$ or $\frac{4}{5}$?

     e. $\frac{1}{4}$ or $\frac{1}{3}$?

❑   Other questions to promote understanding and critical thinking might include the following:

What does the word *fraction* mean?

What do the terms *numerator* and *denominator* signify?

How can you differentiate between a mixed number and a fraction?

How can you identify an improper fraction?

Using manipulatives, explain how you know that $\frac{1}{2}$ is equal to $\frac{3}{6}$.

✈ Alternative Assessment ✈

Observations

Students may be observed during group or individual activity. Observations may provide information about the understanding of a mathematical concept or a behavior that affects it. Each observation should be concept-specific. In other words, one or two concepts at the most should be assessed during one observation.

Some of the attributes that can be assessed in the elementary mathematics classroom are listed below. This is not a complete list. Additional concepts may be added as each unit is introduced.

The following concepts may be considered for observation assessment.

Cooperative Group Task Assessment
- Is sufficient time allotted to ensure that all group members understand the current task?
- Are tasks divided between group members?
- Is the use of group time productive?
- Do members record results accurately?
- Are all group members allowed time for input?
- Do all group members abide by the rules for cooperative efforts?

Individual Task Assessment
- Is the task understood?
- Is a plan in progress?
- Is data organized and interpreted correctly?
- Are patterns used and recognized?
- Is estimation an integral part of each procedure?
- Are manipulatives used effectively to provide assistance in reaching the solution?
- Are plans revised when the original plan proves ineffective?
- Is the student on task?
- Are probing questions asked?
- Is the task completed?
- Can the solution be illustrated and communicated to others?

→ Mathematics for the 21st Century →

Mathematics as Reasoning (Questioning Strategies)

As assessment practices shift for the elementary mathematics classroom, questioning strategies also shift. Instead of asking for the one correct answer, now students seek diverse paths to find multiple solutions. Process, rather than product, is the password for the future.

The *Curriculum and Evaluation Standards for School Mathematics* (1989) and the *Professional Standards for School Mathematics* (1991) both place a strong emphasis on classroom questioning procedures. Asking the right questions is the responsibility of the classroom teacher and is an art to be learned. In the *Professional Standards*, high-order thinking skills are encouraged with questions that reveal a high level of thinking rather than rote memorization.

In the implementation of high order questioning skills, it is wise to prepare a list of questions ahead of time. In the search for high-level thinking responses, ample wait-time should be the rule, rather than the exception. Students should be given the opportunity to listen and think about the question.

Classroom questions should be formulated to create a thought-provoking answer rather than a memorized fact. Questions that ask students to compare and contrast, evaluate, and synthesize will provoke such a response. As difficult as this change in questioning skills may seem at first to the classroom teacher, it becomes a worthwhile task when it is obvious that students are being challenged to think at a higher level.

Innovative questioning techniques are used to encourage the following:
  1. To help students determine if an idea is mathematically correct.

  • How did you reach your conclusion?
  • Why do you think your solution is correct?
  • Does your answer make sense?
  • Can you give another illustration to clarify the solution?

  2. To help students learn reasoning skills.
  • Is this true for all cases?
  • How can you prove that your answer is the correct one?
  • Have you explained all of your assumptions?
  • Will the procedure which you used work for all cases?

3. To help students learn to make mathematical connections.
   - What previously learned strategies were useful in solving this problem?
   - How could you apply this strategy to today's science experiment?
   - What role did mathematics play in the school life of the early colonial settlers?
   - How does this relate to your life?

4. To help students learn to understand, create, and solve problems.
   - Can you restate the problem in your own words?
   - Do you see a pattern?
   - Can you predict what will happen next?
   - If you do not know where to begin, what should you do first?

5. To empower students to work together and make sense of mathematics.
   - Does anyone have a different solution to that same problem?
   - Do you agree or disagree with Joanna's statement?
   - Can you convince the rest of the class that your response makes the most sense?
   - Could you restate your solution in another way?

6. To assist students in self-evaluation.
   - What procedural changes will you make when solving the next problem?
   - What dead-end roads did you follow?
   - In what way does your answer prove your point?
   - How will this strategy help you in another problem-solving situation?
   - What questions do you have before beginning your next problem?

7

Decimals, Percents, and Real Numbers

UNDERSTANDING DECIMALS, PERCENTS, AND REAL NUMBERS

1. Decimals: Place Value and Arithmetic
2. Decimals: Estimation, Mental Computation, and Error Patterns
3. Ratio and Proportion
4. Using Percents
5. Percents: Mental Computation and Estimation
6. Rational, Irrational, and Real Numbers

▼ PROBLEM CHALLENGE: Get it Straight

1. What percent of the numbers from 1 through 100 are formed with only straight lines?

2. What percent of the letters in the alphabet are formed with only straight lines?

2 K O
P G 7 J
H 4 3 M

HANDS-ON MATHEMATICS ACTIVITIES

The following activities are provided to enhance your understanding of decimals, percents, and real numbers.

Decimals: Place Value and Arithmetic

✳ **Key Ideas:**   Decimal numbers are an extension of whole numbers. Their place values are also an extension of the whole-number system.

☞ **Activity 1:   Decimal Representation**

Purpose: To identify decimal numbers represented by decimal pieces.
Materials: Activity Card 7.1 — Decimal Pieces

❑   These are decimal pieces used to represent decimal numbers.

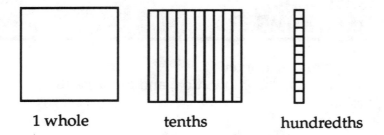

1 whole   tenths   hundredths

❑   Example: What decimal number is represented by the decimal pieces?

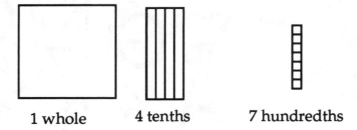

1 whole   4 tenths   7 hundredths

Answer: 1.47

❑   What decimal numbers are represented?

a.

b.

_____

☛   **Activity 2: Representing Decimals**

Purpose: Using decimal pieces to represent decimals.
Materials: Activity Card 7.1 — Decimal Pieces

Decimal numbers are easily represented with decimal pieces.

Example: Represent the decimal 1.43 with decimal pieces.

    1 whole   4 tenths   3 hundredths

Represent each decimal number with decimal pieces:

    a. 0.73   b. 2.80   c. 1.92   d. 5.09

☞   **Activity 3: Expanded Notation**

Purpose: Using decimal pieces in expanded notation.
Materials: Activity Card 7.1 — Decimal Pieces

Writing decimal numbers in expanded notation can help students visualize place value and renaming.

Write each decimal number in expanded notation and compute.
Example: Consider adding two decimal numbers with no renaming.

$$
\begin{array}{rclccc}
 & & & \text{tenths} & & \text{hundredths} \\
0.5\,4 & = & & .5 & + & .04 \\
+\,0.4\,2 & = & & +\,.4 & + & .02 \\
\hline
 & = & & .9 & + & .06 = 0.96
\end{array}
$$

Example: Consider adding two decimals with renaming.

$$
\begin{array}{rclcclccl}
0.3\,5 & = & .3 & + & .05 & = & .3 & + & .05 \\
-\,.1\,7 & = & .1 & + & .07 & = & .1 & + & .07 \\
\hline
 & & & & & & .4 & + & .12 = 0.52
\end{array}
$$

❑   Use decimal pieces to illustrate each computation. Complete each computation in writing, using expanded notation.

a.   0.2 7
    + 0.1 6

b.   0.5 8
    + 0.4 2

c.   0.3 2
    + 0.1 6

d.   0.4 1
    + 0.2 8

☛ **Activity 4:   Reading and Writing Decimals**

Purpose: To understand how to read and write a decimal.

Reading decimal numbers is a little more complicated than reading whole numbers. The procedure for reading a decimal number follows.
1. Read the whole number to the left of the decimal first.
2. Read the decimal as "and".
3. Read the digits to the right of the decimal just as you would a whole number.
4. Label the decimal with the place value of the digit furthest to the right.

Example: Read each decimal.

123.4   567.89

1. "one hundred twenty-three   1. "five hundred sixty-seven
2. and   2. and
3. four   3. eighty-nine
4. tenths"   4. hundredths"

Read and write each of the following decimals:

a. 0.7   b. 2.80   c. 111.92   d. 21.093

 **Journal** _____

Why do you think the understanding of place value is important in the study of decimals?

What comparisons can you make between whole numbers and decimal numbers?

Decimals: Estimation, Mental Computation, and Error Patterns

Key Ideas: Decimal estimation is similar to estimating with fractions or whole numbers. Decimals can be rounded to the nearest whole number so the computation can be completed mentally. We can also use the compatible-numbers strategy to estimate computations with decimals.

☞ **Activity 5: Rounding**

Purpose: To explore the rounding strategy.
Materials: Activity Card 7.1 — Decimal Pieces

The rounding strategy is useful with any computational operation. It involves rounding the decimal to the nearest whole number and computing. Use the decimal piece to represent the decimal. If more than half the piece is shaded, use the next whole number. If less than half the piece is shaded, use the lesser whole number.

Round each decimal to the nearest whole number and compute.

Example: To estimate the product of 3.8 x 7.3, round and multiply, 4 x 7 = 28. *(28 is an approximation of the actual computed product of 27.74.)*

❑   Use the rounding strategy to determine an estimate for each computation:

a. 4.7 + 8.9 =

b. 9.7 – 3 .8 =

c. 3.4 x 8.9 =

d. 12.3 ÷ 3.1 =

☞ **Activity 6: Compatible Numbers**

Purpose: To explore the compatible-numbers strategy.

The compatible-numbers strategy encourages the student to round the decimal to the nearest unit fraction (a unit fraction has a 1 in the numerator). Decimals close to 0.25 are converted to $\frac{1}{4}$, and those close to 0.50 are converted to $\frac{1}{2}$.

Example: Use the compatible-numbers strategy to determine the product of 8.23 x 0.27 and of 12.2 x 0.49.

Estimate	Actual
$8.23 \times 0.27 \approx 8 \times \frac{1}{4} = 2$	$8.23 \times 0.27 = 2.2221$
$12.2 \times 0.49 \approx 12 \times \frac{1}{2} = 6$	$12.2 \times 0.49 = 5.978$

(Note that the larger numbers were rounded.)

❑   Use the rounding and compatible-numbers strategies to determine an estimate for each computation.

a. 4.2 x 8.1 =

b. 9.9 x 3 .3 =

c. 0.24 x 11.8 =

☞   **Activity 7:   More Compatible Numbers**

Purpose: To explore the compatible-numbers strategy.

The compatible-numbers strategy involves rounding decimals to the nearest fraction and estimating the product. The table below displays decimals and equivalent fractions that may be used to obtain estimates.

Table of Equivalent Decimals and Fractions

Decimal	Fraction			Decimal	Fraction		
0.1	$\frac{1}{10}$			0.6	$\frac{6}{10}$	$\frac{3}{5}$	
0.125		$\frac{1}{8}$		0.625		$\frac{5}{8}$	
0.2	$\frac{2}{10}$	$\frac{1}{5}$		0.67			$\frac{2}{3}$
0.25		$\frac{2}{8}$	$\frac{1}{4}$	0.7	$\frac{7}{10}$		
0.3	$\frac{3}{10}$			0.75		$\frac{6}{8}$	$\frac{3}{4}$
0.33			$\frac{1}{3}$	0.8	$\frac{8}{10}$	$\frac{4}{5}$	
0.375		$\frac{3}{8}$		0.875		$\frac{7}{8}$	
0.4	$\frac{4}{10}$	$\frac{2}{5}$		0.9	$\frac{9}{10}$		
0.5	$\frac{5}{10}$	$\frac{4}{8}$	$\frac{1}{2}$	1.0	1		

Example: Use the compatible numbers strategy to determine the product of 12 x .34.

$$12 \times 0.34 \approx 12 \times \frac{1}{3} = 4$$

❏   Use the table, when needed, to estimate each computation.

   a. 14.9 x 0.34 =   b. 99 x 3.3 =   c. 24 x 0.67 =

   d. 23.8 x 0.125 =   e. 20 x 0.81 =   f. 31 x 0.62 =

☞ **Activity 8: Scientific Notation**

Purpose: To understand large numbers written in scientific notation.
Materials: Sand, rice, pennies, and paper

Collect 1,000 of something.

Find 1,000,000 of something. Prove it.

❑ How much space would 1,000,000 of each of the following occupy?

> grains of sand
> grains of rice
> pennies
> sheets of paper

❑ Look at each of the following numbers written in scientific notation:

a. 10^6 b. 10^9 c. 10^{12} d. 10^{-3} e. 10^{-6}

What number does each represent?

☞ **Activity 9: Preventing Errors**

Purpose: Using estimation to prevent decimal errors.

❑ Use rounding or compatible numbers to correctly place the decimal in each of the computations.

a.	14.9	b.	99.3	c.	2.41	d.	9.8
	x 0.34		x 3.3		x 6.78		x 49.5
	5066		32769		163398		4851

Ratio and Proportion

> ✳ **Key Ideas:**   A ratio compares two numbers and is another name for a fraction. A proportion states that two ratios are equal. Proportions are useful when comparing two sets or two measures such as miles per hour or dollars per hour.

☞   **Activity 10:   The Proportion Chart**

Purpose: To use a proportion chart to solve problems.

A proportion chart or table is useful for viewing equivalent ratios. Suppose you are paid eight dollars per hour. A proportion table can be used to view the amount of money you would earn for 2, 3, 4, and 5 hours of work.

Hours	1	2	3	4	5
Dollars	8	16	24	32	40

❑   Complete the proportion table and write two problems that use the data in the table. Create one problem that involves money and a second problem that involves gas mileage.

X	1	2	3	4	5	6	7
Y		150					

Problem 1

Problem 2

☞   **Activity 11:   The Unitary Method**

Purpose: To use the unitary method to solve problems.

❑   Suppose you made 33 dollars in 6 hours. How much money would you make at this rate for 13 hours?

1. Estimate the answer.

2. Make a proportion chart.

3. What is troublesome with the estimate and proportion chart methods?

With the unitary method you determine the amount per unit. In the above problem, for instance, dollars per hour.

$$\frac{33 \text{ dollars}}{6 \text{ hours}} = 5.50 \text{ dollars/hour}$$

$$\frac{5.50 \text{ dollars}}{1 \text{ hour}} \times 13 \text{ hours} = 71.50 \text{ dollars}$$

(Note that you can divide the labels like the numerals. The hours cancel and leave you with dollars, which is the label for our answer.)

4. Solve each of the following problems using the *unitary method.*

a. Jim earns $1,700 in 4 weeks. How much would he earn, at the same rate, for 9 weeks?

b. Sandy drove 347 miles on 11 gallons of gas. How far can she drive on a full tank of 18 gallons?

c. A machine can make 1,723 widgets in 13 hours. How many widgets can the machine make in 40 hours?

☞   **Activity 12:   The Multiplier Method**

   Purpose: To use the multiplier method to solve problems.

❑   Suppose you made 33 dollars in 6 hours. How much money would you make at this rate for 13 hours?

   You used the unitary method in the previous activity.

   With the multiplier method you determine the number of times more.

   In the above problem:

   $$\frac{6 \text{ hours}}{13 \text{ hours}}$$

   $$\frac{6 \text{ hours}}{13 \text{ hours}} \times 33 \text{ dollars} = 71.50 \text{ dollars}$$

   Note that the labels (hours) cancel and leave you with dollars, which is the label for our answer.

❑   Solve each of the following problems using the *multiplier method*.

   a. Jim earns $1,700 in 4 weeks. How much would he earn, at the same rate, for 9 weeks?

   b. Sandy drove 347 miles on 11 gallons of gas. How far can she drive on a full tank of 18 gallons?

   c. A machine can make 1,723 widgets in 13 hours. How many widgets can the machine make in 40 hours?

✎ **Journal**

Why is rounding a useful strategy for elementary students? Where will they use the strategy?

Compare and contrast the unitary method and the multiplier method.

Where might a proportion chart be useful?

Where will knowledge of ratio be beneficial?

Using Percent

 Key Ideas: Percent means per 100. We use percents in many common daily applications.

☛ **Activity 13:   Three types of percent problems**

Purpose: To gain an understanding of simple percent computations.

There are three types of simple percent problems. Each can be solved using a simple proportion method.

$$\frac{\%}{100} = \frac{part}{whole}$$

Example: Type I – How much is 34 percent of 50?

$$\frac{34}{100} = \frac{X}{50} \qquad 100X = (34)(50) \qquad X = 17$$

Example: Type II – 17 is 34 percent of what number?

$$\frac{34}{100} = \frac{17}{X} \qquad 34X = (17)(100) \qquad X = 50$$

Example: Type III – What percent of 50 is 17?

$$\frac{X}{100} = \frac{17}{50} \qquad 50X = (17)(100) \qquad X = 34$$

❑   Solve each problem using the proportion method.

a. What percent is 75 of 300?   b. What percent is 300 of 75?

c. What is 45 percent of 56?   d. What is 230 percent of 80?

e. 60% of what number is 13?   f.   250% of what number is 50?

☞   **Activity 14:   Comparing Interest Rates**

Purpose: To gain an understanding of simple consumer credit.

Simple Interest

Simple interest is calculated using the formula $I = P\,r\,t$, where
   I = the amount of interest
   P = the principal
   r = the rate
   t = the time in years.

❑   What is the interest on $1,000 at 12% interest after 3 years?

$$I = P\,r\,t$$

$$I = \$1{,}000 \times \frac{12}{100} \times 3$$

$$I = \$360$$

The borrower must pay the principal and the interest.

The amount paid is $A = P + I = \$1{,}000 + \$360 = \$1{,}360$

We can adjust the formula to calculate the amount more directly.

$$A = P + I = P + P\,r\,t$$

$$A = P\,(1 + r\,t)$$

$$A = \$1{,}000\left(1 + \frac{12}{100} \times 3\right) = \$1{,}000\,(1.36) = \$1{,}360$$

Compound Interest

Compound interest is more difficult to compute. In the following chart compare simple interest with compound interest on $1,000 for 3 years.

Comparison of Simple and Compound Interest

Years	Simple Interest	Compound interest
1	$I = \$1,000.00 \times \dfrac{12}{100} = \$120$	$I = \$1,000.00 \times \dfrac{12}{100} = \$120$
2	$I = \$1,000.00 \times \dfrac{12}{100} = \$120$	$I = \$1,120.00 \times \dfrac{12}{100} = \$134.40$
3	$I = \$1,000.00 \times \dfrac{12}{100} = \$120$	$I = \$1,254.40 \times \dfrac{12}{100} = \$150.53$

The total interest for 3 years would be $120 + $134.40 + $150.53 =$404.93. The total amount of money is $1,000 + $404.93 = $1,404.93.

We can calculate compound interest more directly with the formula:

$$A = P (1 + i)^n \qquad A = \$1,000 (1 + .12)^3 = \$1,404.93$$

❑   Suppose the inflation rate is 5% for 10 years. Calculate the price of each item, using simple interest and compound interest.

a. Sunday paper $1.00   b. Hamburger $2.50

c. Rent $500.00   d. Tuition $3,000.00

e. Car $10,000.00   f. House $120,000.00

☛ **Activity 15:   One More Comparison of Interest Rates**

Purpose: To gain an understanding of simple consumer credit.

Many institutions calculate compound interest more frequently than once per year. They calculate interest semi-annually, quarterly, monthly, and even daily. The formula for calculating compound interest is

$$A = P\left(1 + \frac{r}{n}\right)^{nt}$$

P = principal

n = Number of times interest is paid per year (or other period)

r = rate of interest

t = time in years

❏   Use your calculator to compute the amount of interest on $1,000 at a 12% rate for 3 years with each way of compounding.

P = Principal	Compounded	r = rate	t = time	n = period
$1,000	annually	12%	3 years	1
$1,000	semi-annually	12%	3 years	2
$1,000	quarterly	12%	3 years	4
$1,000	monthly	12%	3 years	12
$1,000	daily	12%	3 years	360

$$A = P\left(1 + \frac{r}{n}\right)^{nt}$$

annually—A = $1,000 (1.12)^3 = $1,404.93

a. semi-annually   A =   b. quarterly   A =

c. monthly   A =   d. daily   A = set up only

✎ **Journal**_____

Explain your findings concerning interest computations.

What questions do you have about the process of determining interest?

Percents: Mental Computation and Estimation

✳ **Key Ideas:**   Estimating with percents involves changing the percent to a convenient fraction or decimal to complete the mental computation.

☛ **Activity 16:   Rounding and Compatible Numbers**

Purpose: To understand fraction, decimal, and percent equivalents.

Percents can be converted to decimals for rounding or to compatible fractions. Both methods allow for convenient mental computation.

Example: What is 22% of 397?

Rounding Method	Compatible Number Method
0.10 x 400 = 40 40 x 2 = 80 (answer)	$\frac{1}{4}$ x 400 = 100 (answer)

Actual Calculation

$\frac{22}{100}$ x 397 = 87.34 (answer)

Table of Equivalent Percent, Fractions, and Decimals

Percent	Fraction	Decimal	Percent	Fraction	Decimal
10	$\frac{1}{10}$	0.10	60	$\frac{3}{5}$	0.60
12.5	$\frac{1}{8}$	0.125	62.5	$\frac{5}{8}$	0.625
20	$\frac{1}{5}$	0.20	66.7	$\frac{2}{3}$	0.667
25	$\frac{1}{4}$	0.25	70	$\frac{7}{10}$	0.70
30	$\frac{3}{10}$	0.30	75	$\frac{3}{4}$	0.75
33.3	$\frac{1}{3}$	0.333	80	$\frac{4}{5}$	0.80
37.5	$\frac{3}{8}$	0.375	87.5	$\frac{7}{8}$	0.875
40	$\frac{2}{5}$	0.40	90	$\frac{9}{10}$	0.90
50	$\frac{1}{2}$	0.50	100	1	1.00

❏   Use the table, when needed, to estimate each computation:

a. 50% of 44   b. 75% of 400   c. 90% of 90

d. 24% of 120   e. 20% of 888   f. 15% of 252

Rational, Irrational, and Real Numbers

✳ **Key Ideas:** The real-number system is made up of rational and irrational numbers. Rational numbers include integers, whole numbers, and natural numbers.

☞ **Activity 17:   The Real-Number System**

Purpose: Another look at the real-number system.

The real-number system is shown below with a flow chart.

Flow Chart of the Real Number System

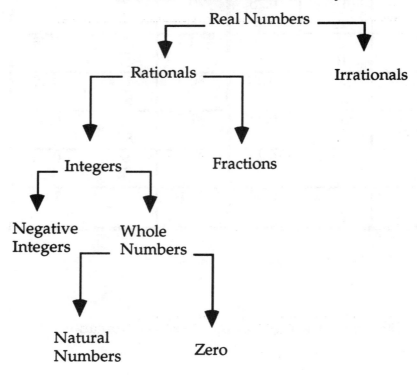

❑   Define and give an example of each term:

   a. Real Number   b. Fraction

   c. Rational Number   d. Negative Integer

   e. Irrational Number   f. Natural Number

   g. Integer   h. Zero

Journal

Illustrate each property with an example.

Addition of real numbers is closed.

Division of real numbers is not closed.

Addition of real numbers is commutative.

Subtraction of real numbers is not commutative.

How would you explain the term *property* to a younger student whom you are tutoring?

✈ EXTENSIONS ✈

☀ **Key Ideas:**   In Extensions, you may revisit some of the concepts and activities presented in this chapter. The following activities allow you to explore some ideas a little further. Sections include Mental Computation, Calculators, Critical Thinking, Alternative Assessment, and Mathematics for the 21st Century.

✈ Mental Computation ✈

☞ **Activity 18:   Decimal Computation**

Purpose: To estimate computations.

Estimate each computation using appropriate strategies.

a. .92 x 0.031

b. 5,201 x 8.51

c. $17.1 \times (2.12 \times 10^5)$

d. 42.123 ÷ 6.7

e. 1.204 ÷ 0.31

f. $(8.5 \times 10^3) \div 2.3$

g. What would the simple interest be on $100,000 borrowed at 10% at the end of 20 years?

✈ Calculators ✈

☞ **Activity 19:   Decimal Computation**

Purpose: To compute decimals using a calculator.
Materials: Calculator

❑   Use your calculator to verify each estimate in activity 18.

a. .92 x 0.031

b. 5,201 x 8.51

c. $17.1 \times (2.12 \times 10^5)$

d. 42.123 + 6.7

e. 1.204 + 0.31

f. $(8.5 \times 10^3) + 2.3$

g. What would the simple interest be on $100,000 borrowed at 10% at the end of 20 years?

✈ Critical Thinking ✈

☛ **Activity 20:   Large and Small Numbers**

Purpose: To use scientific notation.
Materials: Calculator

1. A light year is the distance light travels in one year.

    Use your calculator to determine the distance light travels in one year
    if light travels at the speed of 180,000 miles per second.

    Write your answer in scientific notation.

2. The measure of 100 grains of sand in a line is 1.2 centimeters.

    What is the length of one grain of sand?

    Write your answer in scientific notation.

3. Use your calculator to determine each product:

    a. $(1.2 \times 10^3) \times (4.3 \times 10^4) =$ b. $(2.3 \times 10^4) \times (3.3 \times 10^2) =$

    How can you determine the exponent in the product?

4. Use your calculator to determine each quotient:

    a. $(12.2 \times 10^3) \div (4.3 \times 10^4) =$ b. $(21.3 \times 10^4) \div (3.3 \times 10^2) =$

    How can you determine the exponent in the quotient?

✈ **Alternative Assessment** ✈

Interviews

Interviews with a student can provide a wealth of information about the student's thinking and thinking skills. In order to assess the student's mathematical understanding, the teacher tries to create a picture of what the student sees rather than to discover whether the student can provide the exact correct answer. The purpose of the interview is to discover whether the student really understands the mathematical concepts or is merely memorizing formulas and answers.

An interview should include a series of planned questions. Interviews are time-consuming, but they can provide useful information for diagnosing the needs of students who are having difficulties and for discovering needed changes in the curriculum.

At the beginning of the interview, the student should be placed at ease. Before proceeding with class interviews, it is best to hold a demonstration interview with one student while the class observes. Prior to the demonstration, a thorough explanation of the purpose and use of the interview should be discussed with the entire class. Students feel relaxed and at ease when they understand why the event is taking place and what its importance is for them.

It is imperative that the teacher be a good listener and that any comments be non-judgmental, if trust is to be established. Beginning questions should be broad, leading to more specific questions. Wait-time is important. True thinking involves time.

Interviews held for assessment purposes may be either formal or informal. Formal interviews require questions prepared ahead of time. Informal interviews are those implemented as a regular part of the daily interaction between the teacher and student.

✈ Mathematics for the 21st Century ✈

Developmentally Appropriate Practices

Young children enter schools with a positive attitude toward learning. It is the responsibility of the school to take this positive attitude and provide learning activities that meet the developmental needs of each child. It is imperative that primary teachers include developmentally-appropriate practices that enhance learning and allow students to achieve success.

In the NAEYC publication, *Developmentally-Appropriate Practice in Early Childhood Programs Serving Children From Birth Through Age 8* (Ed. Sue Bredenkamp, National Association for the Education of Young Children, 1987), the following guidelines are suggested:

1. Curriculum goals should be designed to encourage physical, social, intellectual, and emotional growth. Curriculum and instruction should be responsive to individual differences and focus on the development of self-esteem and positive attitudes toward learning in general;
2. Children should have multiple opportunities to use manipulatives that are concrete, real, and relevant to their lives. Discovery learning is promoted, with each child becoming a discoverer;
3. Opportunities for positive interaction with peers in small cooperative groups promotes communication while the child works and plays. The development of social skills is encouraged;
4. Mathematics is taught across the curriculum, and problem solving is an integral part of that curriculum;
5. Parents are included in the learning process;
6. Student progress is reported to parents in a narrative rather than numerical or graded format;
7. The child is allowed to proceed through the curriculum at his/her own appropriate pace.

The effective teacher asks two questions to guide thinking and planning.

1. What can I do in my elementary mathematics classroom to develop and enhance the traits of a lifelong learner in my students?
2. How can I encourage collaboration and cooperation instead of competition between students?

8

Geometry

▼ PROBLEM CHALLENGE: Fast-Draw Math

1. Create two squares by drawing
     five lines.
     six lines.
2. Create two equilateral triangles drawing
     five lines.
     four lines.
3. Create your own problem for
   Fast-Draw Math.

HANDS-ON MATHEMATICS ACTIVITIES

The following activities are provided to enhance your understanding of geometry.

Beginning Geometry

✳ **Key Ideas:** The informal awareness of geometry begins when we start to recognize shapes in our environment such as a baseball, a building block, a brick, an ice cream cone. In a classroom we see a clock on the wall, the corner of the room, the blackboard, and the tile on the floor as evidence of geometry around us. As students begin to recognize geometric shapes, they also begin to put names with those shapes. The vocabulary of geometry can be made meaningful by including hands-on activities that require a high level of student involvement to ensure that student's interest involves requesting the name of the object rather than merely having to memorize its definition.

☞ **Activity 1: Pattern-Piece Pick and Sort**

Purpose: To understand the concept of geometrical shapes and patterns.
Materials: Activity Card 8.1 — Pattern Pieces

Pattern Pieces are a collection of six geometric shapes usually found in six different colors. The shapes represented are square, triangle, rhombus, parallelogram, trapezoid, and hexagon. The sides of all shapes are the same length, except that the trapezoid has one side that is twice as long as the others. The blocks can be placed together to form patterns and illustrate symmetry, congruence, perimeter and area, patterns, graphing, and fractions. Students should be allowed time for free exploration when first given pattern pieces.

The following task incorporates the use of graphing skills and recognition of the geometric shapes. Each person picks up a handful of pattern pieces and sorts them according to shape. On the board or overhead projector, a chart is drawn to record the total number of each pattern piece found. Students are given a copy of the chart. A review of terms might take place prior to this activity. One means of introduction is to hold up each pattern piece and ask if anyone can recall its name.

❑ Grab a handful of pattern pieces and count each type. Record your findings.

Triangle	Square	Parallel-ogram	Trape-zoid	Rhombus	Hexagon

Chapter 8   Geometry   149

☞   **Activity 2: Pattern-Piece Riddles**

Purpose: To understand the concept of geometrical shapes and angles.
Materials: Activity Card 8.1 — Pattern Pieces

❑   The teacher calls the clues one at a time. Students use the pattern pieces
     on their desks and eliminate those that do not fit the specifications given
     in the riddle to determine the solution.

   Who Am I?

   Riddle #1
   I have four sides.
   I have four equal angles.
   I have two pairs of parallel sides.
   Who am I? (square)

   Riddle #2
   I have obtuse angles.
   I am not a parallelogram.
   I have more than four sides.
   Who am I? (hexagon)

   Riddle #3
   I have acute angles.
   All of my sides and angles are congruent.
   I have fewer than 6 sides.
   I have no right angles.
   Who am I? (triangle)

   Riddle #4
   I have at least two obtuse angles.
   I have no right angles.
   I am equal to half of the hexagon.
   Who am I? (trapezoid)

   Riddle #5
   I have two sets of parallel sides.
   I have two obtuse angles.
   I have two acute angles.
   Who am I? (parallelogram or rhombus)

   Students can then prepare a set of clues and take turns presenting
   their riddles to the class.

Plane Figures

 Key Ideas: A set of points in a plane is known as a *plane figure*. Plane figures may be zero-dimensional, one-dimensional, or two-dimensional. A point is zero-dimensional, describing a simple location. A line is one-dimensional, possessing length but no thickness. A two-dimensional figure has area, but no volume.

☛ **Activity 3: Geoboard Construction**

Purpose: To develop an understanding of plane figure construction.
Materials: Activity Card 8.3 — Geoboard Recording Sheet and/or Geoboards with Rubber Bands

❑ **Triangles: Three-sided figures**

1. A triangle that has three equal sides and three equal angles is known as an *equilateral triangle.* Using your Geoboard Recording Sheet, draw three different sizes of equilateral triangles.

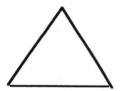

An equilateral triangle has three sides of the same length.

2. A triangle that has no two sides of the same length is called a *scalene triangle.* Using your Geoboard Recording Sheet, draw three scalene triangles.

A scalene triangle has three sides of different lengths.

3. A triangle that has one right angle is called a *right triangle.* Construct three right triangles on your Geoboard Recording Sheet.

A right triangle has one 90° angle.

4. A triangle that has two sides of the same length is known as an *isosceles triangle.*   Draw three isosceles triangles.

An isosceles triangle
has two equal sides.

❑   **Quadrilaterals: Closed figures with four sides.**

5. A square is a quadrilateral that has four equal sides and four equal angles. Draw two squares of different sizes.

A square has four equal
sides and four 90° angles.

6. A rhombus is a quadrilateral with four equal sides. Draw a rhombus.

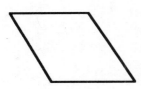

A rhombus has four
equal sides.

7. A parallelogram is a quadrilateral which has two sets of equal sides. Draw two parallelograms.

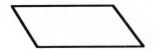

A parallelogram has two
pairs of equal sides.

☛ **Activity 4:   Tangram Shapes**

Purpose: To understand and explore a variety of geometric shapes.
Materials: Activity Card 8.4a — Tangram Pieces
                 Activity Card 8.4b — Tangram Shape Chart

❑   Using your Tangram Pieces and the Tangram Shape Chart, create as many shapes as possible.

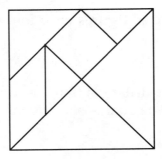

Place your drawings in the appropriate boxes on the Tangram Shape Chart.

Is it possible to fill all the boxes?

Check your solutions with a friend.

Journal

How does the concept of geometry tie in with your everyday life?

Write one fascinating fact about geometry. Tell why you found it fascinating.

Write a story about a triangle who wanted to be a square.

List two different types of quadrilaterals and describe each.

Janet asked why a square can be a rectangle, but a rectangle cannot be a square. How would you clarify the concept of square and rectangle?

Angle Measurement of Polygons

Key Ideas: The sum of the angle measures of any triangle is 180°. The sum of the four measured angles of any convex quadrilateral is 360°. A regular polygon has all sides congruent and all angles congruent.

☞ **Activity 5: Sum of the Angles**

Purpose: To understand the concept of vertex angle measurement of regular polygons (all sides and all vertex angles are congruent).

Materials: Activity Card 4.13 — Protractor and Metric Ruler
Paper

❑ 1. Using your ruler, draw a triangle. Tear off the three corners or vertex angles of the triangle. Nestle the three vertex angles side by side.

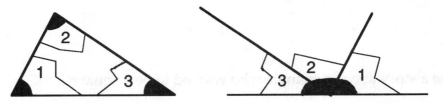

Triangle with each
angle labeled

The three angles of the
triangle arranged to
show 180°

❑ 2. Be aware that the sides of vertex angle 1 and vertex angle 3 will form a straight line. What is the sum of the angles?

❑ 3. Draw a different triangle and repeat the procedure. What is the sum of its angles?

❑ 4. Draw a quadrilateral. Tear off the vertex angles and arrange them as you did for the triangles. What did you find?

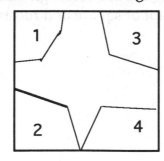

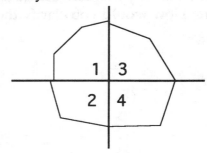

❑   5. You now see that the sum of the angles of a triangle is 180 degrees.
          Now notice that the diagonal that goes from one vertex of a
          quadrilateral to a non-adjacent vertex will divide the quadrilateral into
          two triangles. The sum of the angles of those two triangles is 360
          degrees. This is also the sum of the vertex angles of a quadrilateral.

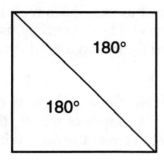

❑   6. The same idea can be used to determine the sum of the angles of every
          polygon. When all the diagonals from one vertex of a pentagon are drawn
          to all the other non-adjacent vertices, 3 triangles are formed. The sum of
          the angles in a triangle is 180°. Therefore, 3 x 180° = 540°.

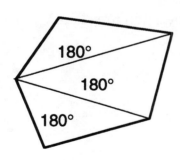

❑   7. Draw a hexagon. Draw all the diagonals from one vertex of the
          hexagon to all the other non-adjacent vertices. What do you discover?

☞   **Activity 6:   Tesselations**

Purpose: To understand the concept of tessellations.
Materials: Activity Card 8.1 — Pattern Pieces
               Activity Card 8.6a — Tessellations
               Activity Card 8.6b — Quadrilaterals

A tessellation is a covering of a plane with one or more shapes with no gap and no overlap. In this chapter, tesselations will be formed by using regular polygons. A regular polygon is a closed figure having all sides the same length and all angles of equal measure.

❑   You have been given the task of tiling your kitchen floor using only one kind and one size of geometric shape. Cut out the shapes of the regular polygons and decide which one will be the best to cover the floor with no gap and no overlap.

In your decision-making process you might want to consider the following questions:

       • Will the equilateral triangle tessellate?
       • Will the square tessellate?
       • Will the pentagon tessellate?
       • Why do these three shapes tessellate or not tessellate?
       • Will the hexagon tessellate?
       • Will the heptagon or octagon tessellate?
       • Will the nonagon, decagon, and dodecagon tessellate?

Draw a picture of the design for your kitchen floor.

Did you know that bees use the regular hexagon for the shape of the cells in their honeycomb?

Irregular polygons that tessellate are discussed in the following chapter.

Journal

Make a general statement about finding the sum of the angles of a polygon.

Draw a pattern illustrating regular polygons that tessellate.

If you were in the home-decoration business, how would the knowledge of tessellations be helpful?

Using the overhead manipulatives, explain tesselations to a younger student. Record the student's reaction in your journal.

Spatial Visualization

> ✳ **Key Ideas:** Spatial visualization includes interpreting illustrations, developing mental images, and visualizing how movement will continue or change in certain images. Spatial visualization skills can be increased with practice and can lead to a heightened understanding of mathematical thinking.

☛ **Activity 7:** **Pentominoes**

Purpose: To understand the concept of spatial visualization.
Materials: Activity Card 3.9 — Color Pieces
Activity Card 8.7 — Pentominoes Key

❑ Using the color pieces in groups of five, determine how many different shapes can be created. There are certain rules that are required:

Rule 1: Every two adjacent sides of the color tile must touch completely.

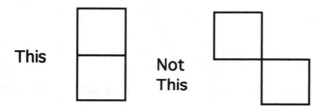

Rule 2: Mirror images count as one.

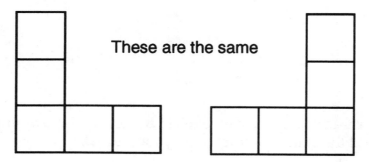

Rule 3: Only five color tiles may be used for each configuration.

Students may work alone or with a partner.
Upon completion, students share their solutions on the overhead projector.

☞   **Activity 8:   Build the Hexagon**

Purpose: To promote spatial visualization, logical reasoning, and understanding of equivalent fractions.

Materials: Activity Card 8.1 — Pattern Pieces

❑   Place a yellow hexagon from the pattern pieces on the overhead projector in front of the class. Ask students to experiment with the pattern pieces on their desks to see how many different ways they can build the hexagon. Allow students to illustrate their solutions on the overhead projector. Request that students call the blocks by their correct names, such as *trapezoid*. Students may at first build the hexagon using one type of pattern piece. Next, if students do not mention using a mixture of pattern pieces, then the teacher builds a mixed hexagon on the overhead. For example: one trapezoid and three triangles equal one hexagon.

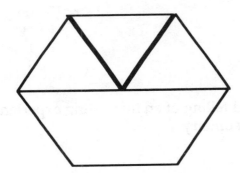

The goal of this activity is not to have each student reach the same conclusion, but rather to encourage varied mathematical thinking. Provide time for students to share their solutions with each other. Ask students how they decided that they had built all the possible combinations.

To tie the activity to an understanding of equivalent fractions, ask students to again refer to the hexagons that they built using only one shape. Build the hexagon with two trapezoids and write

"$\frac{1}{2} + \frac{1}{2} = 1$" on the board.

Using the other combinations, express each one in fraction equivalents.

Journal

Illustrate how each of the following can or cannot be made with triangles:

Square -

Rectangle -

Hexagon -

Write a letter to a friend telling of an interesting experience you had during your study of geometry.

Write a poem about building the hexagon.

✈ EXTENSIONS ✈

✳ **Key Ideas:** In Extensions, you may revisit some of the concepts and activities presented in this chapter. The following activities allow you to explore some ideas a little further. Sections include Mental Computation, Calculators, Critical Thinking, Alternative Assessment, and Mathematics for the 21st Century.

✈ Mental Computation ✈

☞ **Activity 9:   In Your Mind**

Purpose: To promote spatial visualization in mental computations.
Materials: Calculator

When elementary students have assignments, invite them to first mentally compute the answer. Write the result of the mental computation on the right side of the paper and circle it. After the homework is completed, ask students to use their calculators to check and see how close they were to their mental computation. The combination of computing a problem in their heads before solving it and then using a calculator to check it relieves the drudgery of correcting homework by the book. It also enhances the learning process and encourages critical thinking.

❑   Think out the steps needed to help students build a geometrical figure in their minds. Begin with simple figures and work up to complex ones.
Example 1:
    Close your eyes and visualize the following figure in your mind:
        1. I see 2 parallel lines, each 6 inches long.
        2. I see 2 additional lines, perpendicular to the first 2, each 32 inches long.
        3. The lines mentioned in number 2 close off the quadrilateral. What do you see? (Rectangle)
    Discussion follows with questions such as:
        1. Is this the only possible solution?
        2. Could the figure be placed in another position and still meet the criteria?
        3. Did you have to make any adjustments along the way?
Example 2:
    Close your eyes and visualize the following figure in your mind:
        1. I see a triangle.
        2. I see 2 sides that are each 4 inches long.
        3. I see a third side that is also 4 inches long. What do you see? (Equilateral Triangle)

✈ Calculators ✈

✳ **Key Ideas**   Calculators can be beneficial when students are learning to use the formulas for computing area. Students may be supplied with the following calculator formulas on a poster or overhead projector. Then they are asked to solve the problems that follow.

☞ **Activity 10:   Perimeter and Area**

Purpose: To understand the concepts of perimeter and area.
Materials: Calculator

❑   The calculator may be used to determine perimeter. The perimeter of a polygon is the total of the length of all sides.

1. Tanner's yard is shaped like an equilateral triangle. If the perimeter of the yard is 141 feet, what is the length of each side? (47 feet)

2. Emil is planning to fence his backyard to provide running space for his dogs. He measured one side of his rectangular yard and found it to be 87 feet long. The adjoining side is 32 feet long. What is the perimeter of his backyard? (238 feet)

❑   The calculator may also be used to determine area.

The following formulas are for determining area:

Triangle -

$$A = \frac{1}{2} b h$$

Rectangle -

$$A = l w$$

Square -

$$A = s^2$$

Parallelogram -

$$A = b h$$

❑   **Use a calculator to determine the area of each polygon.**

a. Rectangle
Length =   189 cm
Width   =   47 cm

b. Triangle
Base   =   78 cm
Height =   22 cm

c. Parallelogram
Base   =   238 cm
Height =   48 cm

d. Triangle
Base   =   89 cm
Height =   88 cm

e.   A triangle has a base of 24 cm and a height equal to three times the base. What is the area?

✈ Critical Thinking ✈

✳ **Key Ideas**   In the study of geometry, numerous technical geometrical terms are
encountered. In the past, the definitions of these terms as well as the
routine geometric formulas were learned by rote memorization and
often forgotten the next day. In order to promote high-order thinking
skills and understanding, rote memorization does not hold the place
it once did in elementary mathematics. Instead, formulas and
definitions can be placed on posters around the room or on the
blackboard for handy reference. Understanding and application of
the term and the formula are now stressed. Students can actively
learn to understand and classify quadrilaterals using definitions
placed on the overhead and the materials listed below.

 Activity 11:   Which Quadrilateral?

Purpose: To understand quadrilaterals.
Materials: Activity Card 8.6b — Quadrilaterals
                 Activity Card 4.13 — Protractor and Metric Ruler

For each figure on the Activity Card 8.6b Quadrilaterals, measure every
angle and side. Write the measures inside the quadrilateral and cut out the
figure. Use the quadrilaterals to classify those which fit in the categories
that follow. Some quadrilaterals may be placed in more than one group.

List the numbers of all quadrilaterals that belong in each classification:

1. A square   2. A parallelogram

3. A triangle   4. A rectangle

5. A rhombus   6. A trapezoid

7. Only one pair of parallel sides   8. Only one right angle

9. Two pairs of opposite parallel sides   10. Diagonals are perpendicular

✈ Alternative Assessment ✈

Student Self-Assessments

Student self-assessment involves students in the personal assessment of their own mathematical progress. Self-assessment may be an entirely new idea and suggests advance preparation and discussion with each student.

During the first week of the school year, discussion should center on mathematical goals for the year. Some possible goals follow:

1. Understand the mathematical concepts encountered.

2. Be open to implementing new strategies and new ideas.

3. Persist until the problem is solved.

4. Explain your mathematical reasoning to others in clear, concise terms while using manipulatives.

5. Work cooperatively with confidence.

Students need to be trained in the art of questioning techniques in order to correctly implement the art of self-assessment. Some sample questions students may ask themselves follow:

1. Did I clearly understand the problem?

2. Did I think the process through before beginning?

3. Did I create a feasible plan?

4. Did I solve the problem using a reasonable strategy?

5. Does the solution make sense?

6. Is there another way to solve this problem?

What does one do with student self-assessments? They can be placed in the student's portfolio and shared with parents. The teacher should look for agreement and disagreement between the student's self-assessment and the assessment of the teacher. Students can be asked to explain their growth in mathematical concepts using their self-assessments as examples. Students should be asked to regularly assess their own progress and to cite evidence that supports their self-assessments.

SAMPLE STATEMENTS FOR A
SELF-ASSESSMENT QUESTIONNAIRE

Check either "yes" or "no" to indicate your response to each statement.

Statements	Yes	No
1. Mathematics is useful.		
2. I enjoy mathematics.		
3. When a problem is hard, I give up.		
4. I use problem-solving strategies.		
5. I try more than one strategy.		

Group self-assessment can be used periodically to identify progress made toward the achievement of group goals.

SAMPLE QUESTIONS FOR A
GROUP SELF-ASSESSMENT QUESTIONNAIRE

Check "yes", "no", or "maybe" to indicate your response to each question.

Did your group...	Yes	No	Maybe
1. follow directions?			
2. work well together?			
3. allow each member to participate?			
4. implement strategies?			
5. persist until problem was solved?			

✈ Mathematics for the 21st Century ✈

Alternative Assessment

In the report on the future of mathematics education, *Everybody Counts* (Mathematical Sciences Education Board, 1989), the National Research Council stated that "we must ensure that tests measure what is of value, not just what is easy to test." Alternative assessment measures what is of value. Alternative assessment is not a goal in itself, but rather a means by which mathematical teaching and learning can be improved. The old-fashioned Friday Quiz that was given, recorded, and forgotten has now taken a back seat to the concept of alternative assessment. In order to implement alternative assessment, one must first have an assessment plan.

A sample plan is presented below.

1. Decide on goals for the unit.

2. Create a plan, based on the *Curriculum and Evaluation Standards for School Mathematics* (NCTM, 1989).

3. Set up a system of documentation of student achievement which includes portfolios, performance assessment, interviews, journals, observations, open-ended question responses, and student self-assessments.

4. Include manipulatives as a valuable part of assessment. Some states encourage the use of calculators, rulers, base 10 blocks, tangrams, and other manipulatives during assessment tasks.

5. Include cooperative group tasks as a part of the assessment procedures.

6. Share alternative assessment goals and ideas with students, parents, and other teachers.

Standardized and other multiple-choice tests provide a limited amount of information, predominately informing the teacher of what the student has memorized. By implementing alternative assessment, a greater understanding of student progress is gained. Standardized tests provide limited vision of what the student has memorized (like a horse with blinders). Alternative assessment provides wide-angle vision, allowing the teacher to grasp a true picture of the horizon of mathematical understandings and applications which the student has mastered and to what extent this has been accomplished.

Some recommended types of alternative assessment for use in the elementary school mathematics classroom are described briefly below.

A. Portfolios: In a portfolio, a student can collect a variety of quality work to share with his/her parents, teachers, and friends. A portfolio provides a means whereby each student can select his/her own best work to be assessed. Portfolios may contain a wide variety of activities such as projects, reports, poetry, essays, drawings, interviews, and favorite responses to open-ended questions. Portfolios allow the teacher or parent to comprehensively review progress made in the student's mathematical attitudes and understanding.

B. Performance Assessment: Performance assessment involves providing the student with a mathematical project and observing the degree of thoroughness with which he/she completes the task and presents it to the class. Performance assessment can involve either individual or group assessment. It can include the process and the product.

C. Interviews: Interviews with students provide a comfortable environment for the assessment of knowledge and understanding. When encouragement is given and the student is assured that this is a non-judgmental encounter, then feelings, thoughts, and understandings of the mathematical topics can be expressed. Questions should be planned ahead of time in order to provoke thoughtful responses.

D. Journals: Teachers set the pace for journals by requesting that students write a summary at the end of each day or by providing thought-provoking questions to which students respond. It is important that teachers model positive journal-writing techniques by writing in their own journals each time students write. Journals provide important opportunities for communication between student and teacher. Journals provide students with an opportunity to request help and to assess their own abilities in a non-judgmental environment.

E. Observations: Observations allow the teacher to assess students individually and in groups while they work on a given mathematical task. Observations reveal the way students organize data, create plans, complete tasks, explain ideas, make connections, and evaluate the results of a given task.

F. Open-ended Question Responses: Open-ended questions allow students to give a variety of responses. There is not one obvious answer. The diverse paths which students follow are assessed rather than the correct or incorrect answer. Responses to open-ended questions highlight student thinking.

G. Student Self-Assessments: Student self-assessment is a powerful tool that promotes high-order thinking skills, ownership of learning, and self-understanding. Students can evaluate how well they have completed the goals for the unit, how effectively they completed a task, or how well they participated in a group assignment. They can note areas with which they are most comfortable and ones which present problems. Ideas can be shared for future unit plans to include activities for individuals or the whole class. Students who think about, discuss, and assess their own progress in mathematics by providing examples from their own work will have a better understanding of their mathematical thinking. All students should work on worthwhile tasks and be evaluated in a manner that makes sense and is meaningful. Alternative assessment provides the opportunity for this vision to be implemented.

For additional information about alternative assessment see: Webb, N. Ed., *Assessment in the Mathematics Classroom*; Reston, VA: NCTM 1993.

9

Congruence, Symmetry, and Similarities

UNDERSTANDING CONGRUENCE, SYMMETRY, AND SIMILARITIES

1. Congruence and Rigid Motions
2. Symmetry
3. Similarity and Size

▼ PROBLEM CHALLENGE: Checkerboard Squares

How many squares of any size are on a checkerboard?

Hint: You may want to look for patterns and create a table, chart, or an organized list to help you visualize all possible considerations. The answer is not 64.

HANDS-ON MATHEMATICS ACTIVITIES

The following activities are presented to enhance your understanding of congruence, symmetry, and similarities.

Congruence and Rigid Motions

✳ **Key Ideas:**   Congruence, symmetry, and similarity are all three related to motion geometry. In other words, by changing the size of a geometric figure or moving its position, it is possible to tell if it is congruent or symmetric to another geometric figure. When asked if two figures are congruent, a student will usually try to place one on the other. Other ways to move a geometric figure around to determine congruence are called rigid motions. The three basic rigid motions for geometric figures are rotations (turns), translations (slides), and reflections (flips).

☞ **Activity 1: Translation, Rotation, and Reflection**

Purpose: To understand the concepts of translation, rotation, and reflection.

Materials: Activity Card 8.1 — Pattern Pieces
Activity Card 8.3 — Geoboard Recording Sheet

1. A figure can slide along straight lines: Translation (Slide)

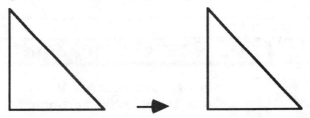

2. A figure can be turned around a point: Rotation (Turn)

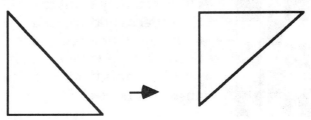

3. A figure can be flipped over a line: Reflection (Flip)

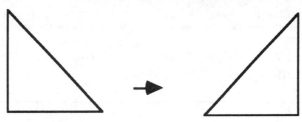

A. Using the trapezoid from the Activity Card 8.1 — Pattern Pieces, illustrate the meaning of a slide. Draw a picture of your activity on the Geoboard Recording Sheet and label it.

B. Once again use the trapezoid and rotate it to the right. Draw a picture of your activity on the Geoboard Recording Sheet and label it.

C. Use the trapezoid and flip it over. Illustrate your activity on the Geoboard Recording Sheet and label the front and back sides of the trapezoid.

D. Repeat the procedure using a triangle, square, and hexagon.

E. Create a geometric design of your own using two of the Pattern Pieces. Illustrate a slide, a rotation, and a flip using your design.

☞ **Activity 2: Congruency Test**

Purpose: To understand the concept of congruence.

Two plane figures are congruent providing one can be moved on top of the other by the process of translation, rotation, or reflection or a combination of any of the three motions.

Look at the figures illustrated below and determine whether the two figures are congruent. Circle either "yes" or "no". List the motion that is illustrated?

a.   ✈   ✈   **Congruent:** Yes   No

                               Motion: _____

b.   ➤➤   ↗   **Congruent:** Yes   No

                               Motion: _____

c.   ▲   ✈   **Congruent:** Yes   No

                               Motion: _____

Symmetry

✳ **Key Ideas:**   When we speak of congruence, we are usually describing a
relationship between two figures which are the same shape and size.
When we speak of symmetry, we are describing the means by which
one single figure can be divided into parts that are the same size and
shape. A design or geometric shape is symmetric when one part is
the mirror image of the other part. A line of symmetry is the point
where a figure can be divided in half so that each half is a mirror
image of the other.

☛ **Activity 3: Mirror Images**

Purpose: To understand the concept of mirror images.
Materials: Activity Card 9.3a — Mirror Cards
            Activity Card 9.3b — Mirror Stand
            Mirrors
            Ruler

First , you will need to put together the Mirror Stand on Activity Card 9.3b
and attach a mirror to that stand.

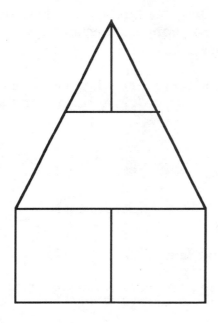

Place a mirror on the bottom line in order to create a mirror image. The
bottom line represents the line of symmetry.
Were you successful in creating a mirror image?

Now, follow the same procedure with the second figure.

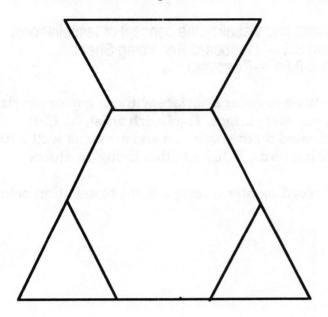

Did it work?

Next, using straight lines and a ruler, draw the letters of the alphabet on a sheet of paper. Use the mirror to decide which letters are symmetrical. List the letters which are symmetrical below.

Now, using your mirror and Activity Card 9.3a, determine which figures are symmetrical.

Finally, create four figures of your own. Using the mirror, determine whether these four figures are mirror images.

☞ **Activity 4: Tessellations**

Purpose: To understand and visualize the concept of tessellations.
Materials: Activity Card 8.3 — Geoboard Recording Sheet
              Activity Card 8.6a — Tessellations

A figure which can be used to cover a surface without gap or overlap can be said to *tessellate* or *tile* that surface. The Dutch artist, M. C. P (1898 - 1972), has fascinated mathematicians and artists as well with his famous tessellations using birds, fish, and other living creatures.

Using the Geoboard Recording Sheet, complete the tessellation below.

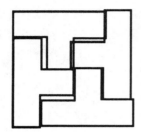

❏   What other letters will tessellate?

Using Activity Card 8.6a — Tessellations, continue the patterns illustrated until you cover an entire sheet of paper. Color your tessellations.

When a combination of two geometric figures form a tessellation, it is called a semi-regular tessellation. Using a square and an octagon, create a semi-regular tessellation.

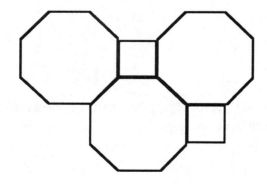

Color your design.

Would your design be appropriate for a kitchen floor?

☞ **Activity 5:   The Game of Hex**

Purpose: To understand the Game of Hex.
Materials: Activity Card 9.5 — Game of Hex

❑   **The Game of Hex**

Hex is a game of deductive reasoning played by two participants on a
game board of eleven by eleven hexagons. See Activity Card 9.5 — Game
of Hex. The two players take turns placing their mark (usually an "x" or
an "o") on any hexagon which is unoccupied. The first player attempts to
form an unbroken line from the left of the board to the right, while the
second player attempts to form an unbroken line from the bottom to the
top of the board. The lines do not have to be straight. The first player to
reach the opposite side is declared the winner.

The Primary Game of Hex

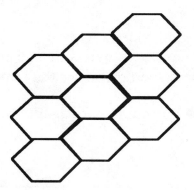

The game can be used for primary grade students using a 3 by 3 or 4 by 4
grid instead of the usual 11 by 11. When the game is finished, students can
discuss strategies that they found useful and consider what different
strategies they would apply the next time.

Similarity and Size

> ✳ **KEY IDEAS:** Similarity deals with changes in size. A change in size uniformly multiplies the sides of a figure with no changes to either the shape or the angles. When a drawing is enlarged, a new picture is obtained in which everything is a different size, but the same shape. A size change can be easily accomplished by using a graph.

☞ **Activity 6:** **Big and Small**

Purpose: To understand the concept of enlarging a picture by using a graph.

Materials: Activity Card 6.3 — One-inch Graph Paper
Activity Card 11.2 — One-centimeter Graph Paper

Copy the geometric figure below onto one-inch graph paper, enlarging the picture one section at a time.

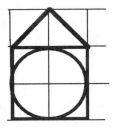

If you had used a magnifying glass, would you see the same results?

Create another figure and try the procedure once again. Next, try it with a friend.

✎ Journal

In what ways can you find examples of symmetry in your daily walk or drive to school?

Draw two illustrations of symmetry found in nature.

Draw one example of symmetry which you have discovered in your classroom.

✈ EXTENSIONS ✈

✳ Key Ideas: In Extensions, you may revisit some of the concepts and activities presented in this chapter. The following activities allow you to explore some ideas a little further. Sections include Mental Computation, Critical Thinking, Alternative Assessment, and Mathematics for the 21st Century.

✈ Mental Computation ✈

☞ **Activity 7:   Half and Half**

Purpose: To enhance spatial visualization using mental computation.

For each figure, make only one cut to create two congruent halves. Hint: the cut does not have to be a straight line, but must be one continuous line.

a.

b.
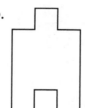

c.
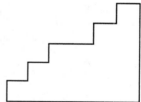

d.

e.

f.

g.
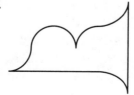

✈ Critical Thinking ✈

Critical thinking activities in the area of Geometry are important and should be a predominant part of the curriculum. Teaching students to critically analyze new concepts as they are presented will enhance their understanding and help them integrate learning into their daily lives.

The concept of the Problem Challenge can be used to emphasize critical thinking. Instead of merely giving out the problem, ask questions similar to those that follow in activity 8.

☞ **Activity 8:   Diagonals and More Diagonals**

Purpose: To understand and apply the concept of diagonal.

Problem Challenge

❑   How many diagonals are there in two hexagons?

　　　1. How many sides does a hexagon have?
　　　2. What else do we know about a hexagon?
　　　3. What strategy was useful in solving the problem?
　　　4. How would you describe a diagonal?

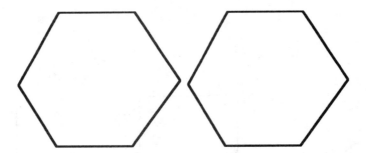

❑   After you solve the problem answer these questions:

　　1. How did you know where to begin?
　　2. Did you follow any blind leads?
　　3. Is there another way to solve the problem?
　　4. If you were planning a shopping center in a nearby town, how might this information help you?
　　5. Were the diagonals easy to count?
　　6. How many diagonals does a 12-sided polygon have?
　　7. How many diagonals does a 24-sided polygon have?
　　8. Do you see a pattern here?

✈ Alternative Assessment ✈

Documentation and Reporting

As the curriculum and the ways to assess it change, reporting to parents, administrators, other schools, and to the students themselves must change. What we report, as well as how it is reported, requires change. A variety of assessment techniques may be used in addition to the usual test scores and grades: portfolios, checklists, observations, journals, interviews, and performance assessment.

In order to facilitate change, the documentation of these new techniques should be recorded in a way that makes it meaningful to the teacher, the student, and the world outside the elementary classroom.

Descriptive reports can shed light on the understanding that is taking place in the classroom. Such reports provide much more information than the mere recording of a test score or letter grade. A descriptive report might include comments on the following:

1. daily student work
2. major project presentations
3. group projects
4. problem challenge of the day/week
5. journal
6. interviews
7. innovative ideas
8. ability to plan
9. ability to ask probing questions
10. ability to think critically when processing new information
11. ability to listen to the ideas of others
12. ability to provide group leadership
13. ability to persist in carrying out a plan
14. ability to evaluate
15. willingness to work cooperatively
16. willingness to try multiple approaches
17. additional student work
18. positive student behaviors
19. criteria used to assess the activities/understandings
20. suggestions for parental assistance

Comments made in descriptive reports should be a faithful reflection of the student's understanding and achievement as evidenced by the activities accomplished.

```
✈ Mathematics for the 21st Century ✈
```

Mathematical Connections

The fourth Standard of the *Curriculum and Evaluation Standards for School Mathematics* (NCTM, 1989) states that students in grades K - 4 and 5 - 8 should be provided with opportunities to make connections to be able to do the following:

1. **Link conceptual and procedural knowledge.**
   When students enter school, they do not have their ideas and thought patterns segregated into academic or subject areas. Therefore, it is important to build on their perspective and expand it to include mathematics. They understand the concrete concept of counting, so it is best to relate the abstract concepts of addition and subtraction to what is already known. In this way they will learn that mathematics is not a set of rules or procedures to be memorized, and they will develop the ability to invent new procedures when necessary.

   Methods which require the students to become active participants in the learning process can be used to accomplish this objective. A series of well-thought-out questions which lead students to answer "how" and "why" is more effective than a lecture.

2. **Recognize the fact that there are relationships between different topics within mathematics.**
   Connections between mathematics topics can also occur. There is no longer a need to teach each individual concept as a separate strand. Problem solving can be intertwined with all areas of the curriculum. Computation, geometry, and measurement, instead of being taught in isolation, can be interwoven. It is important that students be given opportunities to connect ideas both among and within different areas of mathematics. When these connections are lacking, students tend to learn and memorize too many isolated facts and concepts rather than learning the principals of integrated mathematics.

3. **Apply mathematical thinking and modeling to solve problems in other curriculum areas.**
   The *Professional Standards for Teaching Mathematics* (NCTM, 1991) stresses the fact that modern elementary mathematics should emphasize connections between mathematics and other disciplines. It should also provide reflections on the connections between mathematics and science, social studies, language arts, music, and art while engaging all students in tasks which promote those connections.

The K - 4 program provides numerous opportunities to incorporate mathematics into other subject areas and to use other subject areas in mathematics as well. Science and mathematics connect quite naturally. The unit on the Metric System can become a mathematics-science unit. In having students write to share their mathematical thinking and learning experiences, the connection is made to language arts. Including a children's literature book to be read aloud during each unit strengthens the language arts connection. When solving problems, include information on other countries or the past history of our own country to connect with social studies. While studying maps, show that measurement is involved in the use of scale models. When students complete the broad jump in physical education, they use measurement to determine the distance jumped. In art, students can integrate geometry and patterns. Music has a definite beat, and the time as well as the value of the musical notes have mathematical representations.

4. **Use mathematics in their own daily activities while learning to value the role of mathematics in our culture.**
   Another connection should include the interests and activities of the students in the classroom. Whenever possible, it is best to begin a lesson with problems derived from the lives of the students or their environment. This provides a purpose for learning a particular skill or concept and a reason for applying it to their lives.

   In the past, students have often learned mathematics in the classroom with no relation to their lives outside that classroom. Now, it is the teacher's task and responsibility to indicate ways in which mathematics can permeate the lives of students. The newspaper can provide one example. Outside speakers who use mathematics in their careers can also be a positive addition to the classroom. When mathematical ideas are connected to everyday experiences, children tend to become more aware of the usefulness of mathematics.

   In order to experience mathematical connections, students should participate in interactive learning activities. The purpose of this standard is to help students visualize how mathematical ideas are related. Providing students with mathematical connections presents them with a more effective understanding of exactly how mathematics works. Manipulatives and cooperative learning provide opportunities to extend mathematical concepts through discussion and application. Using connections, as highlighted above, will lead to a greater understanding of mathematics and its usefulness as well as a longer retention of mathematical concepts. Persistent attention to the recognition of connections between topics and other disciplines will instill in the students the idea that the mathematical concepts which they are learning are relevant and useful.

10

Measurement

UNDERSTANDING MEASUREMENT

1. Metric Measure
2. Perimeter and Area
3. Area of Quadrilaterals and Triangles

▼ PROBLEM CHALLENGE: Building Perspective

1. A log is 6 feet long.
   How many cuts are needed
   to make 1-foot pieces?

2. Spencer wants to build a fence
   120 feet long. How many fence
   posts are needed if each post
   is 10 feet from the next?

HANDS-ON MATHEMATICS ACTIVITIES

The following activities are provided to enhance your understanding of measurement.

Metric Measure

> ✳ **Key Ideas:** The United States is the only major country in the world that continues to use the English system. Even the English have switched to the metric system. You are probably familiar with some of the metric system since you purchase many items that have been packaged or made with metric measures.

☞ **Activity 1: Measuring Length**

Purpose: To measure length.
Materials: Paper clips

Almost any item can be measured using a non-standard unit of measure. We may find ourselves using a non-standard unit of measure when we need to know the length of an object, but do not have a ruler at hand. Children can gain an understanding of measuring by using non-standard units of measure.

Small or regular paper clips can be used to measure length.

❑   What is the length of this line in paper clips?

_____

(The length is between 3 and 4 regular paper clips in length.)

1. What is the width of this page in paper clips?

2. What is the length of this page in paper clips?

3. What are the advantages of using a paper clip as a unit of measure?

4. What are the disadvantages of using a paper clip as a unit of measure?

☛   **Activity 2: Metric Measure**

Purpose: To measure length with a centimeter ruler.
Materials: Activity Card 4.13 — Centimeter Ruler

The numbered distances on your ruler are centimeter lengths. There are several convenient ways of remembering the length of a centimeter. It is approximately the width of your little finger, the diameter of an M&M, the thickness of a slice of bread, or the width of a paper clip. Perhaps you can think of an example that would be useful to you.

❑   What is the length of this line in centimeters?

_____

(The length is approximately 10 centimeters.)

1. First, estimate the length of the first line below and write it in the chart beside "estimate." Now measure the same line and write it beside "actual." Estimate the next line and enter your estimate. Now measure it. Continue to estimate, measure, estimate, measure to complete the table.

a._____

b._____

c._____

d._____

e._____

f._____

Line	a	b	c	d	e	f
Estimate						
Actual						

2. Why is it helpful for students to estimate the length of each line before measuring?

☞ **Activity 3: A Centimeter Measuring Game**

Purpose: To gain an understanding of centimeter measuring.
Materials: Large washers or counters

This game helps the participants become adept at estimating distances in centimeters.

How to play the game.

1. Two to four players set up the track on a surface such as a large table. Change the dimensions to fit the table if needed. Use large heavy washers at each vertex of the triangular track. Measure distances from the center of each washer. Mark the position of each vertex on the table in case the washers are moved.

2. Each player has a counter or a washer marked with his or her initials. Player one places his washer at vertex 1 and snaps it with his finger, striking his washer with his fingernail, attempting to strike vertex 2.

3. The player attempts to estimate the distance from vertex 1 to the washer within plus or minus 2 centimeters. He continues to snap his washer attempting to strike vertex 2 if he estimates correctly. He again estimates the distance from vertex 1 to his washer. As long as he estimates correctly within plus or minus 2 centimeters, he may continue.

4. If the player does not estimate correctly, he marks the position of his washer and continues from that spot when it is his turn again.

5. Play continues until one person strikes vertex 1.

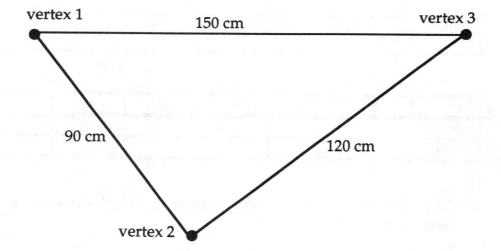

☛ Activity 4: Converting Metric Measures

Purpose: To understand how to read and write a decimal.

The metric prefixes are given in the chart. These prefixes are placed in front of each basic measurement unit: meter for length, gram for mass, and liter for volume, for example.

Conversions within the metric system can be made using the chart.

Prefix	kilo-	hecto-	deka-	(none)	deci-	centi-	milli-
Symbol	k	h	dk		d	c	m
Meaning	1000	100	10	1	0.1	0.01	0.001

Example: Convert 344.7 centimeters to meters. Write 334.7 in the centimeter box. Meters are 2 spaces to the left. Convert 344.7 centimeters to meters by simply moving the decimal point 2 places to the left (the same as dividing by 100)

Prefix	kilo-	hecto-	deka-	Meter	deci-	centi-	milli-
				3.447		344.7	

To change 344.78 cm to mm, move the decimal one space to the right. Notice how the other conversions have been made.

Prefix	kilo-	hecto-	deka-	Meter	deci-	centi-	milli-
	.003447	.03447	.3447	3.447	34.47	344.7	3447.

❑   Make the conversions:

a. 34 km to cm   b. 2.3 dkm to mm   c. 565.7 dm to km

d. 67.54 mm to dm   e. 1234 mm to dm   f. 56.23 cm to m

✎ Journal

Describe what you like best about the metric system.

Work with a friend to create a riddle about the metric system. Record the riddle in your journal.

Perimeter and Area

> **✳ Key Ideas:** Perimeter is the distance around an object. It is measured in units of length such as you used in activities 1 – 4. Area is the amount of surface inside the perimeter. Area is measured in square units.

☞ **Activity 5: Perimeter**

Purpose: To determine the perimeter on the geoboard.
Materials: Geoboard and Rubber Bands

The perimeter of a polygon is found by determining the distance around the outside of the polygon.

The geoboard is useful for determining perimeter. You may use a geoboard or dot paper for the following activities.

Example:
   Find the perimeter of each figure on these geoboards.

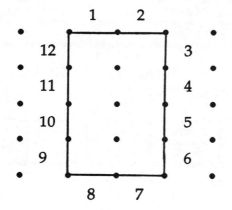 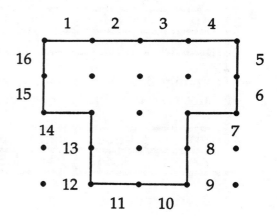

The distance between the pegs on your geoboard or the dots above is 1 unit. To determine the perimeter, it is necessary to simply count the number of units around the outside of the polygon.

The rectangular polygon above left has a perimeter of 12 units.

The polygon on the right has a perimeter of 16 units.

❑ What limitations does the geoboard place on determining perimeter?

Find the perimeter of each polygon.

a
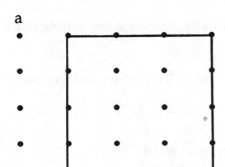

b.
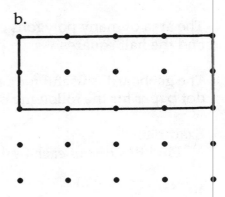

c.
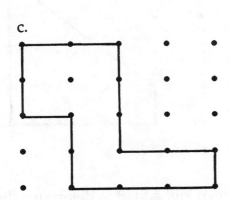

d.
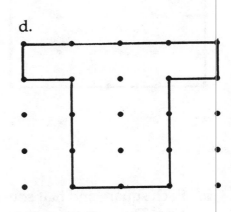

e.
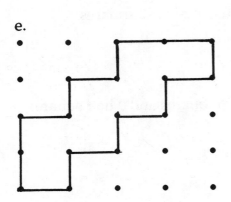

f.
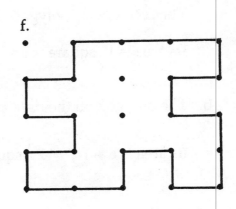

☞ **Activity 6: Area and the Whole-Half Method**

Purpose: To use the whole-half method of finding area.
Materials: Geoboard and Rubber Bands

The area of many polygons can be found by counting the whole squares and the half squares.

The geoboard is useful for determining area. You may use a geoboard or dot paper for the following activities.

Example:
    Find the area of each figure on these geoboards.

a. 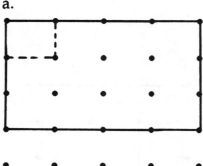   b.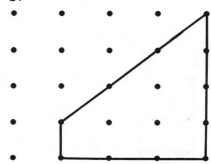

a. Each square and half square is counted and added to determine the area. The number is given the label of square units.

    The rectangular polygon above left contains 12 squares.

    Its area is 12 square units.

b. The polygon on the right contains 6 squares and 3 half squares.

    Its area is $6 + 1\frac{1}{2} = 7\frac{1}{2}$ square units.

Find the area of each polygon using the whole-half method.

a.

b.

c.

d.

e.

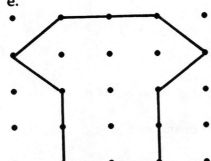

f.

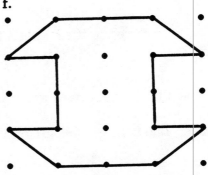

☞ **Activity 7: Area and the Rectangle-Halving Method**

Purpose: To determine the area on the geoboard.
Materials: Geoboard and Rubber Bands

The area of many triangles can be found by making an appropriate rectangle and determining its area. The area of the triangle is one-half the area of the rectangle.

The geoboard is useful for determining area. You may use a geoboard or dot paper for the following activities.

Example:
    Find the area of each triangle.

a.

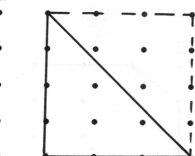

b.

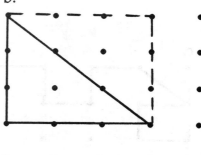

a. On the geoboard above and left, the area of the rectangle is 12.

The triangle has an area one-half that of the rectangle.

The area of the triangle is $\frac{1}{2} \times 12 = 6$ square units.

b. On the geoboard at right, the area of the rectangle is 9.

The triangle has an area one-half that of the rectangle.

The area of the triangle is $\frac{1}{2} \times 9 = 4\frac{1}{2}$ square units.

Find the area of each triangle using the rectangle-halving method.

a.

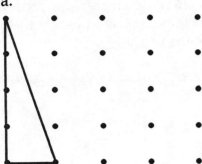

b.

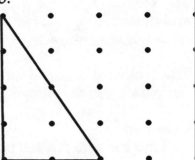

c.

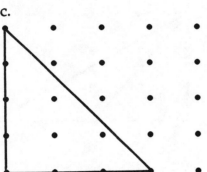

d.

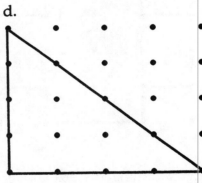

e.

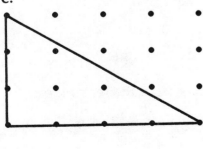

f.

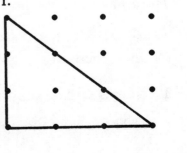

☞   **Activity 8: Area and the Is-Not Method**

Purpose: To determine the area on the geoboard.
Materials: Geoboard and Rubber Bands

The area of any polygon can be found by making an appropriate rectangle and determining its area. Areas outside the polygon but inside the rectangle are subtracted from the area of the rectangle.

The geoboard is useful for determining area. You may use a geoboard or dot paper for the following activities.

Example:
     Find the area of each polygon.

a.

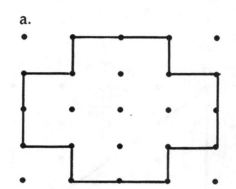

b.

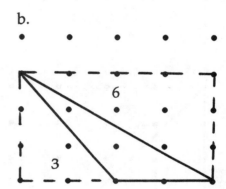

a.   On the geoboard above left, the area of the rectangle is 16.

     The area of the four corners that will be subtracted is 4.

     The area of the polygon is 16 – 4 = 12 square units.

b.   On the geoboard at right, the area of the rectangle is 12.

     Two areas will be subtracted from the area of the rectangle.
        1) The area of the upper right triangle is $\frac{1}{2} \times 12 = 6$.

        2) The area of the lower left triangle is $\frac{1}{2} \times 6 = 3$

     The area of the triangle in question is 12 – 6 – 3 = 3 square units.

Find the area of each polygon using the is-not method.

a.

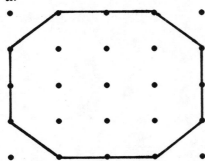

b.

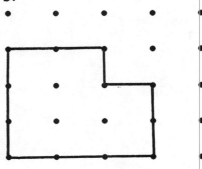

c.

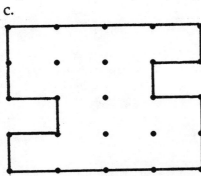

d.

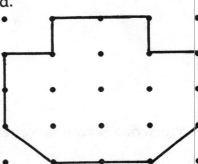

e.

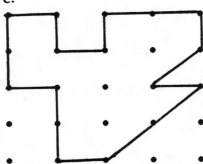

f.

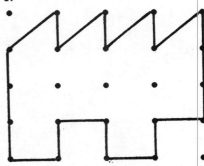

✎ Journal

Illustrate two ways of finding the area of triangles on a geoboard. Record the illustrations in your journal.

1.

2.

Which one is your favorite?

Why?

Area of Quadrilaterals and Triangles

✳ **Key Ideas:**   The formulas used to determine the area of many polygons can be developed on the geoboard.

☞   **Activity 9: The Area of a Square**

Purpose: To develop the formula for determining the area of a square.
Materials: Geoboard and Rubber Bands

The geoboard is useful for developing the formula for the area of a square. You may use a geoboard or dot paper for the following activities. Make each square on your geoboard. Determine the length of two adjoining sides and the area of each square. Write your findings in the chart.

Example:
   Find the length of two adjoining sides and the area of each square.

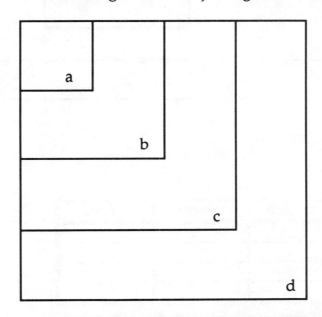

Square	Side	Side	Area
a	1	1	1
b	2		
c	3		
d	4		

❏   What mathematical process can you apply to the two sides to obtain the area? Complete the formula:

Area = side   side

☛ **Activity 10:   The Area of a Rectangle**

Purpose: To develop the formula for determining the area of a rectangle.
Materials: Geoboard and Rubber Bands

The geoboard is useful for developing the formula for the area of a rectangle. You may use a geoboard or dot paper for the following activities.

❑   Make each rectangle on your geoboard. Determine length, width, and area of each rectangle. Write your findings in the chart.

Example:
    Find the width, length, and the area of each rectangle.

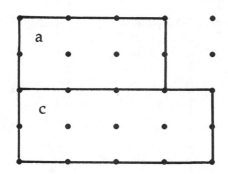 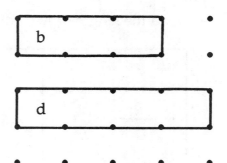

Rectangle	Length	Width	Area
a	3	2	6
b	2		
c	3		
d	4		

❑   What mathematical process using the width and length obtains the area?

Complete the formula:

Area = length   width

☞ **Activity 11:   The Area of a Parallelogram**

Purpose: To develop a formula for the area of a parallelogram.
Materials: Geoboard and Rubber Bands

The geoboard is useful for developing the formula for the area of a parallelogram. You may use a geoboard or dot paper for the following activities.

Make each parallelogram on your geoboard. Determine the length, width, and area of each parallelogram. Write your findings in the chart.

Example:
   Find the length, height, and area of each parallelogram.

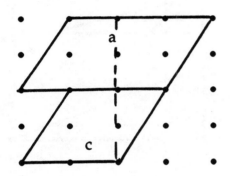
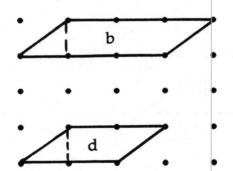

Parallelogram	Length	Height	Area
a	3	2	6
b	3		
c	2		
d	2		

❑   What mathematical process can be applied to the width and length to obtain the area?

Complete the formula:

$$\textbf{Area = length \quad height}$$

☞   **Activity 12:   The Area of a Triangle**

Purpose: To develop the formula for determining the area of a triangle.
Materials: Geoboard and Rubber Bands

The geoboard is useful for developing the formula for the area of a triangle. You may use a geoboard or dot paper for the following activities.

Make each triangle on your geoboard. Determine the base, height, and area of each triangle. Write your findings in the chart.

Example:
    Find the base, height and area of each triangle.

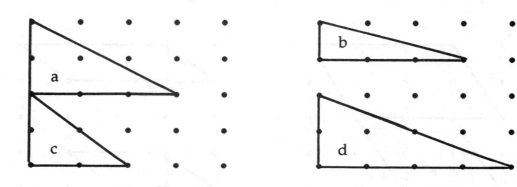

Triangle	Base	Height	Area
a	3	2	6
b	3		
c	2		
d	4		

❑   What mathematical process can be applied to the width and length to obtain the area?

Complete the formula:

$$\textbf{Area} = \quad \textbf{base} \quad\quad \textbf{height}$$

Find the area of each polygon using the formulas.
Confirm your findings using any of the three methods.

a.

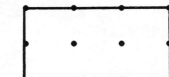

b.

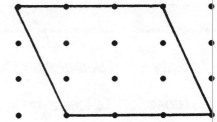

c.

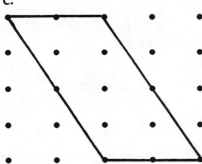

d.

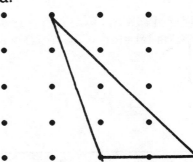

e.

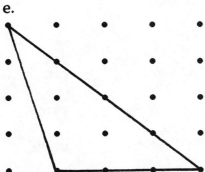

f.

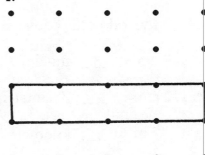

✈ EXTENSIONS ✈

 Key Ideas: In Extensions, you may revisit some of the concepts and activities presented in this chapter. The following activities allow you to explore some ideas a little further. Sections include Critical Thinking, Alternative Assessment, and Mathematics for the 21st Century.

✈ Critical Thinking ✈

☞ **Activity 13:   Measurement in The United States**

Purpose: To look at metric purchases.

The United States continues to rely upon the English or customary measurement system for most everyday measures. There are items, however, that can be purchased using metric measures.

List six items you can purchase that use a metric measure. Do not consider items labeled with ounces and the equivalent grams.

1.   3.

2.   4.

☞ **Activity 14:   Measurement in The United States**

Purpose: To look at measurement conversions.

Make the following conversions (See activity 4):

a. 112 cm =   ___ meters   b. 1,147 m =   ___ centimeters

c. 112 cm =   ___ decimeters   d. 7,897 cm =   ___ yards

e. 1,147 m = ___ kilometers   f. 17,000 feet = ___ miles

g. What difficulties, if any, arise when making conversions within the
   metric system of measurement?

☞ **Activity 15:** Measurement in The United States

Purpose: To look at measurement conversions.

1. Make the following conversions:

a. 139 inches = ___ feet   b. 14 feet = ___ inches

c. 139 inches = ___ yards   d. 17,000 feet = ___ yards

e. 14 feet = ___ yards   f. 17,000 feet = ___ miles

2. Complete the following computations:

a.   2 yards, 2 feet, 8 inches   b.   13 yards, 2 feet, 4 inches
   + 2 yards, 2 feet, 6 inches   − 11 yards, 2 feet, 8 inches

What difficulties, if any, arise when making conversions within the English system of measurement?

☞ **Activity 16:** **Measurement in The United States**

Purpose: To look at converting to the metric system.

The United States continues to rely upon the English or customary measurement system. List five advantages for switching to the metric system and five disadvantages.

Advantages	**Disadvantages**
1.	1.
2.	2.
3.	3.
4.	4.
5.	5.

✈ Alternative Assessment ✈

Conferences

Conferences with students can reveal a vast amount of information about their attitude towards and understanding of mathematics. During a conference, students can receive encouragement from the teacher and, after trust is developed, feel free to ask questions about the topic under current consideration or topics covered in the past.

The teacher should explain the purpose of the conference and demonstrate it thoroughly to the whole class before the procedure is implemented. First, decide the time schedule for the conferences. Will they be held every day after lunch during a thirty-minute study hall time? Will they be held once or twice a week during the last ten minutes of mathematics class? A regular scheduled time and routine for conferences will increase their meaningfulness to both the student and the teacher.

It is a good idea to let the student sign up for the conference. This way it is voluntary rather than procedural. After several weeks, it may be wise to suggest that each class member schedule a conference before the end of the month or grading period. Conferences may be requested by either the teacher or the student.

Assure students that no grade is assigned to a conference, but that this is a time for teacher and student to better visualize mathematical understandings and misunderstandings as well as to exchange ideas for future curriculum change.

For the first conference, offer a selected topic for discussion. Ask students to come prepared to let you know one particular area of mathematics in which they are experiencing either difficulty or joy or both. Another beginning topic might be, "How did you feel about the geometric art activity we did on Thursday?"

During conferences, personal difficulties and other roadblocks may be discussed by the student. This is an acceptable part of the conference schedule. A child who is struggling to solve a difficult personal situation alone cannot easily concentrate on the mathematical task at hand. By allowing time for this verbalization to occur, the roadblock may be removed and a sense of trust and confidence be developed between the student and teacher.

→ Mathematics for the 21st Century →

Implementing Technology in the Classroom

In their 1989 document, the *Curriculum and Evaluation Standards for School Mathematics*, The National Council of Teachers of Mathematics recommended that some areas of the current curriculum receive increased attention and that other areas receive decreased attention. The use of calculators and computers was recommended to receive increased attention in elementary mathematics classrooms.

In reference to the use of calculators, NCTM reiterated that the elementary mathematics teacher should be able to do the following:

- implement calculators as useful tools for learning mathematics;
- make appropriate and continuous use of calculators;
- use calculators to explore patterns and numbers;
- incorporate the use of calculators in problem solving;
- implement the use of calculators in realistic situations; and
- assist students in deciding on the reasonableness of an answer.

Calculators do not replace the need for basic computation skills, basic facts, estimation, and mental computation. Instead, calculators can be used as an alternative to constant paper-and-pencil computation.

Computers hold an important place in the elementary mathematics classroom as a powerful supplement to standard classroom learning. Computer programs can prove beneficial to students in the areas of problem solving, critical thinking, geometry, and number concepts. Many programs present realistic problems for the student to solve.

The use of computers in the elementary classroom provides a meaningful change from the standard operating procedures which involve only computation. Computers also provide students with new ways and means to explore the mathematical content for their grade level.

The careful, creative use of technology can add quality to the curriculum and a sense of joy and accomplishment for students. The integration of calculators and computers into the elementary school mathematics program is vital to the implementation of mathematical reform for the 21st century.

11

Algebra and Coordinate Geometry

UNDERSTANDING ALGEBRA and COORDINATE GEOMETRY

1. Tables and Graphs
2. Writing Formulas
3. Solving Problems with Tables and Graphs
4. Geometry with Coordinates

▼ PROBLEM CHALLENGE: Bottle of Wine

A bottle of wine costs $10.00.
If the wine costs $9.00 more than
the cork and bottle, how much
did the wine cost? How much
did the cork and bottle cost?

HANDS-ON MATHEMATICS ACTIVITIES

The following activities are provided to enhance your understanding of
algebra and coordinate geometry.

Tables and Graphs

> ✳ **Key Ideas:**   Tables and graphs are useful tools for displaying data in an organized way.

☛ **Activity 1: Constructing a Table**

Purpose: To gain an understanding of placing data in an organized table.

Many people are interested in the gas mileage of their car. Mrs. Smith drove 297 miles on 11 gallons of gasoline and determined that she was obtaining 27 miles per gallon. Complete the following table:

Gallons	Miles
1	
2	
3	
4	
5	
6	
7	
8	
9	
10	
11	297
12	

1. Do you expect this car to always obtain this gas mileage? Why?

2. The car's gas tank holds 12 gallons. What is the car's range (the distance the car can travel on one full tank of gas) for a single tank of gas?

3. What advantages does a table have when interpreting data?

☞   **Activity 2: Constructing a Graph**

Purpose: To gain an understanding of constructing a line graph.
Materials: Activity Card 11.2 — One-centimeter Graph Paper

Line graphs should include a title, a label for each axis, and an appropriate
scale for each axis. The independent variable is placed along the x-axis and
the dependent variable is placed along the y-axis.

Complete the following graph using the data from the table in activity 1.
Complete the graph on one-centimeter graph paper.

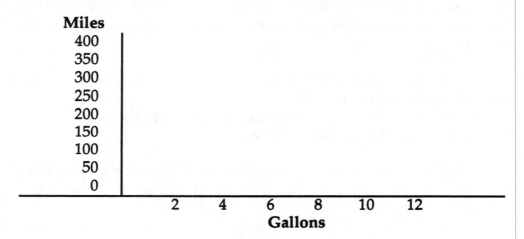

The Miles per Gallon for Linda's Car

1.   What advantages does a graph have over a table?

2.   What is the slope (rise over run or the change in y divided by the
     change in x) of this graph?

3.   What does the slope of the graph indicate?

4.   The x-axis represents the independent (manipulated) variable. Why are
     the number of gallons considered the independent (responding)
     variable?

5.   The y-axis represents the dependent variable. Why is the number of
     miles considered the dependent variable?

Writing Formulas

✳ **Key Ideas: Formulas provide another way of summarizing and presenting data.**

☞ **Activity 3:   Writing Formulas**

Purpose: To gain an understanding of writing formulas.
Materials: Data Table from Activity 1
Graph from Activity 1

Data that forms a straight-line graph such as you made in Activity 2 are easily represented by a formula. Recall the general formula for a straight line: $y = mx$. Remember that y is the dependent variable, and x is the independent variable.

❑ **From the chart in Activity 1 or the graph in Activity 2, we can write a formula representing the data.**
Example: One set of data from the previous activity was
11 gallons and 297 miles.

Using the formula $y = mx$, where $y = 297$ and $x = 11$, we obtain

$$
\begin{aligned}
y &= mx \\
297 &= 11m \\
m &= 297/11 \\
m &= 27
\end{aligned}
$$

1. Do you obtain the same results with other data from the table or graph? Why or why not?

2. What does the number 27 represent?

3. What calculations are needed to determine that $m = 27$ from the table and from the graph?

4. What advantages does a formula have over a table or graph?

Journal

Data can be organized by using a table or a graph. Data may also be represented by a formula. Describe two advantages and two disadvantages of expressing data in a table, graph, or in a formula.

Table

Advantages   Disadvantages

1.   1.

2.   2.

Graph

Advantages   Disadvantages

1.   1.

2.   2.

Formula

Advantages   Disadvantages

1.   1.

2.   2.

Which do you prefer?

Where do you see tables, graphs, and formulas in your daily life?

Solving Problems with Tables and Graphs

✳ **Key Ideas:**   Problems can be solved in a variety of ways, including the use of tables and graphs.

☞   **Activity 4:   Problem Solving with Tables and Graphs**

Purpose: To gain an understanding of tables and graphs.
Materials: Activity Card 11.2 — One-centimeter Graph Paper

The following data are 30 student test scores and their grade-point averages after one semester in college.

Student	1	2	3	4	5	6	7	8	9	10
Test Score	300	600	500	400	800	500	700	600	500	600
GPA	1.5	2.5	3.5	2.5	4.0	3.5	3.5	3.5	3.5	4.0

Student	11	12	13	14	15	16	17	18	19	20
Test Score	400	400	500	300	700	500	500	500	800	600
GPA	3.5	1.5	2.0	2.5	4.0	3.0	2.5	3.5	3.0	2.5

Student	21	22	23	24	25	26	27	28	29	30
Test Score	500	800	500	400	700	700	400	600	500	300
GPA	2.5	3.5	2.0	2.0	3.5	3.0	3.0	3.0	3.0	2.0

Make a table of the scores on the next page. Place the test scores in the first column (independent variable, x-axis) consecutively ordered with the low scores at the bottom and with the high scores at the top. Place the GPA scores in the second column.

Construct a scattergram of data by placing all 30 points on the graph below the table you constructed on the next page. A scattergram is the result of placing all the data on a graph with no line drawn.
Draw one straight "line of best fit" through the point of your scattergram. A line of best fit is your best judgment of where a straight line could be drawn to complete the graph. About half the points should fall above and below the line of best fit.

Write a formula for the line you drew. Remember that $y = mx + b$, where m is the slope and b is the x-intercept.

How does the "line of best fit" help make predictions?

Why are many predictions determined by the line of best fit erroneous?

Complete the table by placing the test scores and grade-point averages in appropriate places.

Table: Test scores of 30 students and their first-semester college GPA.

Test Score	GPA	Test Score	GPA	Test Score	GPA

Complete the graph by placing an x for each piece of data in the appropriate place. Draw one line of best fit through the points.

Graph: Scattergraph of test scores of 30 students and their first-semester college GPA.

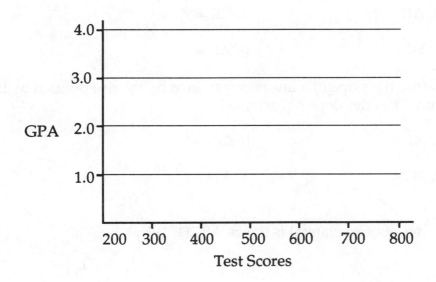

Geometry with Coordinates

✳ Key Ideas: Geometry with coordinates links geometry and algebra.

☞ **Activity 5:   Coordinate Geometry**

Purpose: To gain an understanding of coordinate geometry.
Materials: Activity Card 11.2 — One-centimeter Graph Paper

Below are four coordinates placed on a graph.

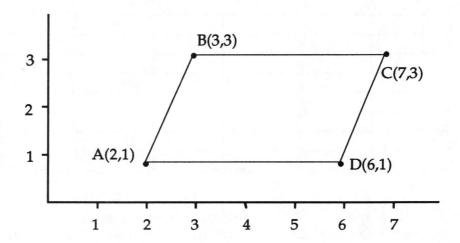

1. Use the distance formula to find the length of the following lines:

    a. AB =   b. CD =

    c. BC =   d. AD =

2. Recall that the slope of a line is determined by the rise divided by the run. Find the slope of each line:

    a. AB =   b. CD =

    c. BC =   d. AD =

3 What kind of quadrilateral is figure ABCD? Why?

Journal

How can a table or a graph help you in problem solving?

Where would you use coordinate geometry?

In Activity 4, what does the slope m (in the formula y = mx + b) of the graph tell you?

In Activity 4 what does b (in the formula y = mx + b) of the graph tell you?

✈ EXTENSIONS ✈

 Key Ideas: In Extensions, you may revisit the concepts and activities presented in this chapter. The following activities allow you to explore some ideas a little further. Sections include Calculators, Critical Thinking, Alternative Assessment, and Mathematics for the 21st Century.

Calculators

☞ **Activity 6:   Temperature Conversions**

Purpose: To use a formula to convert temperature scales.

Use $C = \dfrac{5}{9}(F - 32)$ or $F = \dfrac{9}{5}C + 32$ to convert each temperature.

a. $0°\,C =$ __ $°\,F$ b. $32°\,F =$ __ $°\,C$ c. $75°\,C =$ __ $°\,F$

d. $25°\,C =$ __ $°\,F$ e. $68°\,F =$ __ $°\,C$ f. $212°\,F =$ __ $°\,C$

✈ Critical Thinking ✈

☞ **Activity 7:   Construct a Graph**

Purpose: To construct a graph of the movement of an object.
Materials: Activity Card 11.2 — One-centimeter Graph Paper

A pendulum has a period of 2 seconds, the time for the pendulum to swing from the point of release back to that point. A pendulum is released from its highest point and accelerates until it is traveling at its maximum speed at the bottom of the arc one-half second later; then it decelerates until it reaches its highest point with a speed of zero in another one-half second. It returns to the starting point following this same pattern. Make a graph of the pendulum's velocity over a time of 6 seconds.

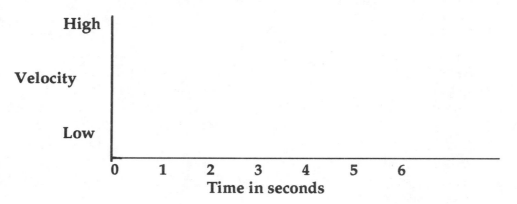

✈ Alternative Assessment ✈

Classroom Management

Effective classroom management is influenced both by what you do and what you do not do. If effective teaching is absent, no amount of classroom management strategies will help. Strategies to implement classroom management are not substitutes for good teaching. Outstanding teaching is, in effect, a preventative: it keeps children so interested that they have no time nor opportunity to misbehave. Good teaching, however, does not prevent all classroom management problems. Sometimes a student is so filled with problems that they simply overflow from his life at home or elsewhere into his classroom. When that happens, it is necessary to be prepared. Keeping order in the classroom is one of the teacher's prime concerns to ensure an atmosphere where maximum learning can take place.

Since alternative assessment is a fairly new concept, students may not be comfortable with it. Careful explanations by the teacher can alleviate student fears. After students begin to experience alternative assessment and find it non-threatening, anxieties lessen.

An often-stated concern on the part of the teacher is: 1) how to manage all the varied forms of alternative assessment; 2) teach, and 3) control classroom behavior at the same time.

A few helpful hints are listed here:

1. Explain to students what type of assessment you are using and why you are using it.
2. Establish rules in your classroom. Let the students participate in the rule-making process.
3. Encourage each student to be responsible for his/her own behavior.
4. While the majority of the class is doing group work, use the opportunity to interview a few individual students.
5. Carefully review your curriculum guides and textbooks to see which areas are the most important to emphasize and connect.
6. Be firm in your expectations for correct classroom behavior. Especially when cooperative group work is involved, it is important to set high standards for behavior and to be firm in carrying out those standards.
7. Express a positive attitude toward alternative assessment.
8. Begin using one or two particular forms of alternative assessment with which you are most comfortable. Whenever possible, team with another teacher who is using the same forms of alternative assessment to enable the sharing of ideas.

✈ Mathematics for the 21st Century ✈

Estimation and Mental Computation

Estimation can be described as an educated guess. It is performed mentally without any aids. It is accomplished quickly, and it produces answers that are sufficient for the moment, though not exact. Mental computation, on the other hand, is finding an exact answer mentally, without the aid of pencil, paper, or manipulatives.

Estimation

According to the *Standards* , elementary mathematics should provide opportunities for students to explore strategies for estimation, understand when it is appropriate to use estimation, discern if the results of their estimation make sense, and apply estimation throughout the elementary mathematics curriculum and in their lives. Students need to develop reasoning and the skill of decision-making when using estimation.

Elementary mathematics activities should be planned to develop an estimation mindset. Children need to understand the meaning of an estimate and when it is appropriate to use an estimate. If children are given frequent practice in estimation, they will learn to value the skill of estimation and to apply it to their lives. Teachers should emphasize computational estimation in a variety of problem-solving situations.

Estimation activities can enhance the understanding of place value. Whenever possible, estimation activities should require students to place the estimated items in groups of ones, tens, and hundreds. Students need to understand that estimates should fall within a reasonable range and do not have to be exact. Specific strategies are useful when teaching estimation. Students should understand and be able to apply the concept of compatible numbers. Compatible numbers are numbers that are friendly and fit together easily, for example numbers like 64 and 36 which add to 100. When adding sets of numbers, it helps for students to pair up the friendly numbers.

Another effective strategy is front-end estimation. Students focus on the front digits, adding only the numbers in the hundreds place. This will give one estimate. Later, students can use this strategy in connection with the rounding strategy. For 28 x 46, one thinks 30 x 50 = 1500 for an estimate.

It is important for students to understand that flexibility is essential in estimation procedures. Students need to be taught to realize that estimation skills are necessary life skills to develop.

Mental Computation

Mental computation is the ability to obtain an exact answer when required without the aid of paper and pencil or calculator. Students need to be inventive in their mental computation strategies, not simply to apply pencil-and-paper strategies. Discussions help students devise and develop strategies.

When first learning mental computation, students need to use numbers that are easy to combine, look for a strategy that is comfortable and convenient, apply their logical reasoning, and apply their previous knowledge about the number system, number concepts, and number sense. Teachers should include mental computation as a regular part of class activities. Mental computation sessions should be short and should promote confidence in the students. Creativity should be encouraged.

Learning to use mental computation has many advantages:

1. First, mental computation is an everyday life skill. The average adult is said to use mental computation 75% of the time.
2. Becoming adept at mental computation can make written computation easier for the average student. Using mental math shortcuts for multiplying with zeros or adding comparable numbers lends understanding to computation concepts.
3. Mental computation increases the understanding of place value and basic computational problems.
4. Becoming proficient in mental computation tends to lead to improved skills in the area of estimation.
5. Mental computation can lead to an awareness of the reasonableness of an answer and the use of logic.
6. Mental computation activities lead to the development of a positive attitude towards mathematics.

To ensure success mental computation, the teacher must committee to the inclusion of mental computation as a regular part each lesson. Every opportunity should be taken to model mental computation skills aloud.

The NCTM *Standards* clearly state that it is imperative for students to learn to choose appropriate methods of calculation. At times paper and pencil are appropriate, while at other times mental computation is more effective. Sometimes an estimate is required, while at other times the use of a calculator is most efficient. Students need multiple opportunities to discuss the method most appropriate for a variety of circumstances and justify their choices. This will provide students with the background to make effective decisions when they are presented with problem-solving situations.

12

Computers

UNDERSTANDING COMPUTERS

1. Computer Use in the Teaching and Learning of Mathematics
2. Programming in the Elementary School
3. The Preview and Use of Software
4. Selected Software

▼ PROBLEM CHALLENGE: The Math Princess

The Princess of Math-Magic land has been imprisoned in the tower by a fire-breathing dragon. To escape, she must solve the Tower Puzzle by finding the fastest way to move the tower (six discs) from the original post to one of the two remaining posts. The discs must have the same arrangement as on the original post, may be moved only one at a time, and a smaller disc must always be placed on top of a larger one. Use Activity Card 12 to solve the Tower Puzzle.

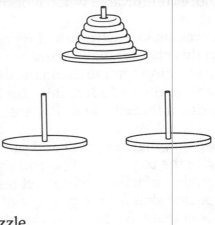

HANDS-ON MATHEMATICS

The following sections are provided to enhance your understanding of computers and computer software.

Computer Use in the Teaching and Learning of Mathematics

This chapter contains ideas concerning the role and potential uses of the computer in the elementary mathematics classroom. The NCTM *Standards* discusses the use of computers as a means to reach the mathematical goals of the future. They state that "a computer should be available in every classroom for demonstration purposes (and) every student should have access to a computer for individual and group work." NCTM supports the use of computers to develop simulating and modeling mathematical situations, supporting problem solving, and developing geometric intuition.

Some elementary schools tend to ignore the use of technology, particularly computers, while others are in the spotlight and on the cutting edge. This chapter contains comments as well as ways and means for the implementation of computers to take place. This chapter reflects, to a greater degree than the remaining chapters, the opinion of the authors.

Computers are not a substitute for excellent teaching. They do, however, provide a valuable instructional tool to help in the task of teaching and learning mathematics in the elementary school. Computers may be used by individuals or by teams of students. Often, when computers are first introduced, students feel more comfortable when working with a partner.

Three major instructional types of software for the classroom will be addressed in this chapter. First, there are tutorials. These programs provide direct instruction for a mathematical skill or concept. All parts of an introductory lesson are usually included: introduction, concept explanation, illustrations, questions (critical thinking and diagnostic), and assessment.

Second, there are drill and practice programs that allow the students to interact with the computer. The drill and practice program usually provides data on the number of trials and correct responses. As a rule, practice is provided on a specific skill for the purpose of developing automatic recall or recognition of ideas that have been previously taught.

Third, there are problem-solving programs and simulations. Problem solving is identified as the number one area for emphasis throughout the elementary mathematics curriculum. Therefore, it is important that students be provided multiple opportunities for problem-solving experiences on the computer. Some of the problem-solving software involves computation, while others apply spatial visualization, simulations, or the use of problem-solving strategies. For problem-solving software to be highly motivating and most valuable, it should be integrated into the problem-solving curriculum.

Programming in the Elementary School

There are several myths that abound concerning programming in the elementary school.

1) The first myth is that teachers must be programming experts to introduce computers into their classrooms. Teachers do need to be computer-literate and comfortable with the use of computers and computer software, but they are not required to be experts in programming. In many schools, programming skills, if taught, are taught by a specialist in the computer lab.

2) The second myth is that the prime purpose for using computers in elementary school mathematics is to teach students to develop their programming skills. The teaching of programming below the junior high or middle school level is highly controversial. There is little agreement on whether it should be taught, much less which language is to be used. The two common languages used are BASIC and Logo. In elementary schools containing a computer lab, Logo is more often used. The commitment to teach programming in the elementary school is great in terms of time, resources, and preparation. It appears that teachers who are comfortable with programming will teach it with success, but those who have neither the time nor the commitment would better invest their time in sampling and evaluating software for effective implementation in the mathematics classroom. To accomplish this task, teachers are not required to be experts, but do need to be knowledgeable and enthusiastic about computers and software to prepare the students for successful computer implementation.

If, however, programming is taught, the teacher should review the following information on the topic of Logo. Logo, a computer programming language for children, was developed during the 1960's and 1970's by a group of computer scientists, educators, and mathematicians at the Massachusetts Institute of Technology. Seymour Papert, a member of the design team, in his book, *Mindstorms: Children, Computers, and Powerful Ideas* (New York: Basic Books, 1980), states that computer activities should provide opportunities for thinking and that the students should be in control of the computer. The majority of computer uses (drill, practice, tutorials, and games) delegate control to the computer. Logo allows the child to hold the controls and receive immediate feedback from the computer. With Logo, a student can draw pictures and shapes while exploring the concepts of points, lines, and angles. As students improve their problem-solving skills and logical thinking, they begin to break large tasks into smaller, more manageable pieces. Logo is simple to learn and most students can begin creating drawings after five to ten minutes of instruction. In some elementary schools, Logo is taught in the computer lab to allow students to draw shapes and examine the properties of those shapes.

In Logo's "Turtle Graphics," a small triangle or small turtle-shape appears on the computer screen. Students can direct the turtle to move around on the screen and to show the path it is taking. To first start Logo, the student inserts a Logo language disk into the disk drive on the computer. The computer screen will show a message such as "Welcome to Logo?" The question mark is an indication that the computer is expecting a Logo command. The student then types "DRAW" to enter the draw mode and the turtle will appear in the center of the screen. In the *draw mode*, the student gives directions to the turtle using a few special commands such as those below.

Command	Abbreviation	Function	Example
FORWARD	FD	moves turtle forward	FD 50
BACK	BK	moves turtle back	BK 20
LEFT	LT	turns turtle to *its* left	LT 80
RIGHT	RT	turns turtle to *its* right	RT 100
CLEARSCREEN	CS	clears the screen	CS

If a student types the command "FD 10," the turtle moves forward 10 spaces. If the student types "RT 20," the turtle turns to its right 20 degrees. While the student continues moving the turtle around the screen, shapes, lines, and angles can be explored.

One of the first projects to be attempted, after introductory procedures are completed, is to draw a square. After time for free exploration, students discover that four lines (of the same length) and four turns (each of ninety degrees) are required. A square can be drawn with eight simple commands.

FD 40 LT 90
FD 40 LT 90
FD 40 LT 90
FD 40 LT 90

Students may notice a pattern and ask for a shortcut. At that time, the REPEAT command may be introduced. This requires the use of square brackets which include the number of times to be repeated and a list of the command to be repeated.

REPEAT 4[FD 40 LT 90]

Students repeat the process to draw other shapes such as triangles and hexagons.

3) The third myth is that teachers must be familiar with hundreds of software programs. It is unnecessary to try hundreds of computer programs. Instead, the teacher should carefully select a small number of quality software programs to implement in depth. It is better to begin with a single quality program which supports the goals of the curriculum, take enough quality time in order to learn it well, prepare the students carefully for the program (without rushing), and make it an integrated part of the mathematics curriculum with connections across other subject areas.

Students can best be prepared for the implementation of mathematics software by letting them know the goals and expectations of the teacher and the ways in which the software connects with their mathematics curriculum and their lives. An explanation should be provided on data to be collected and the means by which students will be evaluated on computer applications.

The Preview and Use of Software

The rapid increase of computers in the schools has forced teachers to become knowledgeable about computers and computer software. Merely having a computer in the classroom does not ensure that the teacher is computer-wise. Ongoing in-service programs are recommended in order to assist teachers in increasing their knowledge and experience with computers until they are comfortable. Teacher education programs now frequently include computer instruction in one or more of the required methods courses. It is imperative that this trend continue. We cannot ask computer-illiterate teachers to prepare students for the technology necessary for the 21st century.

Teachers need to become effective, efficient evaluators of classroom mathematics software. Reviews of software are readily available in professional and technological journals. The objectives of the software should first be compared with the objectives of the mathematics curriculum being taught. The appropriateness of the grade level, validity of the content, correlation with the mathematics curriculum, and the instructional design should be evaluated.

Software evaluation forms are available on the market. A few recommendations for software evaluation are listed below.

1. Try software which has been recommended by a fellow teacher.
2. Request permission from the manufacturer to preview software prior to purchase.
3. Experience the program until you are familiar and comfortable with it. Then, and only then, implement it with the students.
4. During the preview, ask the following questions:
   - Are the directions clear?
   - Do the graphics enhance the concepts being stressed?
   - Are there multiple levels of difficulty to the program?
   - Does it provide a decision-making environment?
   - Is the program user-friendly?
   - Is the menu complete?
   - Is the program content accurate?
   - Is it well designed as well as flexible?
   - Is it appropriate for your grade level?
   - Does it include a warranty?
   - Has it been reviewed or recommended?
   - Will the program correlate with unit goals?
   - Does the manual include discussion questions as well as enrichment activities?

Selected Software

The following pages contain a list of selected software for the elementary mathematics classroom. Each software program is listed once, though many are applicable to more than one chapter.

Each piece of software included below has been used by the authors, highly recommended by an elementary teacher, and/or received an outstanding technology award. The educational software market is increasing daily. By the time of this printing there will undoubtedly be many more examples of quality software available. We encourage teachers, both preservice and in-service, to stay abreast of new software by reading current computer educational journals, previewing education software catalogs, and attending local and state technology conferences.

☞ **PROBLEM SOLVING AND SETS (CHAPTERS 1 AND 2)**

BOUNCE!   Recommended for Grades K - 8.
Students use information-gathering and pattern-recognition skills to predict which bouncing ball will correctly fit into the sequence (Wings for Learning/Sunburst Communications).

THE FACTORY   Recommended for Grades 4 - 12.
This program challenges students to progress through three levels and create geometric "products" on a simulated machine assembly line (Wings for Learning/Sunburst Communications).

GERTRUDE'S PUZZLES   Recommended for Grades 4 - 7.
Friendly Gertrude the Goose helps students learn to recognize patterns and relationships and implement their problem-solving skills. Students are challenged to think analytically while ordering and sorting pieces according to shape and color (The Learning Company).

GERTRUDE'S SECRETS   Recommended for Grades K - 3.
Students learn classification, grouping, and sequencing skills as they manipulate colorful pieces around the screen (The Learning Company).

HANDS-ON MATH   Recommended for Grades 1 - 8.
Students explore mathematical concepts using computer-simulated manipulatives. Problem solving, place value, and fractions are stressed. Manipulatives include colored rods, counters, chips, number tiles, geoboards, and tangrams. A new Spanish version is now available (Gamco Industries, Inc.).

MATH BLASTER PLUS!   Recommended for Grades K - 6.
This program is a combination of problem solving and drill and practice. It
involves students in addition, subtraction, multiplication, division, fractions,
decimals, and percent skills with outer space themes (Davidson & Associates,
Inc.).

MOPTOWN HOTEL   Recommended for Grades 4 - 7.
An advanced version of MOPTOWN PARADE (which follows), this program
stresses the use of thinking and problem-solving skills. Trial-and-error logic is
used to place the moppet characters in the correct sequence (The Learning
Company).

MOPTOWN PARADE   Recommended for Grades K - 3.
A parade of colorful moppet characters assists students in the discovery of
similarities, differences, and patterns (The Learning Company).

MUPPET MATH   Recommended for Grades K - 2.
The muppets lead students to the discovery that mathematics is everywhere.
Problem solving is stressed, and levels of difficulty are presented (Wing for
Learning/ Sunburst Communications).

OREGON TRAIL   Recommended for Grades 5 - 12.
This simulation program provides practice in the development of decision-
making and problem-solving skills. Students apply problem-solving strategies to
activities which take place during this important time in American history
(Educational Resources).

PERFECT FIT   Recommended for Grades K - 2.
Students practice matching shapes, numbers, letters, and toys (Scholastic, Inc.).

PUZZLE TANKS   Recommended for Grades 3 - 8.
Students receive two tanks with a given capacity plus one storage tank. The
challenging task involves filling, emptying, or transferring varied amounts of
materials to reach the specified goal for the storage tank. Logical thinking is
involved (Wings for Learning/Sunburst Communications).

ROCKY'S BOOTS   Recommended for Grades 4 - 8.
Skills in logical thinking are developed while creative problem solving is
encouraged. Simple electronic circuits and circuit design are used to promote the
use of logic (The Learning Company).

SAFARI SEARCH   Recommended for Grades 3 - 12.
Problem-solving strategies are promoted in a unique environment. The use of
logical thinking is stressed (Wings for Learning/Sunburst Communications).

SOLVE IT!   Recommended for Grades 4 - 12.
Students play the role of a detective using a detective agency search. It is
presented in game format (Wings for Learning/Sunburst Communications).

THE FACTORY   Recommended for Grades 4 - 12.
This program challenges students to progress through three levels and create
geometric "products" on a simulated machine assembly-line. A Spanish version,
La Fabrica, is also available (Wings for Learning/Sunburst Communications).

THE GOODELL DIAMOND CAPER   Recommended for Grade 6.
Alice Goodell has lost her million-dollar diamond. She has enlisted your aid in
solving the problems at the Goodell Toy Palace and locating her diamond (Tom
Snyder Productions).

THE MYSTERY OF THE HOTEL VICTORIA   Recommended for Grade 5.
Bert, the hotel owner, has recently hired you to solve The Mystery of the
Vanishing Garden Tools, The Crime-Stopper Watch, and Molly the Maid.
Problem-solving and critical thinking skills are emphasized (Tom Snyder
Productions).

THE POND   Recommended for Grades 2 - 4.
The frog is helped in his jumps along the lily pads by the student, who arranges
the lily pads according to the suggested pattern. There are six different ponds
representing six levels of difficulty (Wings for Learning/ Sunburst
Communications).

THE SUPER FACTORY   Recommended for Grades 6 - 12.
Students research and design products while practicing their problem-solving
skills (Wings for Learning/Sunburst Communications).

THE WHATSIT CORPORATION   Recommended for Grades 6 - 12.
The simulation program incorporates decision-making, calculating, and record-
keeping while students set up a one-product business (Wings for Learning/
Sunburst Communications).

TREASURE MOUNTAIN   Recommended for Grades 2 - 4.
The Master of Mischief has stolen the magic crown and is hoarding all of the gold
from the mountain. Students use their mathematics, science, and reading skills to
solve the riddles posed by the mountain elves (The Learning Company).

WHERE IN AMERICA'S PAST IS CARMEN SANDIEGO?
Recommended for Grades 6 - 12.
Students practice their problem-solving strategies while sharpening their geography skills to look for the mysterious Carmen. This software provides a link between social studies concepts and problem-solving skills. Also recommended are: WHERE IN EUROPE IS CARMEN SANDIEGO?, WHERE IN THE USA IS CARMEN SANDIEGO? WHERE IN TIME PAST IS CARMEN SANDIEGO?, and WHERE IN THE WORLD IS CARMEN SANDIEGO? (Broderbund Software, Inc.).

ZOOKEEPER   Recommended for Grades 1 - 5.
ZOOKEEPER introduces students to over 50 different animals. In a problem-solving atmosphere which integrates mathematical and science skills, students help release animals back into the wild (Davidson & Associates, Inc.).

☞ WHOLE NUMBERS AND NUMBER THEORY (CHAPTERS 3 AND 4)

ANIMAL RESCUE   Recommended for Grades 1 - 2.
Students are challenged to solve a problem in order to rescue an animal from a grumpy troll. Skills involved are weight comparison, linear estimation, pattern recognition, and visual discrimination (Wings for Learning/Sunburst Communications).

ARITHMETIC CRITTERS   Recommended for Grades K - 2.
Practice is provided in writing the numerals 10 through 99. Trucks appear carrying 10 egg boxes each. One last truck appears carrying from 0 – 9 boxes. Students determine the numeral which identifies the total number of egg boxes, using place value and counting skills (Minnesota Educational Computing Corporation).

BALANCING BEAR   Recommended for Grades K - 4.
This program , an introduction to addition and inequalities, takes the student through four difficulty levels (Wings for Learning/Sunburst Communications).

CONQUERING WHOLE NUMBERS   Recommended for Grades 3 - 6.
Practice in computational skills is provided by this program. It takes the student through four levels of difficulty (Wings for Learning/Sunburst Communications).

HOP TO IT!   Recommended for Grades K - 3.
Young mathematicians are encouraged to strengthen their skills of addition and subtraction Three levels of difficulty entice students to compute correctly in order to move the animated characters on the number line (Wings for Learning/Sunburst Communications).

HOT DOG STAND   Recommended for Grades 6 - 12.
Students plan expenses, keep records, and use computational skills to make a
profit from the hot dog stand. The action takes place at the high school football
games (Wings for Learning/Sunburst Communications).

HOW THE WEST WAS ONE + THREE x FOUR   Recommended Grades 4 - 12.
This program highlights the teaching of the order of operations. The significance
of parentheses is stressed (Wings for Learning/Sunburst Communications).

MATH BLASTER   Recommended for Grades 1 - 6.
MATH BLASTER allows students to practice their computation skills in a circus
environment (Davidson & Associates, Inc.).

MATH RABBIT   Recommended for Grades K - 2.
Basic number and counting skills are implemented here. Addition, subtraction,
patterns, and recognizing number relationships are included (The Learning
Company).

MATH SHOP, JR.   Recommended for Grades 1 - 4.
Students assist in the Math Shop by using skills of addition, subtraction,
multiplication, division, estimation, and coin identification. A new Spanish
version is available (Scholastic, Inc.).

MAYA MATH   Recommended for Grades 4 - 8.
Students work as mathematical archeologists in order to solve the mysterious
Maya 20-base number system (Wings for Learning/Sunburst Communications).

MOUNTAIN MONKEY MATH   Recommended for Grades 1 - 4.
Students send monkeys up and down the mountain trail by building number
sentences using addition and subtraction skills. The final destination is Banana
Land! (Wings for Learning/Sunburst Communications).

MUTANOID MATH CHALLENGE   Recommended for Grades 2 - 8.
Mutanoid opponents help students develop computation and problem-solving
skills. Charts, tables, and graphs are included (Educational Resources).

NUMBER CONNECTIONS   Recommended for Grades K - 3.
Number sense and addition/subtraction skills are presented in a challenging
combination of spoken and pictorial representation of numbers. Students are
provided with opportunities to create their own number activities (Wings for
Learning/Sunburst Communications).

NUMBER MUNCHERS   Recommended for Grades 3 - 6.
Students assist the Number Munchers in their hunt for primes, factors, multiples,
equalities, and inequalities while they try to avoid being caught and eaten by a
Toggle (Minnesota Educational Computing Corporation).

SIDEWALK SNEAKERS   Recommended for Grades K - 5.
Number sense grows as students skip count to move their sneakers along the numbered sidewalk. The more difficult levels deal with the use of multiples (Wings for Learning/Sunburst Communications).

STICKYBEAR MATH I AND II   Recommended for Grades 1 - 4.
In STICKBEAR MATH I, students learn to solve addition and subtraction problems. Stickybear Math II assists in the application of multiplication and division skills (Optimum Resource, Inc.).

SUBTRACT WITH BALANCING BEAR   Recommended for Grades K - 4.
Students help Balancing Bear perform his successful balancing act while learning to use subtraction strategies (Wings for Learning/Sunburst Communications).

SUPER SOLVERS OUTNUMBERED   Recommended for Grades 3 - 6.
Problem-solving strategies are used to match clues and decipher the secret code to find the hiding place of the Master of Mischief. Basic facts and problem-solving skills are stressed (The Learning Company).

THE KING'S RULE   Recommended for Grades 4 - 12.
Students attempt to uncover the rule which will allow them to make their way through the king's castle (Wings for Learning/Sunburst Communications).

ZEROING IN   Recommended for Grades 4 - 8.
Students use computation skills and problem-solving strategies to change given numbers to zero. Students may play with a partner or challenge the computer (Wings for Learning/Sunburst Communications).

☞ **INTEGERS (CHAPTER 5)**

BUMBLE GAMES   Recommended for Grades K - 3.
Basic mathematical and geometric principles are implemented using number lines, number pairs, and graph plotting. Students can plot their own designs (The Learning Company).

BUMBLE PLOT   Recommended for Grades 4 - 7.
Students learn problem-solving strategies as they practice the use of positive and negative numbers. Plotting points on a grid and increased understanding of the concepts *greater than* and *less than* are stressed. Students can also create original drawings while practicing mathematics skills (The Learning Company).

MATH BLASTER MYSTERY   Recommended for Grades 5 - 12.
Problem-solving activities include working with positive and negative numbers. Addition, fractions, decimals, and percents are integrated into the mystery situation (Davidson & Associates, Inc.).

TEASERS BY TOBBS   Recommended for Grades 2 - 12.
Tobbs presents addition and multiplication computations with one or more missing whole numbers or integers. Students use problem-solving strategies to eliminate numbers that cannot be added or multiplied to determine the correct number (Wings for Learning/Sunburst Communications).

☛ RATIONAL NUMBERS, DECIMALS, AND PERCENTS (CHAPTERS 6 & 7)

CHALLENGE MATH   Recommended for Grades 2 - 6.
A space intruder and a lovable dinosaur guide students through practice skills for whole-number and decimal operations. It contains varied levels of difficulty (Wings for Learning/Sunburst Communications).

CONQUERING PERCENTS   Recommended for Grades 5 - 8.
Students use their concepts of percents and problem-solving strategies while estimating what percent of a given figure is painted. Players become percent choppers as they locate fractions, ratios, and partial figures which match a targeted percent (Minnesota Educational Computing Corporation).

CONQUERING RATIO AND PROPORTION   Recommended for Grades 5 - 8.
Students explore ratio concepts and apply proportions in order to solve problems which take place in medieval Europe. Knowledge is tested in games that shoot at targets with a catapult by setting the correct ratio of rock weight to force (Minnesota Educational Computing Corporation).

DECIMAL AND FRACTION MAZE   Recommended for Grades 3 - 10.
This program challenges students to practice decimal and fraction skills while climbing hedges, picking up litter, and crossing rivers to move through a maze. Each student's progress is monitored by a statistical program. Now available in a Spanish edition (Gamco Industries, Inc.).

DECIMAL MUNCHERS   Recommended for Grades 4 - 8.
DECIMAL MUNCHERS is designed to assist students in practicing decimal concepts. The Decimal Munchers try to catch the equivalent decimals before they are caught by a Toggle (Minnesota Educational Computing Corporation).

FRACTION MUNCHERS   Recommended for Grades 4 - 8.
FRACTION MUNCHERS is a drill-and-practice program which is designed to reinforce knowledge of fraction types, equivalent fractions, and fraction sizes. The Fraction Munchers try to gobble up equivalent fractions before they are eaten by a Toggle (Minnesota Educational Computing Corporation).

GEARS   Recommended for Grades 6 - 12.
Students learn to combine gears and build a gear factory using mathematical
formulas to predict a desired outcome. GEARS provides practice with ratios and
decimals (Wings for Learning/Sunburst Communications).

GET TO THE POINT   Recommended for Grades 5 - 9.
Three problem-solving games with decimals stress the concepts of ordering and
place value. Students are asked to place randomly-generated decimal numbers
within a given range (Wings for Learning/Sunburst Communications).

<in COMMON> MATHEMATICS   Recommended for Grades 6 - 12.
Practice in fractional and decimal computation is provided in this program.
Estimation is also stressed (Wings for Learning/Sunburst Communications).

MATH SHOP   Recommended for Grades 4 - 8.
Student shopkeepers use computation skills for whole numbers, decimals,
fractions, ratios, coins, and linear measures to handle purchases (Scholastic, Inc.).

NUMBER QUEST   Recommended for Grades 3 - 9.
Three games involve the use of numbers in lines, boxes, and squares. The
program involves graphing skills and the use of whole numbers, fractions, and
decimals (Wings for Learning/Sunburst Communications).

WHAT DO YOU DO WITH A BROKEN CALCULATOR?
                                         Recommended for Grades 2 - 12.
Students are challenged to find a variety of ways to reach a mathematical
conclusion (Wings for Learning/Sunburst Communications).

☛   **GEOMETRY (CHAPTERS 8 AND 9)**

BUILDING PERSPECTIVE   Recommended for Grades 4 - 12.
Students participate in this challenging game of spatial perception while working
with a 3 by 3, 4 by 4, or 5 by 5 area which depicts buildings of varying heights
viewed from the side. Students are asked to visualize what the building looks
like from the top (Wings for Learning/Sunburst Communications).

ELASTIC LINES: THE ELECTRONIC GEOBOARD
                                         Recommended for Grades 4 - 8.
Students are placed in an environment where they can create geometric shapes
and patterns. The concepts of area and perimeter are addressed. The program
consists of an electronic geoboard over which electronic rubber bands can be
stretched (Wings for Learning/Sunburst Communications).

GEOMETRIC preSUPPOSER   Recommended for Grades 5 - 12.
The properties of shapes are explored. Students are led to understand the
concepts of congruence and similarity while constructing and measuring
geometric figures (Wings for Learning/Sunburst Communications).

MATH AND ME   Recommended for Grades K - 2.
MATH AND ME helps children develop early mathematical skills in the areas of
shapes, numbers, patterns, and addition. The concepts *greater than* and *less than*
are presented in a guessing-game format (Davidson & Associates, Inc.).

ROLLER DOG   Recommended for Grades 5 - 12.
Spatial and figural reasoning are applied to the six levels of objects dealing with
spatial rotation The activities reinforce critical thinking skills. The game can be
played by individuals, cooperative groups, or the entire class (Critical Thinking
Press and Software).

STICKYBEAR SHAPES   Recommended for Grades K - 2.
Stickybear shows off using circles, squares, rectangles, and triangles. Students are
given an opportunity to identify a shape and locate it amidst a group of other
varied shapes (Optimum Resource, Inc.).

WHAT'S MY ANGLE?   Recommended for Grades 7 - 12.
What's My Angle teaches students the basic geometry concepts, proofs, and
problem-solving skills. It provides real-life situations involving geometric
applications (Davidson & Associates, Inc.).

☛   **MEASUREMENT (CHAPTER 10)**

ESTIMATION: QUICK SOLVE II   Recommended for Grades 5 - 8.
This program provides practice with estimation skills. Students learn to estimate
with measurement, time, money, and graphs (Minnesota Educational Computing
Corporation).

MATH SHOP SPOTLIGHT: WEIGHTS AND MEASURES
                                         Recommended for Grades 4 - 8.
Provides practice with English and metric measures (Scholastic, Inc.).

MEASURE WORKS, CLOCK WORKS, AND MONEY WORKS
                                        Recommended for Grades 1 - 4.
MEASURE WORKS entices students to compare sizes/heights and recognize
perimeter and area in metric and English measures. CLOCK WORKS provides
practice in telling time, while MONEY WORKS assists students in making
change and designing commemorative money (Minnesota Educational
Computing Corporation).

TREASURE MATHSTORM!   Recommended for Grades 2 - 4.
The Master of Mischief has cast an icy spell on Treasure Mountain. To undo the
spell, students are asked to perform mental mathematics, read clocks, count
money, make change, and recognize equalities and inequalities (The Learning
Company).

☞   ALGEBRA (CHAPTER 11)

ALGE-BLASTER PLUS!   Recommended for Grades 6 - 12.
ALGE-BLASTER PLUS! helps pre-algebra students understand the algebraic
process, practice graphing skills, and apply the basic steps in solving an equation
(Davidson & Associates, Inc.).

ALGEBRA SHOP   Recommended for Grades 6 - 10.
Students apply pre-algebra and algebra problem-solving skills to problems
which include factoring, square roots, integers, fractions, and decimals
(Scholastic, Inc.).

☞   STATISTICS AND PROBABILITY (CHAPTERS 13 AND 14)

BLOCKERS AND FINDERS   Recommended for Grades 1 - 12.
BLOCKERS AND FINDERS helps students to develop the ability to deal with
conjecture and proof in a situation which involves data collection and
organization. Students search for the hidden blockers which may keep the
finders from moving through the grid (Wings for Learning/Sunburst
Communications).

BLOCKERS AND FINDERS II   Recommended for Grades 4 - 12.
Inference and logic skills assist students in locating the detours in the path of the
finders. The software includes multiple levels of difficulty (Wings for
Learning/Sunburst Communications).

DATA INSIGHTS   Recommended for Grades 6 - 12.
This software program deals with six different plotting techniques. Students are
able to select the statistics which they want calculated (Wings for Learning/
Sunburst Communications).

EXPLORING TABLES AND GRAPHS I AND II   Recommended for Grades 3 - 5.
Students practice using picture, bar, and pie graphs along with tables to assist in
their problem-solving endeavors. The same information is illustrated in the
various types of graphs. Suggestions are provided for the creation of additional
graphs (Optimum Resource, Inc.).

FIVE IN A ROW   Recommended for Grades 2 - 8.
Students learn to apply problem solving, mental computation, analysis, and
probability in this game. Addition, subtraction, multiplication, and division at
varying levels are provided (Critical Thinking Press and Software).

PROBABILITY LAB   Recommended for Grades 6 - 12.
The probability concepts are practiced through simulations of coin tossing, wheel
spinning, and selecting marbles. Users can design and conduct a wide range of
experiments (Minnesota Educational Computing Corporation).

PROJECT ZOO   Recommended for Grades 3 - 5.
Three interdisciplinary programs in mathematics and science develop
measurement (English or metric), map making, graphing, and research skills.
Users collect and represent data in statistical graphs in order to plan and design a
zoo to meet the needs of the animals, staff, and visitors (National Geographic
Society).

STATISTICS WORKSHOP   Recommended for Grades 6 - 12.
A data analysis program, this software provides practice plotting bar charts,
histograms, box plots, and scatter plots (Wings for Learning/Sunburst
Communications).

Addresses of the software suppliers mentioned here are listed in Appendix B.

✈ EXTENSIONS ✈

✈ Alternative Assessment ✈

Preparations for Implementation

When an elementary school is convinced to try alternative assessment, there are several steps which will aid in furthering that preliminary preparation. The implementation of alternative assessment is best shared by teachers, administrators, students, and parents. Prior to the implementation, the following suggestions will lead you to consider all the angles. The suggestions are not meant to be all-inclusive, but rather to serve as a jumping-off point to enhance thinking in this arena.

1. Gather the latest research and commentaries available on alternative assessment to be shared across the board. What others have tried and proven (both successful and unsuccessful) can assist in your decision-making process.

2. As the literature is reviewed, prepare a list of questions and concerns for further investigation by individuals or a committee. Consider what percentage of the assessment program will be alternative assessment and what percentage (if any) will be traditional assessment.

3. Instigate discussions on the status of satisfaction/dissatisfaction with the current total school assessment program.

4. Question the faculty, particularly leadership teams such as grade chairpersons and team leaders, along with the administration regarding their commitment to try proven and innovative ideas for alternative assessment purposes.

5. As understanding grows, clearly define school objectives and outcomes for students in the area of alternative assessment. What are the goals? What type of learning is to be assessed? What will happen to the results?

6. Review grade-level curriculum guides. School curriculum which involves whole-language, cooperative grouping, and a hands-on approach to mathematics and science lends itself naturally to alternative assessment. If the approach is "drill and kill", it might better serve your purposes to stick with current testing procedures.

7. Talk to elementary school teachers who have implemented alternative assessment. First-hand experience from a newly implemented plan can enlighten your ideas and save mileage in the decision-making process.

8. Keep parents well informed about the types of assessment being considered and why. Share quality articles and books that provide parents with research on the implementation of alternative assessment in other schools and other areas of the country.

Alternative assessment is not just a new buzz word. It holds a potential for improving student assessment in the schools and clarifying the picture of what student learning is taking place. In order to ensure success in the implementation, faculty, administration, students, and parents need to be well informed and highly committed to begin the adventure into alternative assessment.

✈ Mathematics for the 21st Century ✈

Dealing With Equity and Diversity in the Classroom

Today's elementary schools are required to serve the needs of all children who attend. In our increasingly diverse society, this entails the understanding and support of many varied ethnic and cultural perspectives. It means that the existing negative stereotypes in mathematical ability that relate to females and minorities must be eliminated. American education stresses that the full potential of each child will be developed. This can only occur when elementary teachers are aware and knowledgeable about what is the best way to incorporate equity and diversity into their classrooms.

Equity in the mathematics classroom means providing methods and materials which help all students, especially females and minorities, to understand mathematics and its importance in their futures. Equity is a concept that extends beyond ethnic groups, and includes gender as well. Historically speaking, women have been denied many opportunities which were open to men. The situation is changing, but has a long way to go.

The encouragement of the maximum development of *all* students, regardless of gender or ethnicity, is a worthwhile goal for mathematics teachers. Equitable practices in the elementary mathematics classroom encourage cooperative group activities to complete problem-solving tasks which involve the use of manipulatives. The tasks often demonstrate multiple solutions, and time is not a factor in reaching a solution. Risk-taking and persistence are encouraged. Students are asked to monitor their thinking processes and to make mathematical connections with the real world. Competition is encouraged among cooperative groups, not individuals.

Specific suggestions which promote the understanding of mathematics and its importance in the future of the students, especially females and minorities follow.

- Develop skills for the effective use of manipulative materials at all grade levels.
- Provide activities that develop problem-solving strategies.
- Provide opportunities for students to participate in activities that emphasize mathematical understanding.
- Explore the use of calculators and computers in the classroom.
- Collect and discuss research findings on students' career aspirations.
- Investigate career options available in mathematics-based fields.

The diversity of American society ensures that large numbers of teachers will be confronted with students who come from other cultures that are unfamiliar to the teacher. In order to respond to this diversity, teachers need to do more than learn how the student writes his/her name in the native language. Children have their behavioral patterns shaped by many influences, not just ethnicity. Other factors may be influential as well, such as, teenage mothers, one-parent families, urban or suburban neighborhoods, poverty or wealthy surroundings, one or more non-English speaking parents, latchkey children, parents on drugs and more.

Elementary schools must serve all children who are enrolled. The future stability of our country depends on the creation of citizens who appreciate the perspectives of others and who recognize the fact that their own cultural group is part of a larger, more diverse world.

To establish diversity in the classroom, what is needed is a commitment on the part of teachers to serve the needs of the minority students in their classes in a serious accountable way. Multicultural lessons, whenever possible, should stress the goals listed below.

To help all students:
1. to develop a pride in their own cultural heritage;
2. to develop a respect for cultures that differ from their own;
3. to realize that differences in values are often the major sources for conflicts between groups;
4. to recognize the fact that other cultural perspectives have value in their own right; and
5. experience opportunities to work with students from other cultures.

Classroom procedures which can be readily incorporated into the mathematics classroom can enable students to become more sensitive to diversity. Some of these procedures are:

1. Teachers need to be aware of their own perspectives as well as the perspectives of their students and the differences which lie therein;
2. Teachers need to honestly monitor their own behavior to ascertain whether they are favoring or disfavoring any one group;
3. Methods of teaching should be varied in order to accommodate a variety of learning styles;
4. Students of different backgrounds should be included in each group when the class is divided for cooperative learning activities; and
5. Evaluation procedures should be checked in order to provide assessment which is as free as possible from social and cultural bias.

Equity and cultural diversity form a natural partnership in the elementary mathematics classroom and serve best when they are connected to a curriculum which stresses equality and fairness for *all* children.

13

Statistics

▼ PROBLEM CHALLENGE: Averages

The grade for a marking period depends upon four tests, each of equal value. If Bill has a 70% and an 80% on the first two tests, what is the lowest he can score on test three and still obtain an 85% average for the marking period?

B⁺ A⁺ C⁻ A⁻ F B

HANDS-ON MATHEMATICS ACTIVITIES

The following activities are provided to enhance your understanding of statistics.

Graphs

☞ **Key Ideas:** Graphs are useful tools for organizing data.

☛ **Activity 1: Reading and Interpreting Graphs**

Purpose: To gain an understanding of graphs.

There are three main types of graphs: bar, line, and circle. Recall that each is useful in different applications. The bar graph helps compare values and is useful for discrete data or when several variables exist.

❑   **Look at the bar graph in this activity and answer each question.**

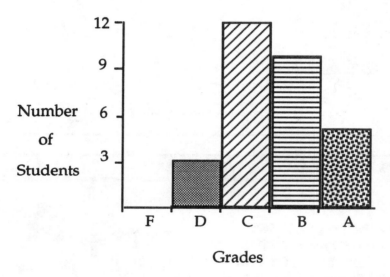

Math Grades for Fourth-Grade Students

1. Why is the bar graph an appropriate graph for this data?

2. How is the bar graph more helpful than the raw data?

3. What information has been lost by presenting data with the graph?

4. How many students are represented by the graph?

5. What conclusion would you draw about the mathematical ability of these students?

☞ **Activity 2: Reading and Interpreting Graphs**

Purpose: To gain an understanding of graphs.

The line graph is useful to show trends over time and for continuous data.

❑   Look at the line graph in this activity and answer each question.

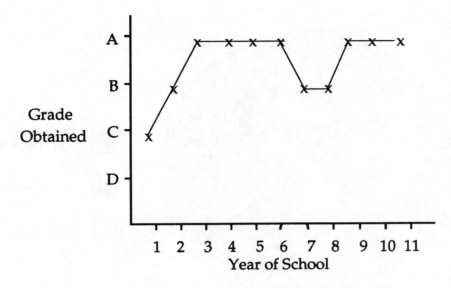

Mathematics Grades for Billy Jones

1. Why is the line graph an appropriate graph for this data?

2. How is the line graph more helpful than the raw data?

3. What information has been lost by presenting data with the graph?

4. What do you predict Billy's mathematics grade will be in his senior year?

☞ **Activity 3: Reading and Interpreting Graphs**

Purpose: To gain an understanding of graphs.

The circle graph is useful when showing parts of a whole.

❑   Look at the circle graph in this activity and answer each question.

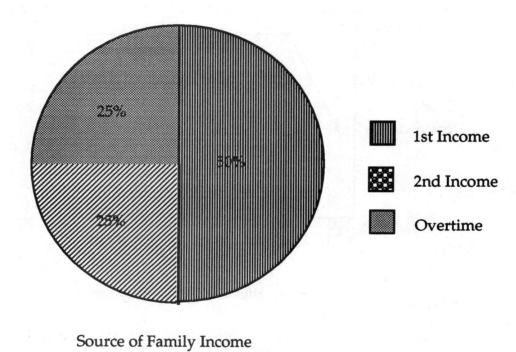

Source of Family Income

1. Why is the circle graph an appropriate graph for this data?

2. How is the circle graph more helpful than the raw data?

3. What information has been lost by presenting data with the graph?

☞ **Activity 4: Constructing Bar Graphs**

Purpose: To gain an understanding of the construction of bar graphs.
Materials: Activity Card 6.3 — One-inch Graph Paper

Bar graphs have the following:
  • an x-axis, usually labeled with the components of the variable being compared
  • a y-axis labeled with the amount of each component on the x-axis,
  • equal-width bars
  • a title for the graph

☐ **Construct a table and bar graph of the following grades:**

C, C, C, C, A, C, B, C, F, B,
C, C, A, B, B, C, C, B, B, A,
C, A, B, C, B, B, F, A, B, A.

☞ **Activity 5: Constructing Line Graphs**

Purpose: To gain an understanding of the construction of line graphs.
Materials: Activity Card 11.2 — One-centimeter Graph Paper

Line graphs have the following:

  • an x-axis usually labeled with the components of the independent variable
  • a y-axis labeled with the components of the dependent variable
  • an appropriate scale with equal size classes along each axis
  • a title for the graph

☐ **Construct a line graph of the daily high temperatures:**

day	1	2	3	4	5	6	7
Temp	95	96	92	90	80	78	90

☛ **Activity 6: Constructing Circle Graphs**

Purpose: To gain an understanding of the construction of circle graphs.
Materials: Activity Card 13.6 — Circle Graph Paper
Activity Card 4.13 — Protractor

Circle graphs have the following:

- a circle consisting of 360°
- a starting point, usually at the 12 o'clock position
- a way of labeling each section
- data that is changed from part to fractions and then to appropriate degrees of the circle
- a title for the graph

❏ **Make a circle graph of the following $1,000 budget:**

Taxes	$300
Shelter	$300
Food	$200
Car	$100
Savings	$100

☛ **Activity 7:   Which Type of Graph?**

Purpose: To gain an understanding of data and graphs.

Look at each type of data presented and select the appropriate type of graph to represent the data.

1. Number of books read by each student in a class   _____

2. Height of each child in a class   _____

3. Height of a child each year between the ages of two and twelve   _____

4. Nationality of each person in the freshman class of students   _____

5. A budget of where your money is spent   _____

☞ **Activity 8:   Frequency Distributions**

Purpose: To gain an understanding of frequency distributions.
Materials: Activity Card 6.3 — One-inch Graph Paper

Frequency distributions are helpful to interpret data such as grades. Place an *x* above the test scores for each student obtaining that test score on the graphs below. The first graph provides space for all individual scores. The second graph uses a range of scores. For example: On the first graph place three *x's* above the score of *70* , since three students scored 70. On the second graph place five *x's* above the scores 70–74.

97, 96, 96, 94, 92, 89, 89, 87, 85, 85,
85, 83, 82, 82, 78, 78, 78, 76, 76, 72,
71, 70, 70, 70, 67, 64, 62, 60, 56, 50

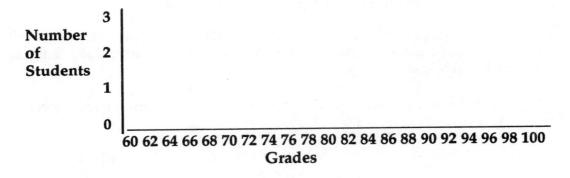

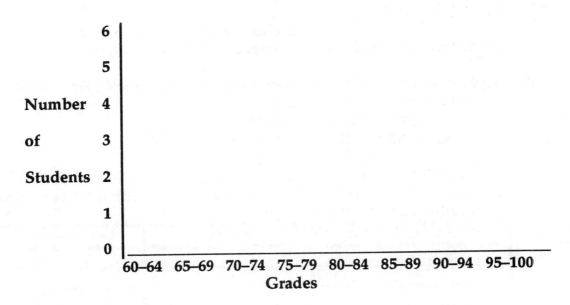

1. What are the highest and lowest scores?
2. What is the most frequently occurring score?
3. Where on each graph are the most frequently occurring scores?

Central Tendency

☞ **Key Ideas:**   Formulas provide another way of summarizing and presenting data. Central-tendency scores indicate that most groups of related scores have the tendency to cluster about a central score. There are several ways of measuring central tendency.

☞ **Activity 9:**   **Mean, Median, and Mode**

Purpose: To gain an understanding of central-tendency scores.

Recall the following:
- The mean of a set of scores is determined by calculating the sum of the scores and dividing that sum by the number of scores.
- The median is the middle score.
- The mode is the most frequently occurring score or scores.

There can be only one mean and one median, but more than one mode can occur. The mean, median, and mode are known as central tendency scores and each is an average.

❑   Determine the mean, median, and mode of the following test scores. Example: Test scores 5, 6, 7, 7, 7, 8, 8, 9, 9, 10.

$$\text{The mean is} \quad 5 + 6 + 7 + 7 + 7 + 8 + 8 + 9 + 9 + 10 = 76$$
$$76 \div 10 = 7.6$$

The median is the middle score between 7 and 8, or 7.5
The mode is the most frequently occurring score, or 7

Determine the mean, median, and mode for the following test scores:

97, 96, 96, 94, 92, 89, 89, 87, 85, 85,
85, 83, 82, 82, 78, 78, 78, 76, 76, 72,
71, 70, 70, 70, 67, 64, 62, 60, 56, 50

List one advantage and one disadvantage for each central-tendency score.

Central-Tendency Score	Advantage	Disadvantage
Mean		
Median		
Mode		

Spread

☞ **Key Ideas:**   Formulas provide another way of summarizing and presenting data. The spread indicates that most scores that are related to each other spread out. The spread of scores can be measured in several ways.

☞ **Activity 10:   Range and Standard Deviation**

Purpose: To gain an understanding of spread scores.
Materials: Activity Card 13.10 — Standard Curve

Recall the following:

*   The range is the number of scores available between the lowest score and the highest score. For a set of test scores, for example, if the lowest score is 90 and the highest score is 100, only ten scores are available for scoring every student who took the test. Large ranges in test scores make grading easier since the scores that are very different are likely to obtain different grades. It is difficult to give different grades to two students, one who scores 92 and the second who scores 93 on the same test. The range of a set of scores is found by the following steps:

    1. finding the high and low scores; and
    2. subtracting the low score from the high score.

*   The standard deviation of a set of scores is useful when related to the mean of that set of scores and the standard curve. The mean, standard deviation, and standard curve permit us to relate different tests to one another. The standard deviation of a set of scores is found using the following steps:

    1. find the mean;
    2. find the deviation of each score from the mean;
    3. square each deviation score;
    4. add the squared deviations and divide by the number of scores; and
    5. determine the square root.

❑   Determine the range and standard deviation of test scores.

Determine the range by subtracting the lowest score from the highest.

Determine the deviation scores by subtracting the mean from every score. These deviation scores are squared. The final step is to add each deviation-squared score and find its square root.

Example: Test scores 4, 4, 6, 6, 7, 7, 8, 8, 10, 10.

Scores	Deviation	Dev Square
10	3	9
10	3	9
8	1	1
8	1	1
7	0	0
7	0	0
6	−1	1
6	−1	1
4	−3	9
4	−3	9
	Sum	40

- The range is $10 - 4 = 6$.
- The standard deviation is
    The sum of the squared deviations is 40.
    The mean squared deviation is $40 + 10 = 4$
    The standard deviation $s = \sqrt{4} = 2$

❑   Determine the range and standard deviation for the following test scores:

97, 96, 96, 94, 92, 89, 89, 87, 85, 85,
85, 83, 82, 82, 78, 78, 78, 76, 76, 72,
71, 70, 70, 70, 67, 64, 62, 60, 56, 50

The graph shows a short method of determining an estimate of the standard deviation for a set of scores. To determine the estimate of the standard deviation, find the range and divide by 4. (The number 4 comes from the chart determined by the size of the sample.)

1. What is the estimate of the standard deviation?
2. What advantages and disadvantages does this estimate have?
3. It is said that a teacher should find the mean and the standard deviation (the estimate will do) for every test administered. Why?

☞   **Activity 11:   Box-and-Whisker Plots**

Purpose: To gain an understanding of box-and-whisker plots.
Materials: Activity Card 13.11—Box-and-Whisker Plot

A box-and-whisker plot graphically displays the data indicating the quartiles.

❑   Make a box-and-whisker plot of the test scores.
Example: For the test scores 4, 4, 5, 6, 6, 7, 7, 8, 8, 9, 10, 10, the box-and-whisker plot would use the quartile scores of 5.5, 7, and 8.5. Recall that the median of all the scores is the 50th percentile or second quartile. The median of the scores below the median of all the scores is the 25th percentile or first quartile. The median of the scores above the median of all the scores is the 75th percentile or third quartile.

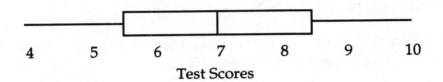

Test Scores

Determine the quartiles for the following test scores and make a box-and-whisker plot.

97, 96, 96, 94, 92, 89, 89, 87, 85, 85,
85, 83, 82, 82, 78, 78, 78, 76, 76, 72,
71, 70, 70, 70, 67, 64, 62, 60, 56, 50

1. How is the box-and-whisker plot helpful to teacher interpreting test scores?

2. Why might it be better to use quartiles instead of deciles?

Standardized Tests

Key Ideas: Educators use standardized tests to measure student progress and evaluate the curriculum. Standardized test scores are an important factor in making these judgments.

☞ **Activity 12: Standardized Test Scores**

Purpose: To gain an understanding of standard scores.

Test results are reported to students, parents, and teachers in a variety of ways. They are useful in making decisions pertaining to the student, to teaching, to the curriculum, and about the administration.

Recall that percentile scores indicate how well a student is achieving compared to his peers. A percentile of 50 indicates the student is scoring better than approximately 50% of similar students.

Recall, also, that stanines report achievement using nine groups. The 50th percentile is equivalent to a stanine of 5.

Percentiles are useful since they are easily explained and understood by parents and nonprofessionals. They are not, however, to be confused with percents. The 50th percentile indicates that the student scored better than about 50% of her peers. It is not a failing score.

The difficulty with percentiles is their accuracy. A student obtaining the 50th percentile on a test will seldom receive the same score upon a retest. The retest score will be either slightly higher or lower than the original score of the 50th percentile.

The 50th percentile is equivalent to a stanine of 5. A stanine of 5 indicates the student scored between the 40th and 60th percentile. Stanines are more realistic since we will never know the student's exact achievement score, only an estimate of his achievement.

❑   The following graph represents one way of creating grade-equivalent scores. A math test is administered to fourth-graders at the beginning of the school year. The same math test is administered to fifth-graders in the middle of the year. The data collected from this test has been placed on the graph. The raw score is the number of questions answered correctly.

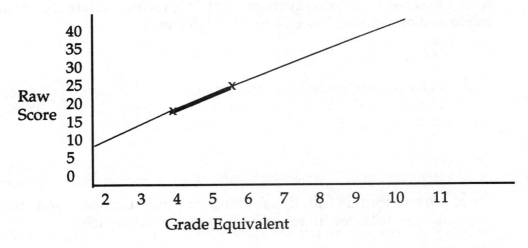

1. What was the raw score of a beginning fourth-grader on this math test?

2. What was the raw score of a middle fifth-grader on this math test?

3. Convert these raw scores to grade equivalents: 5, 10, 15, 20, 25, 30, 35.

    On the graph, the x's indicate real test scores. The average beginning fourth-grader obtained a raw score of 16 on this math test. The average middle fifth-grader obtained a raw score of 22.

4. There are three types of scores on the graph: real, interpolated, and extrapolated. Real data is that data collected and represented on the graph with small "x"s. Interpolated data is represented by the line drawn between the real data (actual scores). Extrapolated data is represented by lines drawn away from the "x"s, both above the real data and below. What is the range of each kind of score? There are two ranges of extrapolated scores.

5. In which of the three types of scores do you have the most confidence?

6. In which of these scores, 2.0, 3.0, 4.0, 5.0, 6.0, 7.0, do you have the least confidence. Why?

✍ Journal

The arithmetic mean is sometimes incorrectly used to show an inflated average. The mode or median better represents some groups of data. Illustrate how you could use the arithmetic mean of thirty class quiz scores to show an inflated average. Hint: High scores inflate the mean. The mode and median are less effected by high scores.

There are two formulas for determining the range. Compare and contrast these two formulas for finding the range of a set of numbers.

Range = high – low

Range = high – low + 1

Which do you think is more accurate?

Why?

As a teacher of children who will assign grades, why should you determine the mean and standard deviation of test scores?

✈ EXTENSIONS ✈

※ **Key Ideas:**   In Extensions, you may revisit some of the concepts and activities presented in this chapter. The following activities allow you to explore some ideas a little further. Sections include Calculators, Critical Thinking, Alternative Assessment, and Mathematics for the 21st Century.

✈ Calculator ✈

✈   **Activity 13:   Standard Deviation**

Purpose: To determine accuracy of estimated standard deviation.
Materials: Calculator

Use your calculator.

Here are some test scores for a class of students.

98	89	83	78	72
96	87	82	78	70
96	87	82	77	68
95	84	81	74	67
92	84	81	74	64
91	84	80	73	62

❑   Determine the following scores using your calculator:

Mean   _____

Mode   _____

Median   _____

Range   _____

Standard Deviation   _____

Divide the range by 4 to determine the estimate of the standard deviation. How does the estimate compare to the actual standard deviation you obtained using your calculator?

✈ Critical Thinking ✈

☞   **Activity 14: Average**
    Purpose: To encourage thought pertaining to mean, median, and mode.

The costs of new houses in Purdy County are as follows:

Mode $100,000
Median $120,000
Mean $130,000

Approximate the graph below. Write the appropriate cost of houses on the x-axis. Place each average on the graph and draw a line representing the number of houses sold at each price. The line should approximate the standard curve.

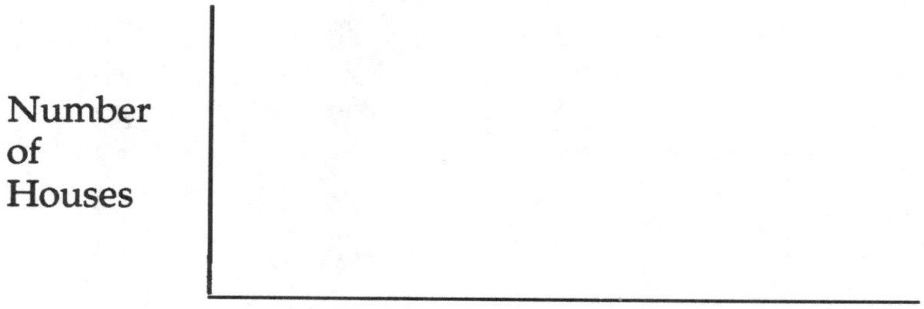

Number
of
Houses

The Cost of Houses in Purdy County

☐   Explain what each of the three average scores tells you about the cost of houses in Purdy County.

Why is the mean cost of houses the highest of the three averages?

What type of person would be interested in the mean cost of housing?

What type of person would be interested in the median cost of housing?

What type of person would be interested in the mode cost of a house?

✦ Alternative Assessment ✦

Checklists

Checklists save time for a busy classroom teacher. In place of writing individual comments about each student daily, a series of checklists may be used. Checklists can be documents that readily provide the teacher with organized information about each student. In *Mathematics Assessment: Myths, Models, Good Questions, and Practical Suggestions* (National Council of Teachers of Mathematics, 1991) a sample checklist is provided which is used by the British Columbia Ministry of Education. This sample checklist includes the following items that can be checked off and dated, with comments added if time permits.

Skills such as the following:
- understands;
- creates a plan;
- implements the plan;
- explains the plan;
- evaluates; and
- extends (all based on Polya's four problem-solving steps).

This checklist provides an assessment of attitudes including the following:
- cooperates;
- shares;
- questions;
- is confident;
- is flexible;
- takes risks;
- accepts advice; and
- stays on task.

 Checklists such as this can become a stepping stone to enable teachers to create checklists that include ideas of their own. In this way the checklist will reflect more personally the goals of the current unit.

In addition to the teacher's checklist, a second checklist can be created for students to use for self-assessment. This checklist can contain many of the same descriptive phrases as those listed above, but can be phrased in a way that makes it more meaningful to the student.

Checklists can be kept in a notebook with a section for each student in the class. This can become a growing, up-to-date record of the progress the student has made during each grading period and the year.

✈ Mathematics for the 21st Century ✈

Beliefs and Attitudes

The mathematical beliefs which students accept as truth can have a profound effect on the outcome of the learning which takes place in the classroom. Many of these beliefs are incorrect and need to be disproved in order to free the students to grow in their mathematical knowledge.

Some of the myths which negatively impact mathematics teaching and learning are the following:

1. There is one right answer for every problem.

   Students tend to think that there is one single correct answer, the one written in the teacher's mathematics book. Stressing the process (how the problem is solved), rather than the product (the answer), helps students, in time, to understand the importance of that process.

2. There is one right way to solve each problem.

   Students often believe that the first person to solve the problem with the correct solution provides the sole way to solve the problem. Asking the question, "Did anyone solve the problem in another way?" will stretch thinking in this area.

3. Students who excel in mathematics must have an excellent memory.

   Through the years mathematics has been synonymous with rote memorization of formulas and theorems. Now, memorization is being de-emphasized, while understanding is emphasized.

4. It is not acceptable to count on one's fingers.

   The use of concrete manipulatives to promote understanding is now recommended. The use of fingers for counting provides yet one more concrete way to reinforce understanding.

5. Mathematics is computation.

   Mathematics was, at one time, thought to be synonymous with computation. In the 1990's, however, problem solving is being stressed as the number one goal for the elementary mathematics classroom. Computation is now one small part of the big picture that is mathematics.

6. Mathematics has never changed in the last 100 years.

We now live in a modern, technological society in which calculators, computers, and problem solving preside. In order to allow students to compete for future jobs, they must be prepared in mathematics for the 21st century. The *Curriculum and Evaluation Standards for School Mathematics* (NCTM, 1989) has been published as a guideline for implementing the needed changes in the elementary mathematics curriculum.

7. Mathematical ability is inherited.

Often parents are overheard saying, "Susie has a hard time with math, but this is not unusual because I was never any good at math either." Mathematical ability is not inherited, and teachers who relieve students of this misinformation will open the doors of opportunity in the field of mathematics to them. Anyone can learn mathematics. The positive "You can do it" attitude of the teacher is a step towards the displacement this myth.

8. Men are better mathematicians than women.

This is an old-fashioned belief which many still hold as truth. Men are not better in mathematics than women. Often women are misled to think that this is true and are thus turned away from a promising career in mathematics. Every effort should be made to correct this misinformation before it causes more damage. Men and women can both be excellent mathematicians.

As you, the teacher, reflect on your own mathematical beliefs and attitudes, you might ask yourself the following questions:

- How do I reflect a positive attitude toward mathematics to my students?

- How can I encourage positive attitudes and beliefs towards mathematics in my elementary classroom?

- How can I encourage both boys and girls to consider career opportunities in mathematics?

- How can I equitably encourage parents to incorporate a positive attitude toward mathematics while working with their children?

14

Probability

UNDERSTANDING PROBABILITY

1. Basic Probability
2. Independent and Dependent Events

▼ PROBLEM CHALLENGE: License Plates

How many license plates can be made using the following:

       1 digit
       2 digits
       6 digits

       1 letter
       2 letters
       6 letters

       3 digits and 3 letters

HANDS-ON MATHEMATICS ACTIVITIES

The following activities are provided to enhance your understanding of probability.

Basic Probability

☞ **Key Ideas:** Probability studies random phenomena that are individually unpredictable, but have a pattern of predictability over the long term.

☞ **Activity 1: Probability Involving Playing Cards**

Purpose: To gain an understanding of the basic probability of drawing certain cards from a regular playing deck.

A deck of regular playing cards contains 52 cards. There are four suits: spades, hearts, diamonds, and clubs. The hearts and diamonds are red, and the spades and clubs are black. Each suit contains 13 cards.

The probability of an event is the number of ways that event can occur compared to the total number of events.

Example: What is the probability of drawing a red card from the deck? There are 26 red cards and 52 cards in the deck.

$$\frac{26}{52} = \frac{1}{2}$$

The probability of drawing a red card from the deck is $\frac{1}{2}$.

❑   What is the probability of making the following draws:

1. heart?

2. four?

3. red four?

4. four of hearts?

☞   **Activity 2:** Tree Diagrams

Purpose: To gain an understanding of probability using tree diagrams.

Tree diagrams can be used to show the probability that certain events will happen by displaying all of the possible events.

Example: I hold four cards: the 2 of spades, the 2 of hearts, the 2 of diamonds, and the 2 of clubs. If I draw two of these four cards, what is the probability that they will both be black?

1st draw	2nd draw	Color	Color	Number of draw	Both black
2 spade	2 heart	black	red	1	no
2 spade	2 diamond	black	red	2	no
2 spade	2 club	black	black	3	yes
2 heart	2 spade	red	black	4	no
2 heart	2 diamond	red	red	5	no
2 heart	2 club	red	black	6	no
2 diamond	2 spade	red	black	7	no
2 diamond	2 heart	red	red	8	no
2 diamond	2 club	red	black	9	no
2 club	2 spade	black	black	10	yes
2 club	2 heart	black	red	11	no
2 club	2 diamond	black	red	12	no

The probability of drawing two black cards from these four cards is

$$\frac{2}{12} \text{ or } \frac{1}{6}$$

❏   When holding the 2 of spades, the 2 of hearts, the 2 of diamonds, and the 2 of clubs, what is the probability of drawing:

1. 2 red cards?

2. 1 red and 1 black?

3. If the first of two cards you draw is black, what is the probability of drawing 2 black cards?

☞ **Activity 3: Drawings**

Purpose: To gain an understanding of applying tree diagrams to drawings.

A university contest has narrowed down the winners to the final six people. Two of the final six people are married to each other. Two names will be drawn and declared winners to go on a Caribbean cruise.

Use a tree diagram to determine

      1. the probability of the husband winning.

      2. the probability of the wife winning.

      3. the probability of neither of them winning.

      4. the probability of both of them winning.

☞ **Activity 4:   Numbered Cubes**

Purpose: To gain an understanding of probability using number cubes.
Materials: Activity Card 3.22 — Number Cubes

A game involves rolling the two number cubes as often as you want. After each roll, the two numbers on the number cubes are added. The purpose of the game is to come closest to the number 25 without going over. You must always roll both number cubes and add the numbers. The sum of the second roll of both number cubes is added to the sum of the first roll.

You have rolled three times and have a total of 21.
If you roll once more, what is the probability of

1. improving your score? (Remember, scores over 25 are losers.)

2. rolling exactly 25?

3. exceeding 25?

Independent and Dependent Events

☞ **Key Ideas:** The probability of an event occurring depends upon the type of event. Independent events (number of drawings where the first number drawn is replaced) have different probabilities from dependent events (number of drawings where the first number drawn is not replaced).

☞ **Activity 5:   Lottery–Pick 3**

Purpose: To understand the probability of independent events.

Three containers each contain 10 balls. The balls in each container are numbered with one number from 1 to 10. A person draws one ball from each container to determine the winner.

1. What is the probability of the number 111 being drawn?

2. If the first number drawn is 1, what is the probability of the next two numbers also being 1?

3. If the first two numbers drawn are 1, what is the probability of the third number also being 1?

☞ **Activity 6:   Lottery – Pick 4**

Purpose: To understand the probability of independent events.

Four containers each contain 10 balls. The balls in each container are numbered with one number from 1 to 10. A person draws one ball from each container to determine the winner.

1. What is the probability of the number 9876 being drawn?

2. If the first number drawn is 9, what is the probability of the next three numbers being 876?

3. If the first two numbers drawn are 9 and 8, what is the probability of the next numbers being 7 and 6?

☞ **Activity 7: Lottery – Pick 6**

Purpose: To gain an understanding of the probability of dependent events.

A can contains 20 balls numbered from 1 to 20. A person draws six numbers without putting the numbers back.

What is the probability of the numbers 2, 4, 6, 8, 10, and 12 being drawn?

☞ **Activity 8: Drawings**

Purpose: To gain an understanding of probability of independent and dependent events.

In a hat are 4 black beads and 3 red beads. One bead is drawn and replaced. Then a second bead is drawn.

What is the probability of drawing

1. 2 black beads?

2. 2 red beads?

3. a black and a red bead?

In a hat are 4 black beads and 3 red beads. One bead is drawn and not replaced. Then a second bead is drawn.

What is the probability of drawing

1. 2 black beads?

2. 2 red beads?

3. a black and a red bead?

Journal

Compare the difference between independent and dependent events.

Give examples of independent and dependent events.

Which lottery, Pick 3, Pick 4, or Pick 6 would you play first?

Why?

Do you think state governments should be in the lottery business given the fact that most of the players, and therefore the money made, comes from the poor?

✈ EXTENSIONS ✈

Critical Thinking

✳ **Key Ideas:** Lotteries are a way of raising money in many states. A closer look at
the probabilities reveals that state lotteries are extremely profitable.

☞ **Activity 9:   A Look at State Lotteries**

Purpose: To determine the probability of winning money in a lottery.

Many states operate daily and weekly lotteries. The daily lotteries usually
involve winning relatively small sums of money such as $500. Weekly
lotteries involve winning larger sums of money (millions of dollars).

Consider the weekly lottery in the state of Florida, where six numbers are
selected from 1 through 42. The numbers drawn are not replaced.

1. If you buy one ticket, what is your probability of winning?
2. If tickets cost $1.00 each, how much money will the state of Florida
   collect, assuming all numbers are sold?
3. Some numbers are more popular than other numbers, and some
   numbers are not chosen in one given lottery. How does this fact
   affect the probabilities of winning?
4. The state of Florida pays the winner of the lottery $7,000,000. What
   percentage of the money collected is being paid to the winner?
5. Is the percentage of money returned to the winner of the Florida
   State lottery a good deal, considering that Las Vegas returns
   approximately 90% , race tracks return approximately 80%, and a
   bookie returns approximately 70% of the money collected?
6. The winner of the lottery is not given the $7,000,000 all at once; it is
   paid over a period of 20 years. How much money does the winner
   receive each year? The winner does not receive the whole amount
   of money each year. Why not?
7. The State of Florida holds the $7,000,000 and pays it out over 20
   years. Assuming the state can collect 8% interest, what amount of
   money is made in interest every year? What amount is paid to the
   winner? Who really wins the lottery?

Alternative Assessment

Parent Newsletters

A monthly or bimonthly newsletter can be a useful tool for sharing student achievements with parents. Parents are interested in what their children are accomplishing and will welcome the opportunity to read your comments about the way in which assignments are being assessed.

The unit being studied can be briefly summarized for the benefit of the parents. This can be followed by a list of key activities which have taken place during the unit. Then samples of student work and student thinking can be presented. Several samples of student responses (including pictures) to an open-ended question could be an integral part of the newsletter. Short quotes from student journals (used with the student's permission), written interviews, and reports of group projects can be useful additions.

The parent newsletter is an excellent medium for providing parents with definitions of the varied means of alternative assessment which are currently being implemented in the classroom. Articles on the topic which appear in professional journals can be summarized or excerpts reprinted to provide the interested parent with a sound knowledge base for alternative assessment.

As connections are made with other subject areas, items such as poems, stories, riddles, and items of historical significance may be added to the newsletter. The newsletter is, in fact, both a letter from the teacher to the parent and an illustration of student achievement.

The newsletter can highlight other subject areas to give the parents a running review of what is taking place in the classroom. This is also an opportunity to enlighten parents on dates for future projects. The parent newsletter can be a positive tool for the sharing of student achievement and the assessment of that achievement. The parent newsletter is a positive line between the student and the teacher in the classroom and the family support group at home.

Mathematics for the 21st Century

Parent Involvement

The active involvement of parents in their children's education can be a plus for all those involved: children, parents, and teachers. If parents are identified as partners with the teacher in the education program of their child, positive results can happen.

Parent Involvement: Service to the School

Numerous parents work on a volunteer basis in the school. Many schools encourage this, but with the changing demographics, large numbers of parents who were once at home are now working. It is up to the schools to find another way for working parents to become actively involved in their child's school and classroom activities. When the principal makes a statement to the parent community that she feels the strength of the school is based upon the participation of parents, a strong message is delivered. The principal could go a step further and request that each parent dedicate one day a year for volunteer service. This might be to accompany the class on a field trip, work at a Saturday School Fair, assist behind stage for a drama or music production, tutor students in another classroom, or participate in career-day activities. When parents volunteer in the schools in any capacity, a clear message is sent to the child, which says "I care."

Parent Involvement: School/Home Relationships

Parents may actively participate in the school/home connection by taking the time to be aware of their child's assignments and of current units which are being studied. Providing information to enable parents to discuss mathematical ideas and concepts in a positive manner is an added benefit.

Parent Involvement: Support of Learning Activities at Home

Parents can provide an enriched mathematics environment in their home in order to promote quality learning of mathematics beyond the elementary mathematics classroom. Teachers can provide articles of interest, suggestions for the use of problem solving and manipulatives at home, and puzzles for the entire family to enjoy. Teachers can work to create an awareness in parents regarding the way in which negative stereotypes can affect a child. Parents should be encouraged to develop positive attitudes in their children. School-sponsored *Family Math* nights are positive ways to enhance parent interest in the way their children learn mathematics.

Specific Activities to Enhance Parental Involvement:

1. Make parents feel welcome in the classroom and in the school.

2. Keep communication lines open.

3. Encourage volunteer parents to work with children rather than correcting papers or completing other routine paper work.

4. Mention to the student how pleased you are to have his/her parent helping in your class.

5. Model positive attitudes towards mathematics for volunteers to copy.

6. Provide clear directions as to the task you wish parents to complete. Provide all materials necessary for the task.

7. Ask for suggestions or ideas from the volunteer. Everyone appreciates their ideas being valued.

8. Plan a school-wide Parent Volunteer Appreciation Luncheon. Follow it up with a personal thank-you note of your own.

Advantages of Having Parents Involved:

1. Parents, teachers, and students work together to create a strong partnership to nurture the learning of mathematics.

2. Parents who feel good about their school involvement will actively promote your school in the community at large.

3. Positive attitudes towards mathematics are enhanced when fun activities are shared in the classroom and the home.

4. Fewer problem situations occur when parents and teachers are working together as a team.

5. Children whose parents volunteer in the school receive the clear message that school is important to their parents and to them.

It is vital that schools provide a broad list of opportunities for parents to volunteer. The opportunities should be described in detail to ensure that parents can select the activities in which they are most comfortable. Parent volunteers are a precious resource and one which each school should carefully protect.

Appendix A
Solutions
Answers to Selected Odd Numbered Activities

Chapter 1

Problem Challenge

d	q	d
d	q	q
d	n	n

Activity 1: License Plate Number 16908
Only digits 0, 1, 6, 8, and 9 make sense upside down.

Activity 3: 5 darts hitting 9, 9, 9, 6, and 2

Activity 5:

	3	5	
7	1	8	2
	4	6	

or a horizontal or vertical flip

Activity 7: One example of a Guess and Check:

Right	Wrong	Money	
5	21	–$0.65	Guess
8	18	–$0.16	Guess
10	**16**	**$0**	**Correct**

Activity 9:

Blue eyed people	2	4	6	8	10	12	**14**
Total people	5	10	15	20	25	30	**35**

Activity 11: 1. 28 Handshakes
2. 42 People

Activity 15:

Day	1	2	3	4	5	6
Money	**1¢**	**2¢**	**4¢**	**8¢**	**16¢**	**32¢**

Day	7	8	9	10	11	12	
Money	**64¢**	**$1.28**	**$2.56**	**$5.12**	**$10.24**	**$20.48**	= **$40.95**

Activity 17: a. 11, b. 24, c. 0, d. 50, e. between $28 and $35.

Chapter 2

Problem Challenge

△ Red	○ Green	▭ Blue	□ Yel
▭ Yel	□ Blue	△ Green	○ Red
□ Green	▭ Red	○ Yellow	△ Blue
○ Blue	△ Yel	□ Red	▭ Green

Activity 3:   1. Determine the intersection of each.

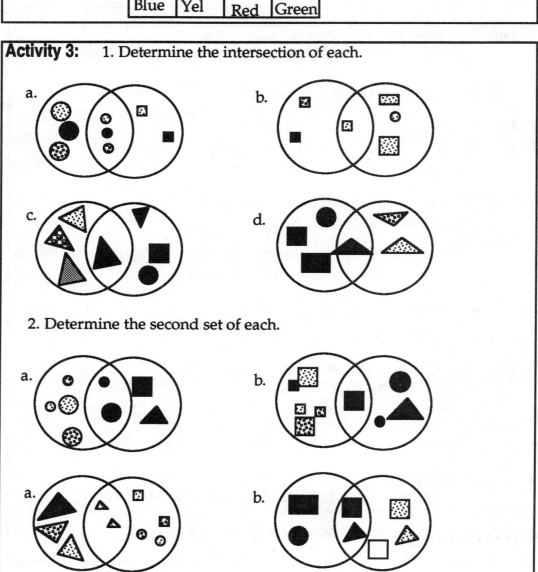

a.

b.

c.

d.

2. Determine the second set of each.

a.

b.

a.

b.

79

| Activity 5: | Row 6 sum = 105 and Row 8 sum = 252 |
| Activity 7: | Take one coin from can labeled 1 nickel and 1 dime. If you pull a nickel, the can must contain 2 nickels since it is mislabeled. If you pull a dime, the can must contain 2 dimes. |

Chapter 3

Problem Challenge

- Guess and Check: 7 trikes = 21 wheels. 4 fewer wheels means 4 fewer trikes: 3 trikes and 4 bikes.

- Table

bikes	7	6	5	**4**	3	2	1	0
trikes	0	1	2	**3**	4	5	6	7
wheels	14	15	16	**17**	18	19	20	21

- Algebra   B + T = 7 and 2B + 3T = 17, where
  B = number of bikes and T = number of trikes

Activity 1:

1a. 37	b. 63	c. 1656	d. 2650
2a. 24	b. 44	c. 94	d. 934
3a. 23	b. 87	c. 813	d. 2322
4a. XCIX	b. CCLXXVI	c. CMXLIV	d. MMCMXLIV

Activity 3:

1a. (8 x 20) + (4 x 1) = 164
1b. (9 x 20) + (7 x 1) = 187
1c. (13 x 20) + (8 x 1) = 268
1d. (14 x 20) + (14 x 1) = 294

Activity 5: a

Step 1 Set up	Step 2 Add the ones	Step 3 Trade	Step 4 Add the tens
19 • ooooo oooo + 15 • oooo	ooooo ooooo oooo 19 • + 15 • _____	1 • 19 • + 15 • _____ 1 oooo	19 + 15 _____ 31 ••• oooo

Similarly for b, c, and d.

Activity 7:

a.
$$
\begin{array}{}
2 \\
2_4 \quad 3 \\
18_2 \quad 17_0 \\
6_8 \quad 7_7 \\
16_4 \quad 1_8 \\
19_3 \quad 13_1 \\
18_1 \quad 2_3 \\
+\ 8_9 \quad 5_8 \\
4 \quad 9 \qquad 8
\end{array}
$$

b.
$$
\begin{array}{}
4 \\
4_8 \quad 5 \\
19_7 \quad 15_0 \\
13_0 \quad 5_5 \\
5_5 \quad 19_4 \\
3_8 \quad 18_2 \\
1_9 \quad 4_6 \\
19_8 \quad 17_3 \\
3 \quad 8 \qquad 3
\end{array}
$$

Activity 9:   1. 20

2a.
xxxxxxxxx
xxxxxxxxx
xxxxxxxxx

3 x 9

b.
xxxxxx
xxxxxx
xxxxxx
xxxxxx
xxxxxx
xxxxxx

6 x 7

Activity 11:

2	9	
0 2	0 9	1
0 6	2 7	3

6	7	
2 4	2 8	4
3 6	4 2	6

3	8	
0 3	0 8	1
0 6	1 6	2

7	4	
2 1	1 2	3
5 6	3 2	8

Activity 13: 42 color pieces make seven groups of 6.

Activity 15: 1.a.

This addend represents 7	This is 3

This is 3	This addend represents 7

2.a.

2	2	2	2
4		4	

General Statement: $a + b = b + a$ for all whole numbers a and b and $a \times b = b \times a$ for all whole numbers a and b.

Activity 19:
a. $30 + 80 = 110$ b. $50 + 40 = 90$
c. $90 \times 20 = 1800$ d. $80 \times 20 = 1600$

Activity 21:
a. $100 + 200 + 200 + 300 = 800$;
    $800 + 50 + 20 + 20 + 20 = 910$
b. $200 + 600 + 100 + 300 = 1200$;
    $1200 + 50 + 100 + 20 + 50 = 1420$
c. $100 + 200 + 100 + 100 + 300 = 800$;
    $800 + 100 + 50 + 20 + 80 + 60 = 1110$
d. $300 + 500 + 200 + 400 = 1400$;
    $1400 + 90 + 40 + 90 + 60 = 1680$

Activity 25: a.

$$
\begin{array}{rcrcr}
45 & = & 40 & + & 5 \\
+\ 67 & = & 60 & + & 7 \\
\hline
& & 100 & + & 12 \quad = \quad 112
\end{array}
$$

$$
\begin{array}{rcrcrcrcr}
45 & = & & 40 & + & 5 & = & 30 & + & 15 \\
-\ 28 & = & -(& 20 & + & 8) & = & -\ 20 & - & 8 \\
\hline
& & & & & & & 10 & + & 7 \quad = \quad 17
\end{array}
$$

Activity 27: $542 \times 63 = 34{,}146$

Chapter 4

Problem Challenge

- Guess and Check: 30 pigs and 10 chickens.
  $120 + 20 = 140$ legs.
  20 legs too many. 10 fewer pigs.
  20 pigs and 20 chickens = 120 legs
- Table   pigs   10   20   30
  Chickens   30   20   10
  Legs   100   120   140
- Algebra $P + C = 40$ and $4P + 2C = 120$
  Where P = number of pigs and C = number of chickens

Activity 1:   XXXXXXXXXXXXXXXXXX (1 x 18) or (18 x 1)

XXXXXXXXX
XXXXXXXXX (2 x 9) or (9 x 2)

XXXXXX
XXXXXX
XXXXXX (3 x 6) or (6 x 3)

Activity 3:
1. 1 has 1 factor, 4 has 3 factors, 9 has 3 factors, 16 has 5 factors, 25 has 3 factors, 36 has 9 factors, 49 has 3 factors, and 64 has 9 factors.
2. Each number forms non-square rectangular arrays with 2 factors and a square with 1 factor.
3. They form a square array

Activity 5:
1. Adds 5 to previous number, counting by 5, ends in 0 or 5, etc.
2. The ones digit is a 0 or 5 or ends in 0 or 5

Activity 7:
1. Adds 9 to previous number, counting by 9, tens digits count from 0 to 9 while ones digits count from 9 to 0, etc.
2. The sum is 9
3. Sum of digits has to be 9

Activity 9:
1. Adds 6 to previous number, counting by 6, product always even, etc.
2. The sum is 3, 6, or 9
3. Must be even and sum of digits equal to 3, 6, or 9 or a .. multiple of 3, 6, or 9.
   2 and 3 rule both have to apply.

Activity 11: a.

$$
\begin{array}{cccc}
 & & & 3 \\
 & & 9 & 3 \\
 & 18 & & \\
36 & & 2 & \\
 & 2 & & \\
\end{array}
$$

$$
\begin{array}{cccc}
 & & & 3 \\
 & 9 & & 3 \\
36 & & & \\
 & 4 & & 2 \\
 & & & 2 \\
\end{array}
$$

$$
\begin{array}{cccc}
 & & 6 & 3 \\
 & 12 & & 2 \\
36 & & 2 & \\
 & 3 & & \\
\end{array}
$$

$$
\begin{array}{cccc}
 & & 3 & \\
 & 6 & 2 & \\
36 & & & \\
 & 6 & 3 & \\
 & & 2 & \\
\end{array}
$$

Activity 13: a.

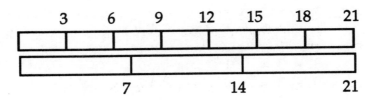

Activity 15: 5 Rule: Divide number by 2 and multiply by 10.

Example: $12 \times 5 = \dfrac{12}{2} \times 10 = 6 \times 10 = 60$.

Activity 17:
1. The ones place digit is 1 less than factor being multiplied by 9.
2. The sum is 9.
3. The ones digit of product is one less than factor being multiplied by 9 and sum of digits in product must be 9.

284

Chapter 5

Problem Challenge

+4	−10	0
−6	−2	2
−4	+6	−8

Activity 1:   a. Many answers.

   o o o   or • o o o o where • = 1 and o = − 1.

Activity 3:

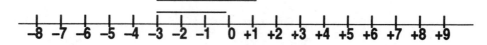

Activity 5:
```
 + 10 + − 5 = − 2
 +  5 + − 5 = − 1
      0 + − 5 =   0
 −  5 + − 5 = + 1
 − 10 + − 5 = + 2

      3 + 3 =    1
      0 + 3 =    0
 −  3 + 3 = − 1
 −  3 + 3 = − 2
```

Chapter 6

Problem Challenge

Using the four basic processes of addition, subtraction, multiplication and division.

1. $4 - 4 + 4/4$
2. $4/4 + 4/4$
3. $(4 + 4 + 4) \div 4$
4. $4 + 4(4 - 4)$
5. $(4 \times 4 + 4) \div 4$
6. $[(4 + 4) \div 4] + 4$
7. $4 + 4 - 4/4$
8. $4 + 4 + 4 - 4$
9. $4 + 4 + 4/4$
10. $(44 - 4) \div 4$
11.
12. $(4 - 4/4) \times 4$
13.
14.
15. $4 \times 4 - 4/4$
16. $4 \times 4 + 4 - 4$
17. $4 \times 4 + 4/4$
18.
19.
20. $(4 + 4/4) \times 4$

Using the factorial, where $4! = 4 \times 3 \times 2 \times 1 = 24$

6. $4! \div 4 + 4 - 4$
11. $(4! + 4! - 4) \div 4$
13. $(4! + 4! + 4) \div 4$
14.
18.
19. $4! - 4 - 4/4$

Using square root, where $\sqrt{4} = 2$

6. $4 + \sqrt{4} + 4 - 4$
14. $4 + 4 + 4 + \sqrt{4}$
18. $4! - \sqrt{4} - \sqrt{4} - \sqrt{4}$

Activity 1:   1) 4   2) 4   3) 2   4) 2

Activity 7:   a. 2   b. 2   c. 3   d. 3

Activity 11:   a. $\frac{1}{3} \approx 0.33 = 33\%$ b. $\frac{4}{5} = 0.80 = 80\%$

c. $\frac{9}{10} = 0.90 = 90\%$ d. $\frac{3}{4} = 0.75 = 75\%$

e. $\frac{2}{5} = 0.40 = 40\%$ f. $\frac{7}{8} = 0.875 = 87.5\%$

Problem Challenge

Straight line numbers = 12%   1, 4, 7, 11, 14, 17, 41, 44, 47, 71, 74, 77
Straight letters =15/26 = 58%   A, E, F, H, I, K, L M, N, T, V, W, X, Y, Z

Activity 1:   a. 1.65   b. 1.82

Activity 5:   a. $5 + 9 = 14$ b. $10 - 4 = 6$ c. $3 \times 9 = 27$ d. $12 + 3 = 4$

Activity 7:   a. $15 \times \frac{1}{3} = 5$ b. $100 \times 3.3 = 330$ c. $24 \times \frac{2}{3} = 16$

d. $24 \times \frac{1}{8} = 3$ e. $20 \times \frac{4}{5} = 16$ f. $30 \times .6 = 18$

Activity 9:   a. $15 \times \frac{1}{3} = 5$ b. $100 \times 3.3 = 330$

c. $2 \times 7 = 14$ d. $10 \times 50 = 500$

Activity 11:   a. $\frac{1700}{4} = \frac{x}{9} = \$3825$ b. $\frac{347}{11} = \frac{x}{18} \approx 567.8$

c. $\frac{1723}{13} = \frac{x}{40} \approx 5302$

Activity 13:   a. $\frac{\%}{100} = \frac{75}{300} = 225$ b. $\frac{\%}{100} = \frac{300}{75} = 400\%$

c. $\frac{45}{100} = \frac{x}{56} = 25.2$ d. $\frac{230}{100} = \frac{x}{80} = 184$

e. $\frac{60}{100} = \frac{13}{x} \approx 21.67$ f. $\frac{250}{100} = \frac{50}{x} = 20$

Activity 15: $A = P \left(1 + \frac{r}{n}\right) nt$

semi-annually: $A = \$1000 \left(1 + \frac{.12}{2}\right)^{6} \approx \$1418.52$

quarterly: $A = \$1000 \left(1 + \frac{.12}{4}\right)^{12} \approx \$1425.76$

monthly: $A = \$1000 \left(1 + \frac{.12}{12}\right)^{36} \approx \$1430.77$

Daily $A = \$1000 \left(1 + \frac{.12}{360}\right) 1080$

Chapter 8

Problem Challenge

1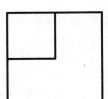

2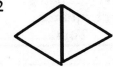

Activity 11: 1. 1 and 3
3. None
5. 2, 3, and 5
7. 4 and 8
9. 1, 2, 3, 5, 7, 9, and 10

2. 1, 2, 3, 5, 7, 9, and 10
4. 1, 3, 7, and 10
6. 4 and 8
8. 4 and 6
10. 1, 2, 3 and 5

Problem Challenge

There are:
8 x 8 one-by-one squares. ....(64)
7 x 7 two-by-two squares ....(49)
6 x 6 three-by-three squares ....(36)
5 x 5 four-by-four squares ....(25)
4 x 4 five-by-five squares....................(16)
3 x 3 six-by-six squares ....(9)
2 x 2 seven-by-seven squares...............(4)
1 x 1 eight-by-eight squares ....(1)

Total 204

Activity 7:

Problem Challenge
1) five cuts
2) 13 posts

Activity 1:
1) about 8 paper clips wide
2) about 10 paper clips long
3) readily available in most desks, inexpensive, easy to carry
4) not a standard measure, not all paper clips the same length, difficult to measure long distances.

Activity 5:
a) 14 units   b) 12 units
c) 16 units   d) 16 units
e) 16 units   f) 22 units

Activity 7:
a) $\frac{1}{2} \times 4 = 2$ square units b) $\frac{1}{2} \times 8 = 4$ square units

c) $\frac{1}{2} \times 12 = 6$ square units d) $\frac{1}{2} \times 16 = 8$ square units

e) $\frac{1}{2} \times 12 = 6$ square units f) $\frac{1}{2} \times 9 = 4\frac{1}{2}$ square units

Activity 9: Area of a square is side x side or A = s x s

Activity 11: Area of a parallelogram = length x height

Activity 13:
Examples:
1) soda (liters)   2) film (35 millimeters)
3) aspirin (milligrams) 4) inoculation (milliliters)

Activity 15:
a) $11\frac{7}{12}$ feet   b) 168 inches

c) $3\frac{31}{36}$ yards   d) $5{,}666\frac{2}{3}$ yards

e) $4\frac{2}{3}$ yards   f) $3\frac{1160}{5280} = 3\frac{29}{132}$ miles

Chapter 11

Problem Challenge

The wine costs $9.50.
The cork and bottle cost $.50

Activity 1: 1) 27 miles per gallon.
2) 12 x 27 = 324 miles
3) Information visible and easy to interpret.

Activity 3 1) Yes. Same relationship between the pairs of data.
2) The constant of miles per gallon
3) Must still use a formula.
4) A formula, if appropriate, is good for all data. A table is limited by space.

Activity 5: 1) $AB = \sqrt{5}$ $CD = \sqrt{5}$
     $BC = 4$ $AD = 4$
2) $AB = 2$ $CD = 2$
     $BC = 0$ $AD = 0$
3) A parallelogram is a quadrilateral with both pairs of opposite sides parallel.

Activity 7:

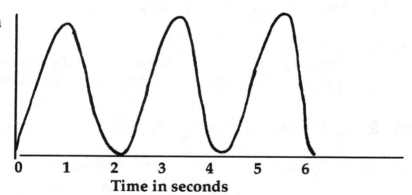

Remember that the period is 2 seconds in duration.

Chapter 12

Problem Challenge

Use the *Solve a Simpler Problem* and *Find a Pattern* strategies.

One disc requires one move	1
Two discs require three moves	3
Three discs require eight moves	7

See the pattern of double the previous answer and add one.

Four discs require $2 \times 7 + 1 = 15$	15
Five discs require $2 \times 15 + 1 = 31$	31
Six discs require $2 \times 31 + 1 = 63$	63

The solution may also be obtained using the formula $2^n - 1$, where n denotes the number of discs.

Chapter 13

Problem Challenge

1st test	70
2nd test	80
4th test	100 (an assumption)
total	250

Bill needs 340 of 400 for an 85 average ($4 \times 85 = 340$),
$340 - 250 = 90$
Bill needs at least a 90 on test 3, assuming he obtains 100% on test 4, to have an average of 85%.

Activity 1:
1) Graph can be used to make comparisons.
2) Graph forms a picture that summarizes the data and is easily remembered.
3) Individual scores are lost.
4) 30 students.
5) Average to above average ability or an easy test

Activity 3:
1) Circle graphs are useful for showing the whole with parts.
2) Graph forms a picture that summarizes the data and is easily remembered.
3) None, when the percents are written on the graph.

292

Activity 5:

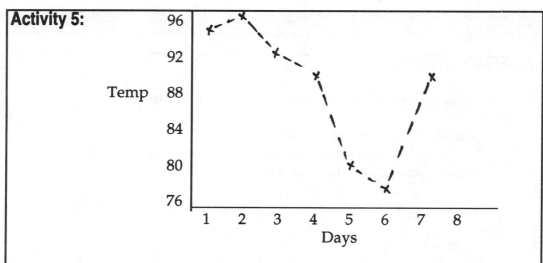

Activity 7: 1) Bar graph with individual students displayed.
2) Bar graph with individual students displayed.
3) Line graph connecting yearly heights.
4) Circle graph of whole class.
5) Circle graph of total amount of money.

Activity 9: mean = 78, median = 78, and mode = 70, 78, and 85.
The mean has the advantage of representing every score.
The disadvantage of using the mean is that it is affected by extreme high or low scores.
The median has the advantage of representing the middle class. It is not affected as much as the mean by extreme scores.
The median does not represent all scores.
The mode represents a large group of scores.
The mode may be useless, such as in the example above where there are three modes.

Activity 11:

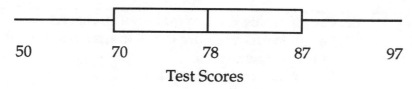

Test Scores

1) The range of scores is shown along with the median. It is a useful way of comparing sets of data.
2) Deciles give too many groups for classroom use where total student populations are about 30. Deciles might be more useful for very large groups such as the total population of the school.

Activity 13: mean ≈ 81, median = 81.5, and mode = 84.
Range = 98 − 62 = 36
Estimate of standard deviation is 36 ÷ 4 = 9.

Chapter 14

Problem Challenge

1 digit = 10 license plates
2 digits = 10 x 10 =100 license plates
6 digits = 10^6 = 1,000,000 license plates
1 letter = 26 license plates
2 letters = 26 x 26 =676 license plates
6 letters = 26^6 = 308,915,776 license plates
3 digits and 3 letters = 10^3 x 26^3 = 17,576,000

Activity 1:
1) 13 of 52 or $\frac{1}{4}$

2) 4 of 52 or $\frac{1}{13}$

3) 2 of 52 or $\frac{1}{26}$

4) 1 of 52 or $\frac{1}{52}$

Activity 3:
1) 1 of 3
2) 1 of 3
3) 6 of 15 or 2 of 5
4) 1 of 15

Activity 5:
1. 1 of 1000
2. 1 of 100
3. 1 of 10

Activity 7:
20 x 19 x 18 x 17 x 16 x 15 = 27,907,200
1 of 27,907,200

Appendix B
Resources for Mathematics Manipulatives

Addison Wesley
Supplemental Publishing Co.
Rt 128
Reading, MA 01867
(800) 447–2226

Aims Educational Foundation
PO Box 8120
Fresno, CA 93747-8120
(209) 255–4094
FAX (209) 255–6396

Carson-Dellosa Publishing company, Inc.
Dept. 9271
PO Box 3566Greensboro, NC 27425-5665
(800) 321–0943
FAX (919) 632–0087

Creative Publications
5040 West 111th Street
Oak Lawn, IL 60453
(800) 624–0822
FAX (919) 425–9790

Creative Teaching Associates
PO Box 7766
Fresno, CA 93747
(800) 767–4CTA
FAX (209) 291–2953

Cuisenaire Company of America
PO Box 5026
White Plains, NY 10602-5026
(800) 237–3142
FAX (800) 551–RODS

Dale Seymour Publications
PO Box 10888
Palo Alto, CA 94303-0879
(800) 872–1100
FAX (415) 324–3424

Delta Education
PO Box 950
Hudson, NH 03051-9940
(800) 442–5444
FAX (603) 595–8580

Didax Inc., Educational Resources
One Centennial Drive
Peabody, MA 01960
(800) 458–0024
FAX (508) 532–9277

Good Apple
1204 Buchanan
Box 299
Carthage, IL 62321-0299
(800) 435–7234
FAX (217) 357–3987

Key Curriculum Press
Martin Luther King, Jr. Way
PO Box 2304
Berkley CA 94702
(800) 338–7638
FAX (800) 541–2442

National Council of Teachers of Mathematics
1906 Association Drive
Reston, VA 22091
(800) 235–7566
FAX (703) 476–2970

Appendix C
Resources for Computer Software

Broderbund
Educational Learning Systems, Inc.
2874 Remington Green Circle
Tallahassee, FL 32308
(904) 386-3708
FAX (904) 385-8067

Critical Thinking Press and Software
PO Box 448
Pacific Grove, CA 939950
(800) 458-4849
FAX (408) 372-3230

Davidson and Associates, Inc.
Attn.: Educational Sales
PO Box 2961
Torrance, CA 90509
(800) 545-7677
FAX (310) 793-0601

Educational Resources
1550 Executive Dr.
Elgin, IL 60123
(800) 624-2426
FAX (708) 888-8499

Gamco Industries
PO Box 1911
Big Springs, TX 79721
(800) 351-1404
FAX (915) 267-7480

Minnesota Educational Computing Corporation (MECC)
Brookdale Corporate Center
6160 Summit Dr.
Minneapolis, MN 55430
(800) 685-6322
FAX (612) 569-1551

National Geographic Society
Department 91, Educational Services
Washington, DC 20036
(800)-368-2728
FAX (301) 921-1575

Optimum Resource
(Formerly Weekly Reader)
PO Box 23317
Hilton Head SC 29925
(800) 327-1473
FAX (803) 785-7031

Scholastic, Inc.
PO Box 7502
Jefferson City, MO 65102-9968
(800) 541-5513
FAX (314) 635-5881

The Learning Company
6493 Kaiser Dr.
Fremont, CA 94555
(800) 852-2255
FAX (510) 792-9628

Tom Snyder Productions, Inc.
80 Coolidge Hill Rd
Watertown, MA 02172
(800) 342-0236
FAX (617) 876-0033

Wings for Learning/Sunburst Communications
Customer Info Services
1600 Green Hills Rd
PO Box 660002
Scotts Valley, CA 95067-0002
(800) 321-7511
FAX (408) 438-4214

Appendix D
Selected Readings from the *Arithmetic Teacher*

Problem Solving and Sets (Chapters 1 and 2)

Balka, Don S. "Digit Delight: Problem Solving Activities Using 0 through 9." *Arithmetic Teacher* 36 #3 (November, 1988): 42–45.

Bledsoe, Gloria J. "Hook Your Students on Problem Solving." *Arithmetic Teacher* 37 #4 (December, 1989): 16–20.

Brown, Sue "Integrating Manipulatives and Computers in Problem Solving Experiences" *Arithmetic Teacher* 38 #2 (October, 1990): 8–10.

Burns, Marilyn "Introducing Division Through Problem Solving Experiences." *Arithmetic Teacher* 38 #8 (April, 1991): 6–12.

Callahan, Leroy G. (Ed.) "Research Report: Problem Solving and Learning Disabilities." *Arithmetic Teacher* 34 #8 (April, 1987): 35.

Campbell, Patricia F. & Bamberger, Honi J. "Implementing the Standards: The Visions of Problem Solving in the Standards." *Arithmetic Teacher* 37 #9 (May, 1990): 14–17.

Cemen, Pamala B. "Developing a Problem Solving Lesson." *Arithmetic Teacher* 37 #2 (October, 1989): 14–19.

Comstock, Margaret & Demana, Franklin. "The Calculator is a Problem-Solving Concept Developer." *Arithmetic Teacher* 34 #6 (February, 1987): 48-51.

Dougherty, Barbara & Crites, Terry "Applying Number Sense to Problem Solving." *Arithmetic Teacher* 36 #6 (February, 1989): 22–25.

Ford, Margaret I. "A Strategy for Problem Solvers." *Arithmetic Teacher* 38 #3 (November, 1990): 35–38.

Frank, Martha L. "Problem Solving and Mathematical Beliefs." *Arithmetic Teacher* 35 #5 (January, 1988): 26-27.

Harel, Guersgon & Behr, Merlyn "Ed's Strategy for Solving Division Problems." *Arithmetic Teacher* 39 #3 (November, 1991): 38–40.

Hazelwood, Donald G. et al. "Suzuki Meets Polya: Teaching Mathematics to Young Students" *Arithmetic Teacher* 37 #3 (November, 1989): 8–10.

Huinker, DeAnn M. "Multiplication and Division Word Problems: Improving Students' Understanding ." *Arithmetic Teacher* 37 #2 (October, 1989): 8–12.

Johnson, James E. "So You Think You Might Be Wrong? Confirmation Bias in Problem Solving." *Arithmetic Teacher* 34 #9 (May 1987): 13-16.

Langbort, Carol "Jar Lids—An Unusual Math Manipulative." *Arithmetic Teacher* 36 #3 (November, 1988): 22-25.

300

Lappan, Glenda "Implementing the Professional Standards for Teaching Mathematics: What Do We Have and Where Do We Go from Here?" *Arithmetic Teacher* 40 #9 (May, 1993): 524–527.

Lobato, Joanne "Making Connections: A Case for Proportionality" *Arithmetic Teacher* 40 #6 (February, 1993): 347–351.

Kersh, Mildred & McDonald, Jacqueline "How Do I Solve Thee, Let Me Count the Ways." *Arithmetic Teacher* 39 #2 (October, 1991): 38–41.

Kroll, Diana L. et al. "Cooperative Problem Solving: But What about Grading." *Arithmetic Teacher* 39 #6 (February, 1992): 17–23.

Mahlios, Jan "Word Problems: When Do I Add or Subtract." *Arithmetic Teacher* 36 #3 (November, 1988): 48–52.

Matz, Karl A. & Leier, Cynthia "Word Problems and the Language Connection." *Arithmetic Teacher* 39 #8 (April, 1992): 14–17.

Nibbelink, William H. et al. "Problem Solving in the Elementary Grades: Textbook Practices and Achievement Trends Over the Past Thirty Years." *Arithmetic Teacher* 35 #1 (September, 1987): 34-37.

Silverman, Frederick L. et al. "Student-Generated Story Problems." *Arithmetic Teacher* 39 #8 (April, 1992): 6–12.

Sowder, Larry "Research into Practice: Story Problems and Students' Strategies." *Arithmetic Teacher* 36 #9 (May, 1989): 25–26.

Sowder, Judith & Sowder, Larry "Creating a Problem Solving Atmosphere." *Arithmetic Teacher* 36 #1 (September, 1988): 46–47.

Szetela, Walter. "The Problem of Evaluation in Problem Solving: Can We Find Solutions?" *Arithmetic Teacher* 35 #3 (November, 1987): 36-41.

Talton, Carolyn F. "Let's Solve the Problem before We Find the Answer." *Arithmetic Teacher* 36 #1 (September, 1988): 40–45.

Thompson, Charles. "Implementing the *Standards*:. Number Sense and Numeration in Grades K–8" *Arithmetic Teacher* 37 #1 (September, 1989): 22-24.

Van de Walle, John "Problem Solving Tips for Teachers." *Arithmetic Teacher* 35 #4 (December, 1987): 26-27.

Van de Walle, John A, and Holbrook, Helen. "Patterns, Thinking, and Problem Solving." *Arithmetic Teacher* 34 #8 (April, 1987): 6-12.

Woodward, Ernest "Problem Solving in the Preservice Classroom." *Arithmetic Teacher* 39 #3 (November, 1991): 41–43.

Whole Numbers and Number Theory (Chapter 3 and 4)

Curcio, Frances et al. "Divide and Conquer: Unit Strips to the Rescue." *Arithmetic Teacher* 35 #4 (December, 1987): 6-12.

Duncan, David & Litwiller, Bonnie. "Number-Lattice Polygons and Patterns: Sums and Products." *Arithmetic Teacher* 37 #5 (May, 1990): 14-15.

Gluck, Doris H. "Helping Students Understand Place Value." *Arithmetic Teacher* 38 #7 (March, 1991): 10–13.

Graeber, Anna O. "Research Into Practice: Misconceptions about Multiplication and Division." *Arithmetic Teacher* 40 #7 (March, 1993): 408–411.

Graeber, Anna O. & Baker, Kay M. "Little into Big Is the Way It Always Is." *Arithmetic Teacher* 39 #8 (April, 1992): 18–21.

Joslyn, Ruth "Using concrete Models to Teach Large-Number Concepts." *Arithmetic Teacher* 38 #3(November, 1990): 6-9.

Hope, Jack "Promoting Number Sense in School." *Arithmetic Teacher* 35 #8(February, 1989): 12–16.

Killion, Kurt & Steffe, Leslie P. "Research into Practice: Children's Multiplication." *Arithmetic Teacher* 37 #1 (September, 1989): 34–36.

Krusen, Kim "A Historical Reconstruction of Our Number System." *Arithmetic Teacher* 38 #7 (March, 1991): 46–48.

Litwiller, Bonnie & Duncan, David "Polygons on a Number Lattice: Sums, Products, and Differences." *Arithmetic Teacher* 37 #3(November, 1989): 39-43.

Markowitz, Zvia et al. "Research into Practice: Number Sense and Nonsense." *Arithmetic Teacher* 36 #6 (February, 1989): 53–55.

Rathmell, Edward C. and Leutzinger, Larry P. "Implementing the Standards: Number Representations and Relationships." *Arithmetic Teacher* 38 #7 (March, 1991): 20–23.

Schultz, James "Area Models—Spanning the Mathematics of Grades 3–9." *Arithmetic Teacher* 39 #2(October, 1991): 42-46.

Trafton, Paul & Zawojewski, Judith "Implementing the Standards: Meanings of Operations." *Arithmetic Teacher* 38 #3(November, 1990): 38-40.

Sowder, Judith "Mental Computation and Number Sense." *Arithmetic Teacher* 37 #7(March, 1990): 18-20.

Turkel, Susan and Newman, Claire. "Developing Number Sense." *Arithmetic Teacher* 35 #6(February, 1988): 53-55.

Van de, John "The Early Development of Number Relations." *Arithmetic Teacher* 35 #6(February, 1988): 15-21.

Whitin, David J. "Number Sense and the Importance of Asking "Why?" *Arithmetic Teacher* 36 #6 (February, 1989): 26–29.

Integers, Rational Numbers, and Decimals, Percents and Real Numbers (Chapters 5 – 7)

Bezuk, Nadine "Fractions in the Early Childhood Mathematics Curriculum." *Arithmetic Teacher* 35 #6 (February, 1988): 56-60.

Cemen, Pamela Byrd "Teacher To Teacher: Adding and Subtrracting Integers on the Number Line." *Arithmetic Teacher* 40 #7 (March, 1993): 388–389.

Cramer, Kathleen and Bezek, Nadine "Multiplication of Fractions: Teaching for Understanding." *Arithmetic Teacher* 39 #3 (November, 1991): 34–37

Fulkerson, Paul "Getting the Most from a Problem." *Arithmetic Teacher* 40 #3 (November, 1992): 178–179.

Hauber, Mary Ann "Percents: Developing Meaning Through Models." *Arithmetic Teacher* 40 #3 (December, 1992): 232–234.

Hiebert, James "Research Report: Decimal Fractions." *Arithmetic Teacher* 34 #7(March, 1987): 22-23.

Klein, Paul "Remembering How to Read Decimals." *Arithmetic Teacher* 37 #7(May, 1990): 31.

Mack, Nancy "Research Into Practice: Making Connections to Understand Fractions" *Arithmetic Teacher* 340 #6 (February, 1993): 362–365.

Ott, Jack "A Unified Approach to Multiplying Fractions." *Arithmetic Teacher* 37 #7(March, 1990): 47-49.

Ott, Jack M. et al. "Understanding Partitive Division of Fractions." *Arithmetic Teacher* 39 #2 (October, 1991): 7–11.

Pothier, Yvonne & Sawada, Daiyo "Partitioning: An Approach to Fractions." *Arithmetic Teacher* 38 #4(December, 1990): 23-32.

Rees, Jocelyn "Two-sided Pies: Help for Improper Fractions and Mixed Numbers." *Arithmetic Teacher* 35 #4(December, 1987): 28-32.

Ryoti, Don "Computer Corner." *Arithmetic Teacher* 34 #7(March, 1989): 50-52.

Schultz, James "Area Models—Spanning the Mathematics of Grades 3—9." *Arithmetic Teacher* 39 #2(October, 1991): 42-46.

Sowder, Judith and Sowder, Larry, Ed. "Using Money to Teach About the Decimal System." *Arithmetic Teacher* 36 #4(December, 1988): 42-43.

Steiner, Evelyn "Division of Fractions: Developing Conceptual Sense with Dollars and Cents." *Arithmetic Teacher* 35 #9(May, 1987): 36-42.

Usnick, Virginia & Lamphere, Patricia "Teaching Mathematics with Technology." *Arithmetic Teacher* 38 #4(December, 1990): 40-43.

Geometry, Congruence, Symmetry and Similarities (Chapters 8 and 9)

Battista, Michael T. and Clemets, Douglas H. "Research into Practice: Using Spatial Imagery in Geometric Reasoning." *Arithmetic Teacher* 39 #3 (November, 1991): 18–21.

Bright, George & Harvey, John "Learning and Fun with Geometry Games." *Arithmetic Teacher* 35 #8(April, 1988): 22-26.

303

Bidwell, James K. "Using Reflections to Find Symmetric and Asymmetric Patterns." *Arithmetic Teacher* 34 #7(March, 1987): 10-15.

Clauss, Judith "Pentagonal Tessellations." *Arithmetic Teacher* 38 #5(January, 1991): 52-56.

Del-Grande, John "Spatial Sense." *Arithmetic Teacher* 37 #6(February, 1990): 14-20.

Dunkels, Andrejs "Making and Exploring Tangrams." *Arithmetic Teacher* 37 #96 (February, 1990): 38-42.

Heukerott, Pamela "Origami: Paper Folding—The Algorithmic Way." *Arithmetic Teacher* 35 #5(January, 1988): 4-8.

Jamski, William "Six Hard Pieces." *Arithmetic Teacher* 37 #2(October, 1989): 34-35.

Kaiser, Barbara "Explorations with Tessellating Polygons." *Arithmetic Teacher* 36 #4(December, 1988): 19–24.

Larke, Patricia "Geometric Extravaganza: Spicing Up Geometry." *Arithmetic Teacher* 36 #1(September, 1988): 36-38.

Morrow, Lorna J. "Implementing the Standards: Geometry through the Standards." *Arithmetic Teacher* 38 #8 (April, 1991): 21–25.

Moses, Barbara "Developing Spatial thinking in the Middle Grades: Designing a Space Station." *Arithmetic Teacher* 37 #6(February, 1990): 59-63.

Newman, Claire & Turkel, Susan "Integrating Arithmetic and Geometry with Numbered Points on a Circle." *Arithmetic Teacher* 36 #5(January, 1989): 28-30.

Onslow, Barry "Pentominoes Revisited." *Arithmetic Teacher* 37 #9 (May, 1990): 5–9.

Owens, Douglas "Research into Practice: Spatial Abilities." *Arithmetic Teacher* 37 #6(February, 1990): 48–51.

Prentice, Gerard "Flexible Straws." *Arithmetic Teacher* 37 #3(November, 1989): 4-5.

Rowan, Richard "Implementing the Standards: Spatial Sense: The Geometry Standards in K–8 Mathematics." *Arithmetic Teacher* 37 #6(February, 1990): 24-26.

Rubenstein, Rheta, et al. "Angle Sense: A Valuable Connector" *Arithmetic Teacher* 40 #6 (February, 1993): 352–357.

Schultz, James E. "Area Models - Spanning the Mathematics of Grades 3-9." *Arithmetic Teacher* 39 #2 (October, 1991): 42-46.

Sgroi, Richard "Communicating about Spatial Relationships." *Arithmetic Teacher* 37 #6(February, 1990): 21-23.

Souza, Ronald "Golfing with a Protractor." *Arithmetic Teacher* 35 #8(April, 1988): 52-56.

Thiessen, Diane and Matthias, Margaret "Selected Books for Geometry." *Arithmetic Teacher* 37 #4 (December, 1989): 47–51.

Wheatley, Grayson "Research into Practice: Spatial Sense and the Construction of Abstract Units in Tiling." *Arithmetic Teacher* 39 #8(April, 1992): 42-45.

Willicutt, Bob "Triangular Tiles for Your Patio?" *Arithmetic Teacher* 34 #9(May, 1987): 34-35.

Wills, Herbert "Magic with Magic Squares." *Arithmetic Teacher* 36 #8(April, 1989): 44-49.

Wilson, Patricia & Adams, Verna "A Dynamic Way to Teach Angle and Angle Measurement." *Arithmetic Teacher* 39 #5(January, 1992): 6-13.

Woodward, Ernest et al. "A Fifth-Grade Similarity Unit." *Arithmetic Teacher* 39 #8(April, 1992): 22-25.

Yackel, Erna & Wheatley, Grayson "Promoting Visual Imagery in Young Pupils." *Arithmetic Teacher* 37 #6(February, 1990): 52-58.

Zaslavsky, Claudia "Symmetry in American Folk Art." *Arithmetic Teacher* 38 #1(September, 1990): 6-12.

Zollman, Alan "Low Tech, 196, and the Geometry of the Calculator Keys." *Arithmetic Teacher* 37 #5(January, 1990): 30-33.

Measurement Algebra and Coordinate Geometry (Chapters 10 and 11)

Andrade, Gloria S. "Teaching Students to Tell Time." *Arithmetic Teacher* 37 #2(October, 1989): 22–26.

Berman, Barbara, and Friederwitzer, Fredda "Algebra Can Be Elementary ...When It's Concrete." *Arithmetic Teacher* 36 #8 (April, 1989): 21-24.

Kieran, Carolyn "Research into Practice: Helping to Make the Transition to Algebra." *Arithmetic Teacher* 38 #7 (March, 1991): 46–48.

Linquist, Mary-Montgomery "Implementing the Standards: the Measurement Standards." *Arithmetic Teacher* 34 #9(May, 1987): 34-35.

Fay, Nancy and Tsairides, Catherine "Metric Mall." *Arithmetic Teacher* 37 #1(September, 1989): 6–11.

Harrison, William. "What Lies Behind Measurement." *Arithmetic Teacher* 35 #9(Mar 1987): 19–21.

Neufeld, Allen "Body Measurement." *Arithmetic Teacher* 35 #9(May, 1989): 12-15.

Kastner, Bernice "Number Sense: The Role of Measurement Applications." *Arithmetic Teacher* 36 #5(February, 1989): 40-45.

Kouba, Vicky et al. "Results of the Fourth NAEP Assessment of Mathematics: Measurement, Geometry, Data Interpretation, Attitudes, and Other Topics." *Arithmetic Teacher* 35 #9(May, 1988): 10-16.

Nibbelink, William H. "Teaching Equations." *Arithmetic Teacher* 38 #3 (November, 1990): 48-50.

Computers (Chapter 12)

Abel, Jean et al. "Popsicle Sticks, computers, and Calculators: Important Considerations." *Arithmetic Teacher* 34 #9(May, 1987): 8–12.

Bainswanger, Richard. "Discovering Division with Logo." *Arithmetic Teacher* 36 #4(December, 1988): 44-49.

Baker, Delores et al. "Teaching Mathematics with Technology." *Arithmetic Teacher* 38 #1(September, 1990): 44-45.

Battista, Michael & Clements, Douglas "A Case for a Logo-based Elementary School Geometry Curriculum." *Arithmetic Teacher* 36 #3(November, 1988): 11-17.

Bitter, Gart & Edwards, Nancy "Teaching Mathematics with Technology: Finding Number Patterns." *Arithmetic Teacher* 37 #4(December, 1989): 52-54.

Bradley, Claudette "Teaching Mathematics With Technology: Making a Navajo Blanket Design with Logo." *Arithmetic Teacher* 40 #9 (May, 1993): 520–523.

Bright, George "Teaching Mathematics with Technology: Numerical Relationships." *Arithmetic Teacher* 36 #6(February, 1989): 56-58.

Brown, Sue "Integrating Manipulatives and Computers in Problem-Solving Experiences." *Arithmetic Teacher* 38 #2(October, 1990): 8-10.

Browning, Christine A. and Channell, Dwayne E. "A "Handy" Database Activity for the Middle School Classroom." *Arithmetic Teacher* 40 #4 (December, 1992): 235–238.

Evered, Lisa "How Does a Computer Subtract." *Arithmetic Teacher* 37 #4(December, 1989): 55-57.

Forish-Ferguson, Laura "Two Technological Fables." *Arithmetic Teacher* 37 #3(November, 1989): 50-51.

Greer, John & Greer, Bonnie "Public Domain Software: A Formula for Better Classroom computing." *Arithmetic Teacher* 36 #1 (September, 1988): 26–30.

Johnson, Carole & Swoop, Karen "Boys and Girls Interest in Using Computers: Important Classroom Considerations." *Arithmetic Teacher* 35 #1(September, 1987): 14-16.

Joseph, Helen "Teaching Mathematics With Technology: Build Parental Support for Mathematics with Family Computers." *Arithmetic Teacher* 40 #7 (March, 1993): 408–415.

Sgroi, Richard J. "Systematic Trial and Error Using Spreadsheets." *Arithmetic Teacher* 39 #7 (March, 1992): 8–12.

Wiebe, James "Teaching Mathematics with Technology: Teacher-Made Overhead Manipulatives." *Arithmetic Teacher* 37 #7(March, 1990): 44-46.

Williams, David "A Calculator-Integrated Curriculum: The Time is Now."
Arithmetic Teacher 34 #6(February, 1987): 8-9.

Statistics and Probability (Chapters 13 and 14)

Allinger, Glenn, Ed. et al . "Reviewing and Viewing." *Arithmetic Teacher*
36 #1(September, 1988): 50-53.

Chancellor, Dinah, Ed. "Calendar Mathematics." *Arithmetic Teacher* 39
#6(March, 1992): 16-17.

Lappan, Glenda "Research into Practice - Teaching Statistics: Mean,
Median, and Mode." *Arithmetic Teacher* 35 #7. (March, 1988): 25-26.

Parker, Janet & Widmer, Connie, Ed. "Teaching Mathematics with
Technology: Statistics and Graphing." *Arithmetic Teacher* 39
#8(April, 1992): 48-52.

Schultz, James "Area Models—Spanning the Mathematics of Grades 3–9."
Arithmetic Teacher 39 #2(October, 1991): 42-46.

Shulte, Albert "Research Report: Learning Probability Concepts in
elementary School Mathematics." *Arithmetic Teacher* 34 #5(January,
1987): 32-33.

Vissa, Jeanne "Probability and Combinations for Third Graders."
Arithmetic Teacher 36 #4(December, 1988): 33-37.

Vissa, Jeanne "Sampling Treats from a School of Fish." *Arithmetic Teacher*
34 #7(March, 1989): 36-37.

Other Articles of Interest

Callahan, Leroy G. (Ed.) "Research Report: Metacognition and School
Mathematics." *Arithmetic Teacher* 34 #9 (May, 1987): 22-23.

Chancellor, Dinah "Higher-Order Thinking: A "Basic" Skill for Everyone."
Arithmetic Teacher 38 #6 (February, 1991): 48–50.

Comstock, Margaret, and Demana, Franklin "The Calculator is a Problem-
solving Concept Developer." *Arithmetic Teacher* 34 #6 (February,
1987): 48-51.

Demana, Franklin & Osborne, Alan "Choosing a Calculator: Four-
Function Foul-ups." *Arithmetic Teacher* 35 #7(February, 1988): 2–3.

Friel, Susan L. "Implementing the Professional Standards for Teaching
Mathematics: Teachers Building on Student's Thinking." *Arithmetic
Teacher* 39 #7 (March, 1992): 32–37.

Garofalo, Joe & Mtetwa, David K. "Implementing the Standards:
Mathematics as Reasoning." *Arithmetic Teacher* 37 #5 (January,
1990): 16–18.

Hiatt, Arthur A. "Activities for Calculators." *Arithmetic Teacher* 38 #6
(February, 1987): 38-43.

Jacobs, Heida Hayes "One Point of View: Mathematics Integration: A Common-Sense Approach to curriculum development" *Arithmetic Teacher* 40 #6 (February, 1993): 301.

Kliman, Marlene "Integrating Mathematics and Literature in the Elementary Classroom." *Arithmetic Teacher* 40 #6 (February, 1993): 318–322.

Midkiff, Ruby Bostick. "Stepping Stones to Mathematical Understanding." *Arithmetic Teacher* 40 #6 (February, 1993): 303–305.

Orman, Sheryl A. "Mathematics Backpacks: Making the Home-School Connection" *Arithmetic Teacher* 40 #6 (February, 1993): 306–310.

Reys, Barbara, J. & Reys, Robert E. "Implementing the Standards: Estimation—Direction from the Standards." *Arithmetic Teacher* 37 #7 (March, 1990): 22–25.

Reys, Robert E. and Reys, Barbara J. (Ed.) "Estimation and Mental Computation." *Arithmetic Teacher* 34 #9 (May, 1987): 24-25.

Slovin, Hannah "Number of the Day." *Arithmetic Teacher* 39 #7 (March, 1992): 29–31.

Sowder, Judith & Sowder, Larry "Research into Practice: integrating Assessment and Instruction." *Arithmetic Teacher* 36 #3 (November, 1988): 43–55.

Spiker, Joan, and Kurtz, Ray "Teaching Primary-Grade Mathematics Skills with Calculators." *Arithmetic Teacher* 34 #6 (February, 1987): 24-27.

Suydam, Marilyn N. "Research Reports: What Are Calculators Good For?" *Arithmetic Teacher* 34 #6 (February, 1987): 22.

Vonder-Embse, Charles B. et al. "The AAN Calculator: A Tool for Enhancing Instruction." *Arithmetic Teacher* 35 #7 (March, 1988): 12-17.

Wiebe, James H. "Calculators and the Mathematics Curriculum." *Arithmetic Teacher* 34 #6 (February, 1987): 57-60.

Wilde, Sandra "Learning to Write about Mathematics." *Arithmetic Teacher* 38 #6 (February, 1991): 38–43.

Yvon, Bernard R. "A Compelling Case for Calculators." *Arithmetic Teacher* 34 #6 (February, 1987): 16-19.

Other Publications of Interest

Mathematical Sciences Education Board (1990). *Counting on You: Actions supporting mathematics teaching standards.* Washington: National Academy Press.

National Commission on Excellence in Education (1983). *A Nation at risk: The imperative for educational reform.* Washington: U.S. Government Printing Office.

National Council of Teachers of Mathematics (1989). *Curriculum and evaluation standards for school mathematics.* Reston (VA): NCTM.

National Council of Teachers of Mathematics (1991). *Professional standards for teaching mathematics.* Reston (VA): NCTM.

National Council of Teachers of Mathematics (1993). *Assessment in the mathematics classroom* Reston (VA): NCTM.

National Research Council (1989). *Everybody counts: A report to the nation on the future of mathematics education.* Washington: National Academy Press.

Stenmark, J.K. (1989). *Assessment alternatives in mathematics: An overview of assessment techniques that promote learning.* Berkeley: University of California.

Stenmark, J.K. (1991). *Mathematics assessment: Myths, models, good questions, and practical suggestions.* Reston (VA): NCTM.

Appendix E
Activity Cards

* An asterisk denotes a color card that is out of numerical sequence and placed at the end of this appendix

Chapter 1   Problem Solving

Chapter 2   Sets

Chapter 3   Whole Numbers

Mayberry and Bath, Student Resource Manual to accompany Mathematics for Elementary Teachers: An Interactive Approach by Sonnabend.

310

Mayberry and Bath, Student Resource Manual to accompany Mathematics for Elementary
Teachers: An Interactive Approach by Sonnabend.

NO NEW CARDS

Activity Card 1.1 *License Plate*

Upside down tag

Original tag

6	3 ,	7	8	3

Difference

Mayberry and Bath, Student Resource Manual to accompany Mathematics for Elementary Teachers: An Interactive Approach by Sonnabend.

Activity Card 1.2 *Toothpick Puzzle*

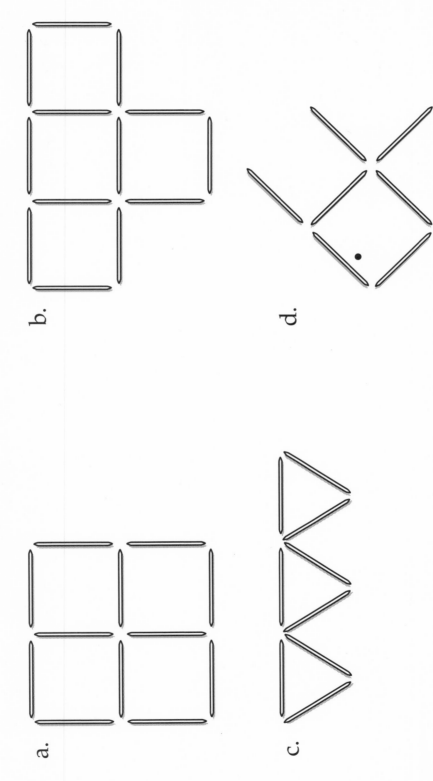

a.

b.

c.

d.

Mayberry and Bath, Student Resource Manual to accompany Mathematics for Elementary Teachers: An Interactive Approach by Sonnabend.

Activity Card 1.5 *Magic Box*

Place the numbers 1–8 so that no consecutive numbers touch at any side or corner.

Mayberry and Bath, Student Resource Manual to accompany Mathematics for Elementary
Teachers: An Interactive Approach by Sonnabend.

Activity Card 1.6 *Guess and Check Strategy*

	Trial #1	Trial #2	Trial #3	Trial #4	Trial #5
Cathy					
Jennifer					
Total	24	24	24	24	24
Comments	Cathy has 8 more than Jennifer.

Mayberry and Bath, Student Resource Manual to accompany Mathematics for Elementary
Teachers: An Interactive Approach by Sonnabend.

Activity Card 1.7 *Homework*

Note: +.08 for each correct answer
       −.05 for each incorrect answer
       26 problems completed (no money due either one)

How many problems correct? _____

	Trial #1		Trial #2		Trial #3		Trial #4	
# Problems correct								
Cost								
# Problems incorrect								
Cost								
Total correct / Total cost								

Hint: Total cost should be zero.

Mayberry and Bath, Student Resource Manual to accompany Mathematics for Elementary
Teachers: An Interactive Approach by Sonnabend.

Activity Card 1.8 *Court Jester's Coins*

5¢	5¢	5¢		1¢	1¢	1¢

# coins	# moves
2	
3	
4	
5	
6	

Mayberry and Bath, Student Resource Manual to accompany Mathematics for Elementary
Teachers: An Interactive Approach by Sonnabend.

Activity Card 1.9 *Blue Eyes*

Blue eyes	2						
Other colors	3						
Total	5	10					35
Comments:							

Mayberry and Bath, Student Resource Manual to accompany Mathematics for Elementary
Teachers: An Interactive Approach by Sonnabend.

Activity Card 1.10a *Elevator Problem*

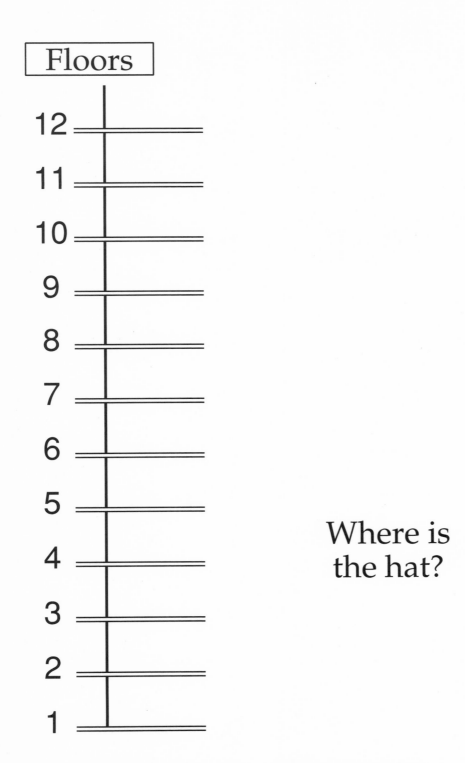

Floors
12
11
10
9
8
7
6
5
4
3
2
1

Where is the hat?

Mayberry and Bath, Student Resource Manual to accompany Mathematics for Elementary Teachers: An Interactive Approach by Sonnabend.

Activity Card 1.10b *Fish Problem*

Head   Body   Tail

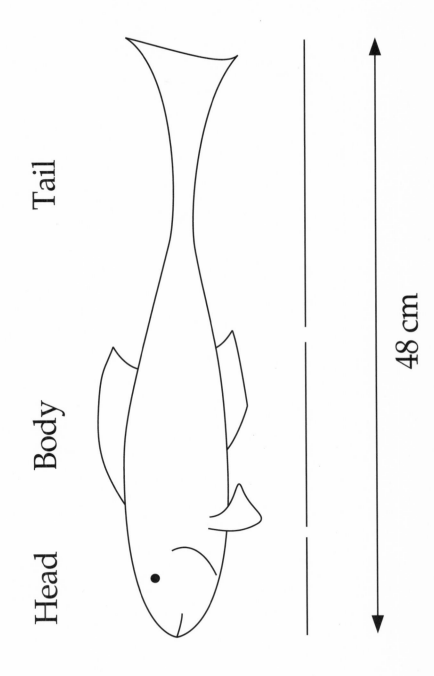

48 cm

Mayberry and Bath, Student Resource Manual to accompany Mathematics for Elementary
Teachers: An Interactive Approach by Sonnabend.

Activity Card 1.11a *Handshake*

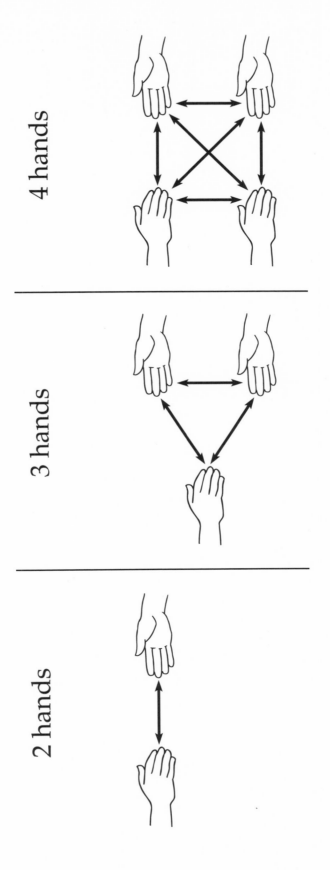

2 hands

3 hands

4 hands

Continue pattern

Mayberry and Bath, Student Resource Manual to accompany Mathematics for Elementary
Teachers: An Interactive Approach by Sonnabend.

Activity Card 1.11b *The Birthday Party*

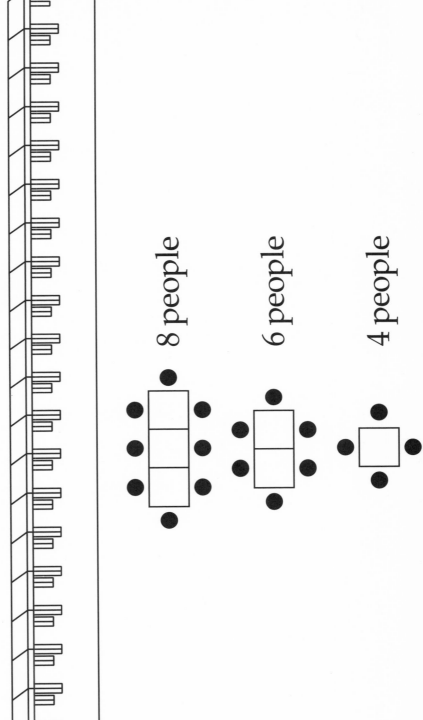

8 people

6 people

4 people

Mayberry and Bath, Student Resource Manual to accompany Mathematics for Elementary Teachers: An Interactive Approach by Sonnabend.

Activity Card 1.13 *Game Board*

Mustard-Ketchup-Relish Recording Sheet

Mustard = 1 digit correct, but in wrong place

Ketchup = 1 digit correct, and in right place

Relish = no digit correct

Number Chosen				Response		
				Mustard	Ketchup	Relish
1.						
2.						
3.						
4.						
5.						
6.						
7.						
8.						

Number Chosen				Response		
				Mustard	Ketchup	Relish
1.						
2.						
3.						
4.						
5.						
6.						
7.						
8.						

Number Chosen				Response		
				Mustard	Ketchup	Relish
1.						
2.						
3.						
4.						
5.						
6.						
7.						
8.						

Number Chosen				Response		
				Mustard	Ketchup	Relish
1.						
2.						
3.						
4.						
5.						
6.						
7.						
8.						

Mayberry and Bath, Student Resource Manual to accompany Mathematics for Elementary Teachers: An Interactive Approach by Sonnabend.

Activity Card 1.14 *Logic Puzzle*

Name Music	Angelica	Bob	Carlos	Damaris
Country				
Rock 'n Roll				
Jazz				
Classical				

Mayberry and Bath, Student Resource Manual to accompany Mathematics for Elementary
Teachers: An Interactive Approach by Sonnabend.

Activity Card 1.15 *Dogsitting Dilemma*

Hour #	Amount Earned
1	1¢
2	2¢
3	4¢
4	8¢
5	
6	
7	
8	
9	
10	
11	
12	
TOTAL	

or $36.00?

Which is the better deal?

Mayberry and Bath, Student Resource Manual to accompany Mathematics for Elementary
Teachers: An Interactive Approach by Sonnabend.

Activity Card 2.2 *Two-circle Venn Diagram*

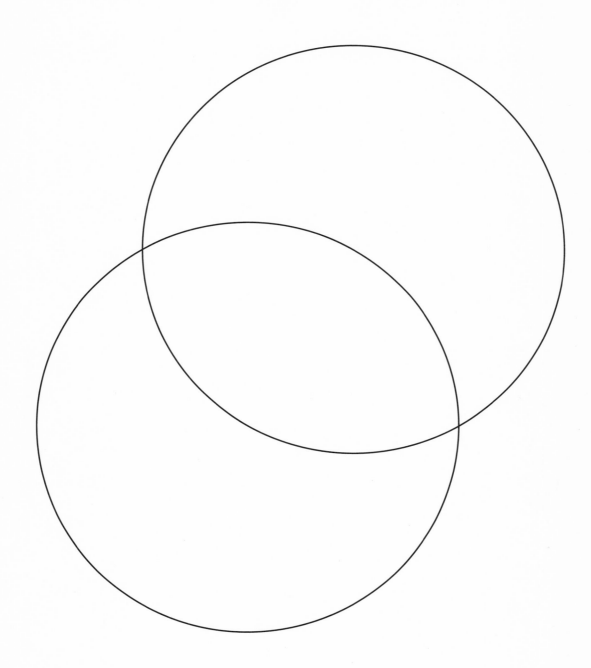

Mayberry and Bath, Student Resource Manual to accompany Mathematics for Elementary
Teachers: An Interactive Approach by Sonnabend.

Activity Card 2.4 *Three-circle Venn Diagram*

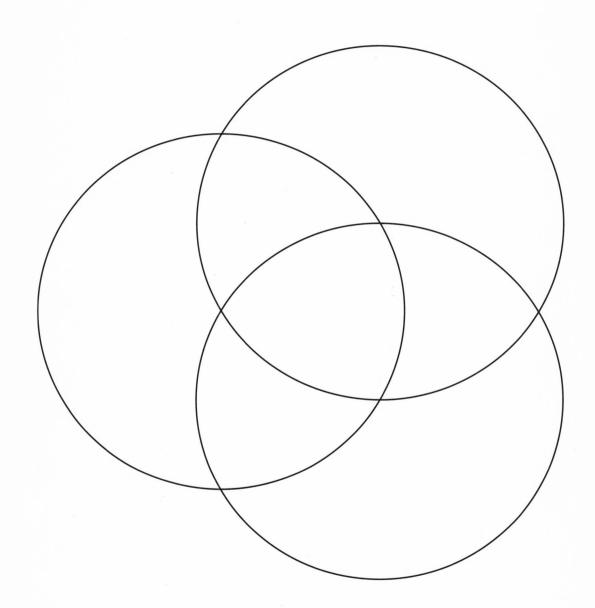

Mayberry and Bath, Student Resource Manual to accompany Mathematics for Elementary
Teachers: An Interactive Approach by Sonnabend.

Activity Card 3.2a *Place Value Mat*

thousands	hundreds	tens	ones

Mayberry and Bath, Student Resource Manual to accompany Mathematics for Elementary
Teachers: An Interactive Approach by Sonnabend.

Activity Card 3.2b *Base Five Coins*

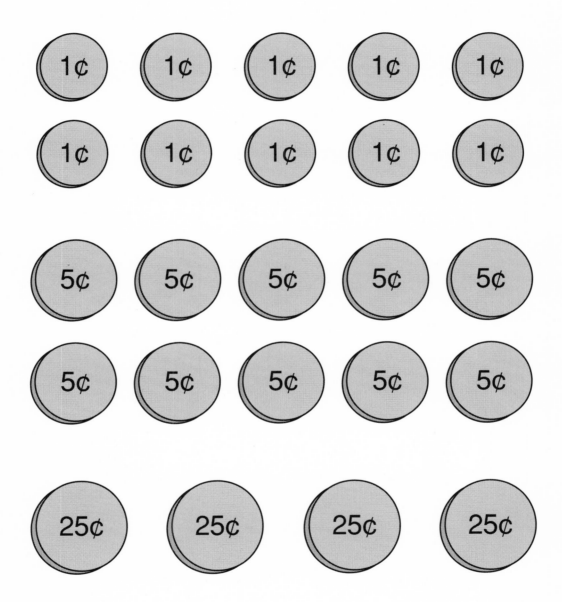

Mayberry and Bath, Student Resource Manual to accompany Mathematics for Elementary
Teachers: An Interactive Approach by Sonnabend.

Activity Card 4.4 *Multiplication Tables*

2

$2 \times 0 = 0$
$2 \times 1 = 2$
$2 \times 2 = 4$
$2 \times 3 = 6$
$2 \times 4 = 8$
$2 \times 5 = 10$
$2 \times 6 = 12$
$2 \times 7 = 14$
$2 \times 8 = 16$
$2 \times 9 = 18$

3

$3 \times 0 = 0$
$3 \times 1 = 3$
$3 \times 2 = 6$
$3 \times 3 = 9$
$3 \times 4 = 12$
$3 \times 5 = 15$
$3 \times 6 = 18$
$3 \times 7 = 21$
$3 \times 8 = 24$
$3 \times 9 = 27$

5

$5 \times 0 = 0$
$5 \times 1 = 5$
$5 \times 2 = 10$
$5 \times 3 = 15$
$5 \times 4 = 20$
$5 \times 5 = 25$
$5 \times 6 = 30$
$5 \times 7 = 35$
$5 \times 8 = 40$
$5 \times 9 = 45$

6

$6 \times 0 = 0$
$6 \times 1 = 6$
$6 \times 2 = 12$
$6 \times 3 = 18$
$6 \times 4 = 24$
$6 \times 5 = 30$
$6 \times 6 = 36$
$6 \times 7 = 42$
$6 \times 8 = 48$
$6 \times 9 = 54$

7

$7 \times 0 = 0$
$7 \times 1 = 7$
$7 \times 2 = 14$
$7 \times 3 = 21$
$7 \times 4 = 28$
$7 \times 5 = 35$
$7 \times 6 = 42$
$7 \times 7 = 49$
$7 \times 8 = 56$
$7 \times 9 = 63$

9

$9 \times 0 = 0$
$9 \times 1 = 9$
$9 \times 2 = 18$
$9 \times 3 = 27$
$9 \times 4 = 36$
$9 \times 5 = 45$
$9 \times 6 = 54$
$9 \times 7 = 63$
$9 \times 8 = 72$
$9 \times 9 = 84$

10

$10 \times 0 = 0$
$10 \times 1 = 10$
$10 \times 2 = 20$
$10 \times 3 = 30$
$10 \times 4 = 40$
$10 \times 5 = 50$
$10 \times 6 = 60$
$10 \times 7 = 70$
$10 \times 8 = 80$
$10 \times 9 = 90$

11

$11 \times 0 = 0$
$11 \times 1 = 11$
$11 \times 2 = 22$
$11 \times 3 = 33$
$11 \times 4 = 44$
$11 \times 5 = 55$
$11 \times 6 = 66$
$11 \times 7 = 77$
$11 \times 8 = 88$
$11 \times 9 = 99$

Mayberry and Bath, Student Resource Manual to accompany Mathematics for Elementary Teachers: An Interactive Approach by Sonnabend.

Activity Card 4.10 *Hundreds Chart*

1	2	3	4	5	6	7	8	9	10
11	12	13	14	15	16	17	18	19	20
21	22	23	24	25	26	27	28	29	30
31	32	33	34	35	36	37	38	39	40
41	42	43	44	45	46	47	48	49	50
51	52	53	54	55	56	57	58	59	60
61	62	63	64	65	66	67	68	69	70
71	72	73	74	75	76	77	78	79	80
81	82	83	84	85	86	87	88	89	90
91	92	93	94	95	96	97	98	99	100

Mayberry and Bath, Student Resource Manual to accompany Mathematics for Elementary Teachers: An Interactive Approach by Sonnabend.

Activity Card 4.13 *Protractor and Metric Ruler*

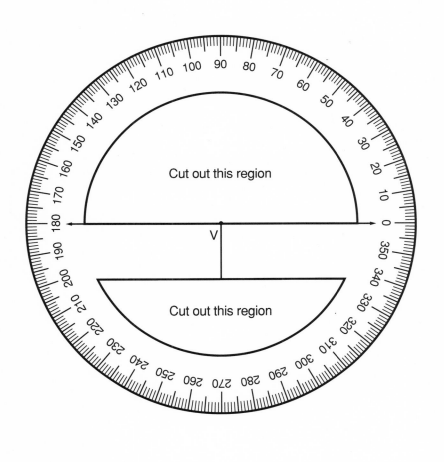

Mayberry and Bath, Student Resource Manual to accompany Mathematics for Elementary
Teachers: An Interactive Approach by Sonnabend.

Activity Card 5.4
Thermometer and Vertical Number Line

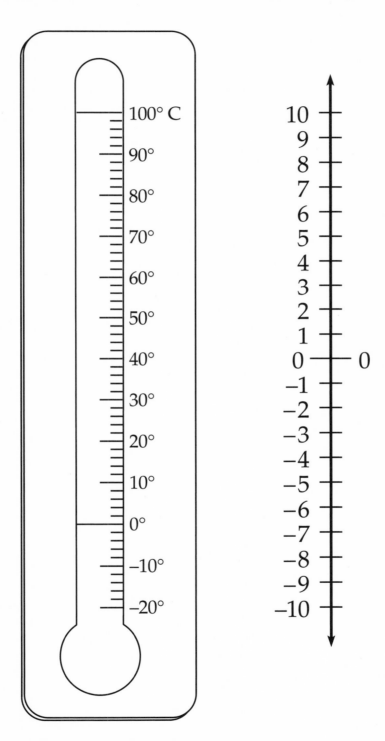

Activity Card 8.3 *Geoboard Recording Sheet*

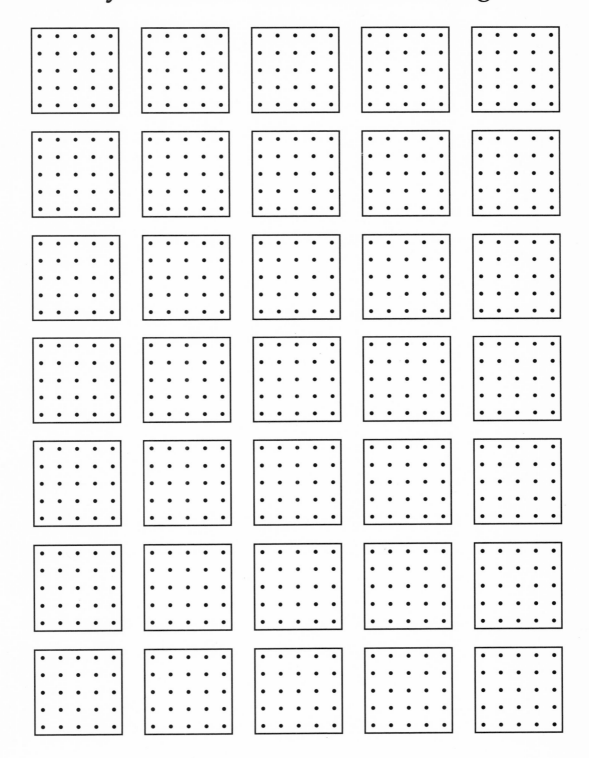

Mayberry and Bath, Student Resource Manual to accompany Mathematics for Elementary
Teachers: An Interactive Approach by Sonnabend.

Activity Card 8.4a *Tangram Pieces*

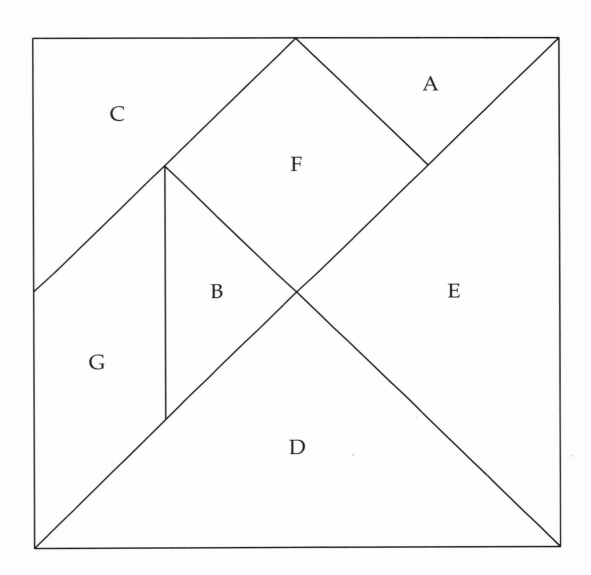

Mayberry and Bath, Student Resource Manual to accompany Mathematics for Elementary
Teachers: An Interactive Approach by Sonnabend.

Activity Card 8.4b *Tangram Shape Chart*

Number of pieces used \ Shape Made	Square	Triangle	Rectangle	Trapezoid	Parallelogram	Rhombus	Pentagon	Hexagon	Other
1									
2									
3									
4									
5									
6									
7									
8									

Mayberry and Bath, Student Resource Manual to accompany Mathematics for Elementary Teachers: An Interactive Approach by Sonnabend.

Activity Card 8.6a *Tessellations*

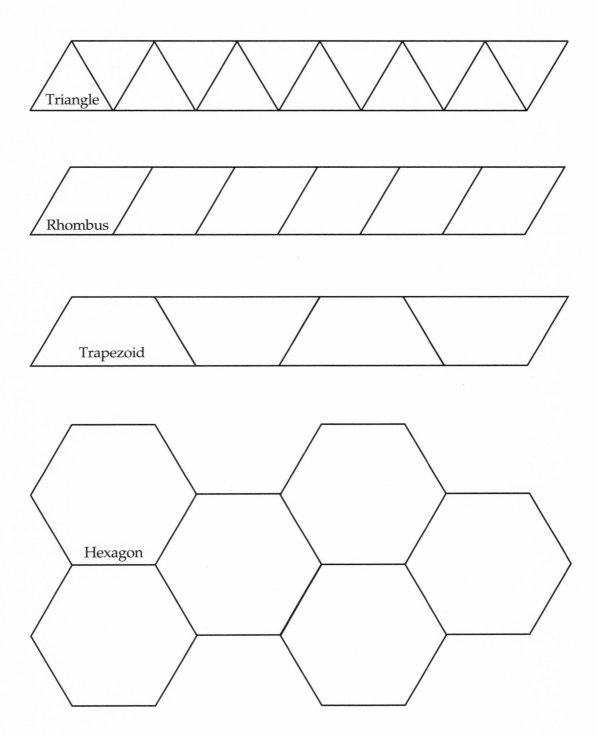

Triangle

Rhombus

Trapezoid

Hexagon

Activity Card 8.6b *Quadrilaterals*

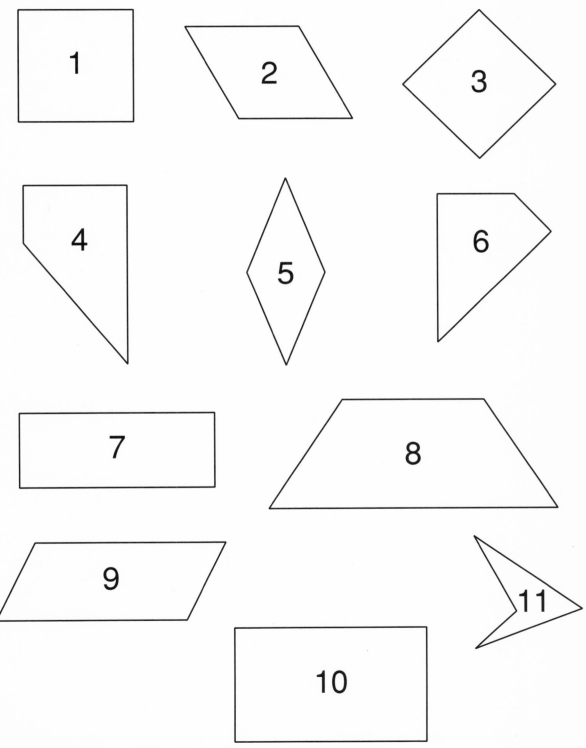

Activity Card 8.7 *Pentominoes Key*

Here are the twelve possibilities for placement of five tiles:

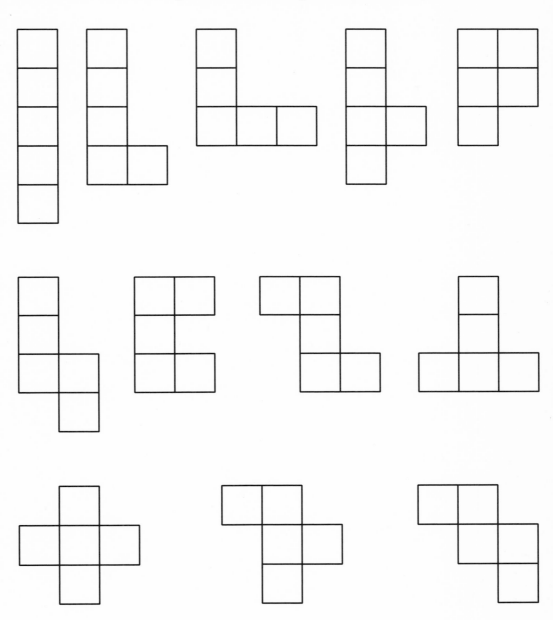

Mayberry and Bath, Student Resource Manual to accompany Mathematics for Elementary
Teachers: An Interactive Approach by Sonnabend.

Activity Card 9.3a *Mirror Cards*

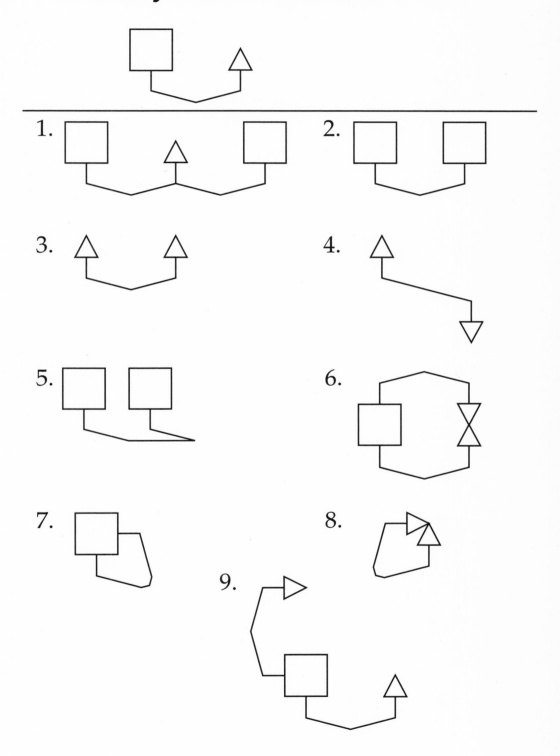

Activity Card 9.3b *Mirror Stand*

1. Cut along all marked lines.

2. Crease firmly on the fold lines
   and glue frame together using
   flaps A and B.

3. Glue the back of a mirror to the stand.

A

Glue the back of your mirror here

B

Mayberry and Bath, Student Resource Manual to accompany Mathematics for Elementary
Teachers: An Interactive Approach by Sonnabend.

Activity Card 9.5 *Game of Hex*

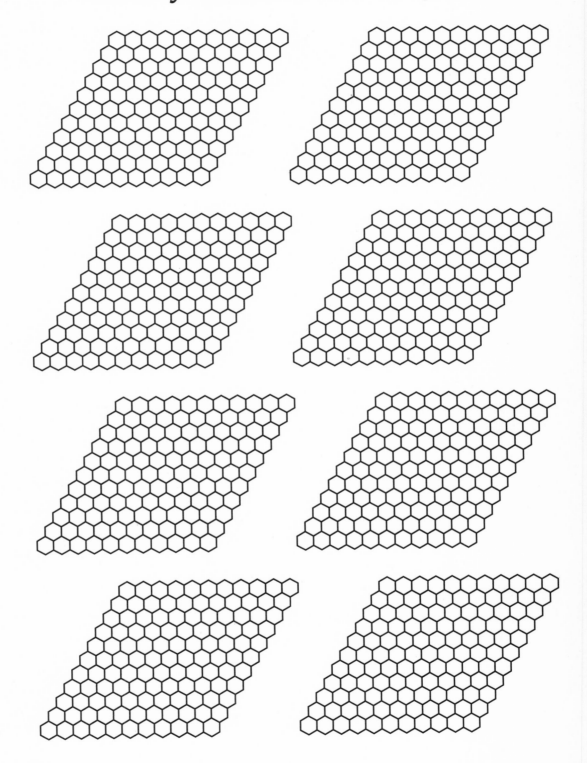

Mayberry and Bath, Student Resource Manual to accompany Mathematics for Elementary
Teachers: An Interactive Approach by Sonnabend.

Activity Card 11.2 *One-Centimeter Graph Paper*

Mayberry and Bath, Student Resource Manual to accompany Mathematics for Elementary
Teachers: An Interactive Approach by Sonnabend.

Activity Card 12 *The Tower Puzzle*

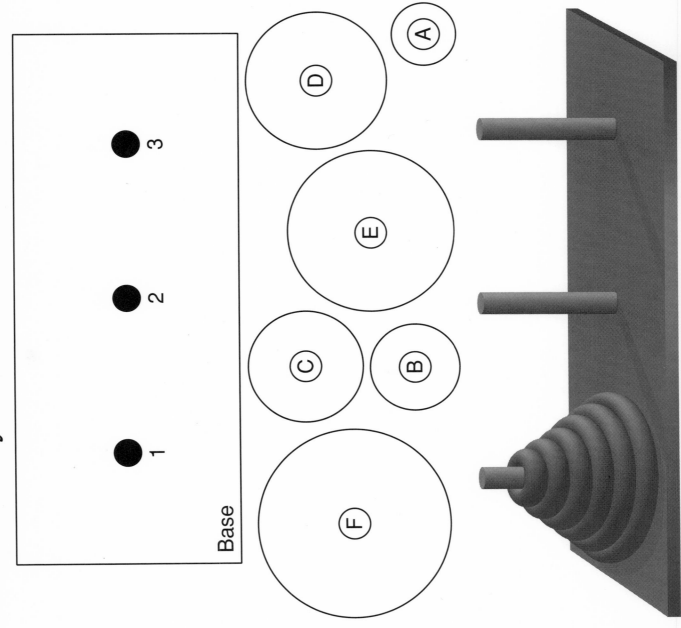

Base

3

2

1

A

D

E

C

B

F

Mayberry and Bath, Student Resource Manual to accompany Mathematics for Elementary Teachers: An Interactive Approach by Sonnabend.

Activity Card 13.6 *Circle Graph Paper*

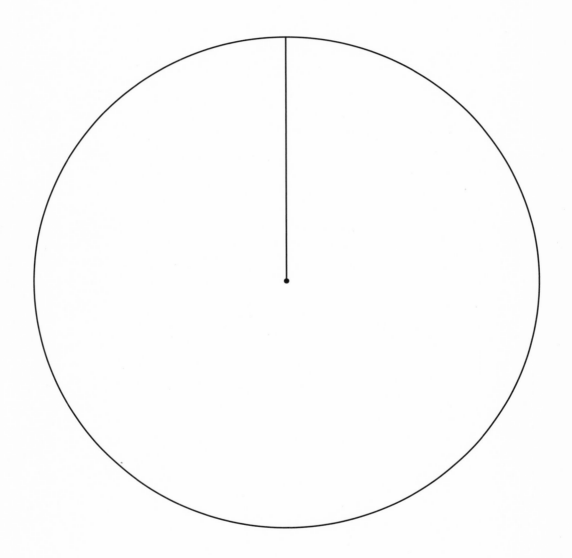

Activity Card 13.10 *Standard Curve*

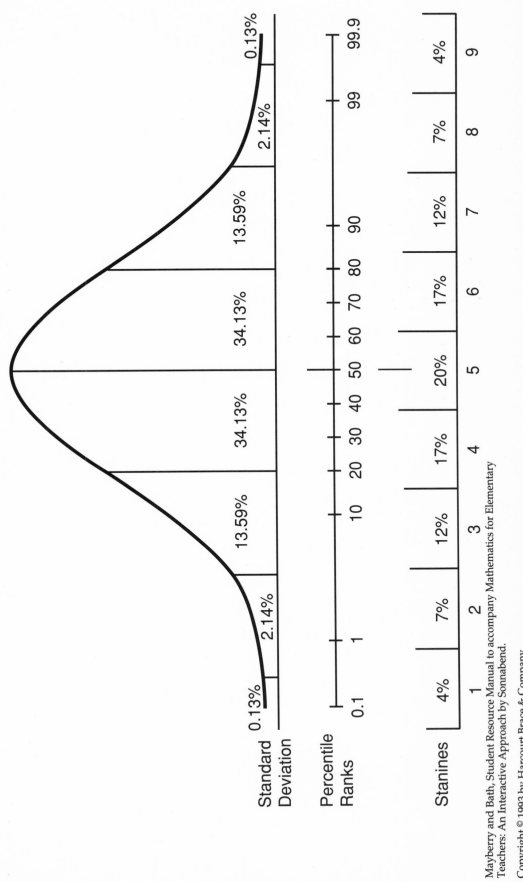

Mayberry and Bath, Student Resource Manual to accompany Mathematics for Elementary
Teachers: An Interactive Approach by Sonnabend.

Activity Card 13.11 *Box and Whisker Plot*

Mayberry and Bath, Student Resource Manual to accompany Mathematics for Elementary
Teachers: An Interactive Approach by Sonnabend.

Activity Card 1.3 *Dart Board*

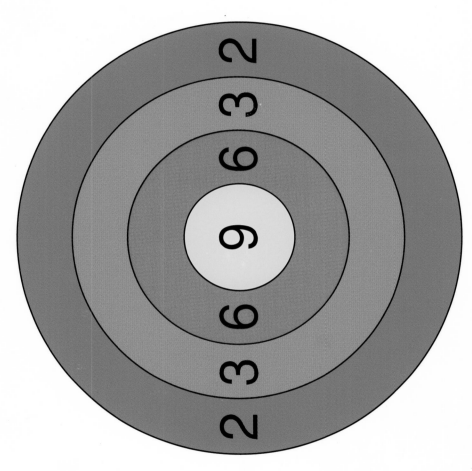

Mayberry and Bath, Student Resource Manual to accompany Mathematics for Elementary Teachers: An Interactive Approach by Sonnabend.

Activity Card 1.4 *Hidden Cube*

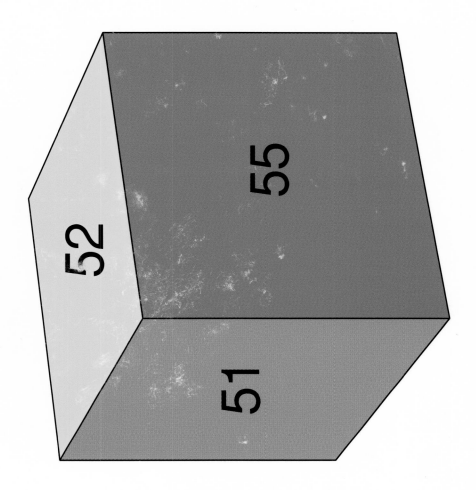

Mayberry and Bath, Student Resource Manual to accompany Mathematics for Elementary
Teachers: An Interactive Approach by Sonnabend.

Activity Card 1.12 *Base Ten Pieces*

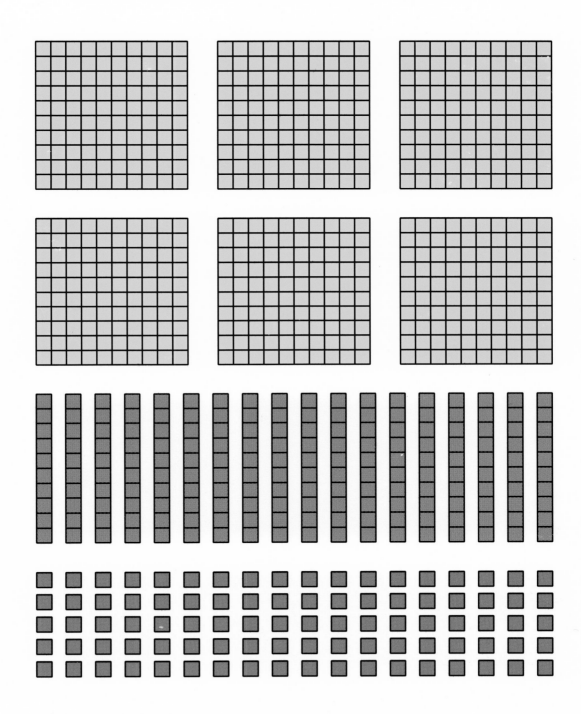

Activity Card 1.16 *Counters*

Remove these chips. Save for use later in the chapter.

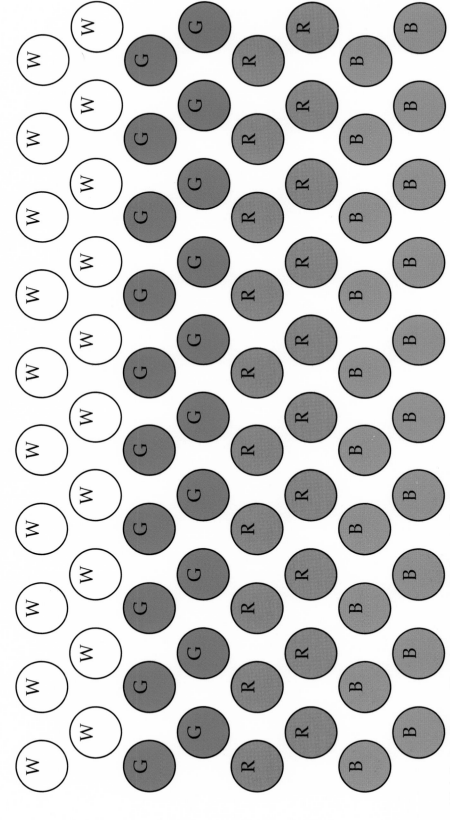

Mayberry and Bath, Student Resource Manual to accompany Mathematics for Elementary
Teachers: An Interactive Approach by Sonnabend.

Activity Card 2.1 *Attribute Pieces*

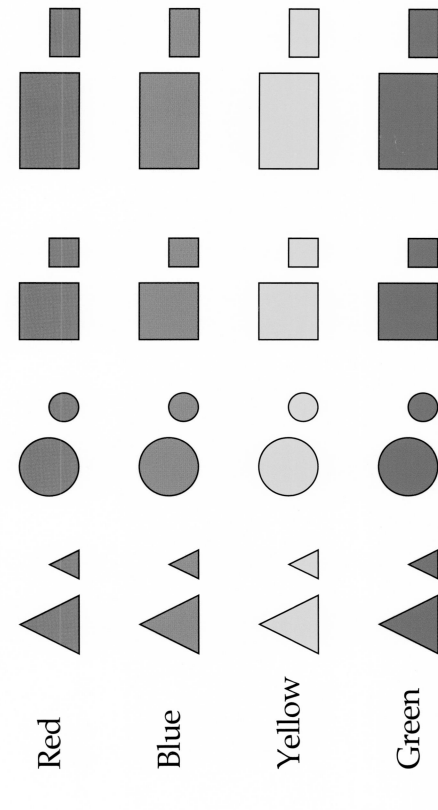

Red

Blue

Yellow

Green

Mayberry and Bath, Student Resource Manual to accompany Mathematics for Elementary
Teachers: An Interactive Approach by Sonnabend.

Activity Card 3.4 *Centimeter Strips*

cm strips

| 1 | 1 | 1 | 1 | 1 | 1 | 1 | 1 |

| 1 | 1 | 1 | 1 | 1 | 1 | 1 |

| 1 | 1 | 1 | 1 | 1 | 1 | 1 |

| 2 cm | 2 cm | 2 cm | 2 cm | 2 cm | 2 cm |

| 2 cm | 2 cm | 2 cm | 2 cm | 2 cm | 2 cm |

| 3 cm | 3 cm | 3 cm | 3 cm |

| 3 cm | 3 cm | 3 cm | 3 cm |

| 3 cm | 3 cm |

| 4 cm | 4 cm | 4 cm |

| 4 cm | 4 cm | 4 cm |

| 5 cm | 5 cm |

| 5 cm | 5 cm |

| 6 cm | 6 cm |

| 6 cm | 6 cm |

| 7 cm |

| 7 cm |

| 7 cm |

| 7 cm |

| 8 cm |

| 8 cm |

| 8 cm |

| 8 cm |

| 9 cm |

| 9 cm |

| 9 cm |

| 9 cm |

| 10 cm |

| 10 cm |

| 10 cm |

| 10 cm |

Mayberry and Bath, Student Resource Manual to accompany Mathematics for Elementary
Teachers: An Interactive Approach by Sonnabend.

Activity Card 3.9 *Color Pieces*

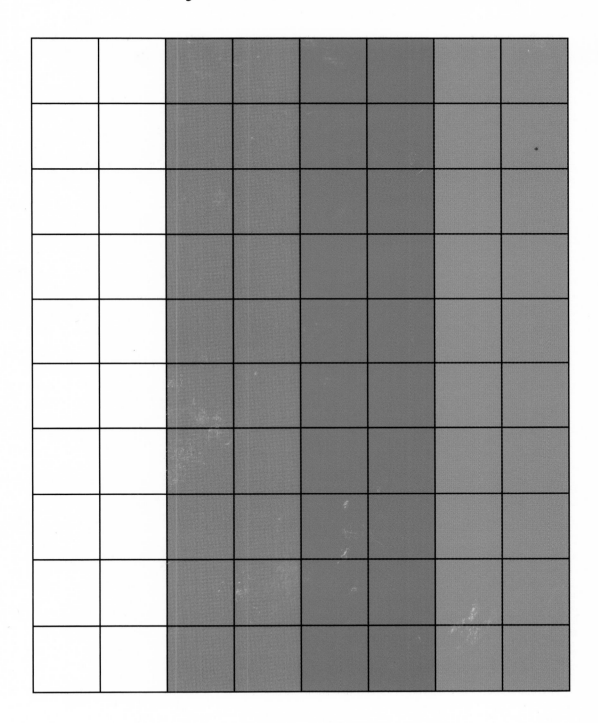

Activity Card 3.22 *Number Cubes*

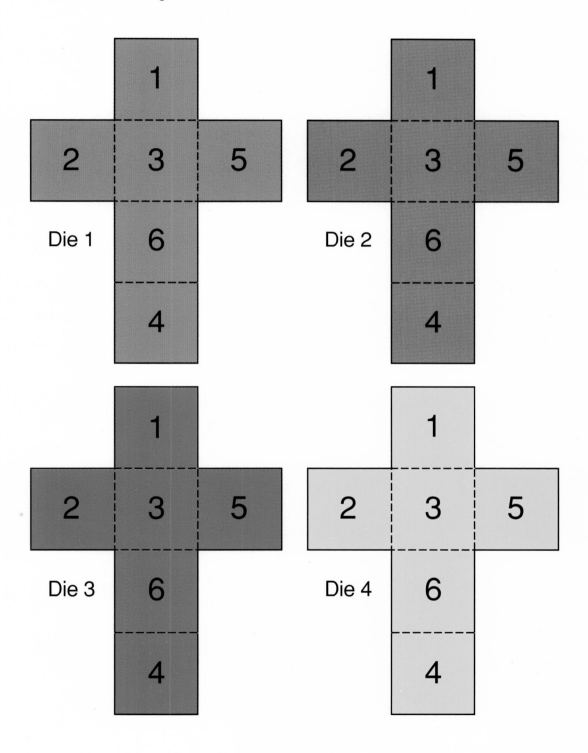

Die 1

Die 2

Die 3

Die 4

Activity Card 6.4a *Fraction Pieces*

1

$\frac{1}{2}$	$\frac{1}{2}$

$\frac{1}{3}$	$\frac{1}{3}$	$\frac{1}{3}$

$\frac{1}{4}$	$\frac{1}{4}$	$\frac{1}{4}$	$\frac{1}{4}$

$\frac{1}{6}$	$\frac{1}{6}$	$\frac{1}{6}$	$\frac{1}{6}$	$\frac{1}{6}$	$\frac{1}{6}$

$\frac{1}{8}$	$\frac{1}{8}$	$\frac{1}{8}$	$\frac{1}{8}$	$\frac{1}{8}$	$\frac{1}{8}$	$\frac{1}{8}$	$\frac{1}{8}$

$\frac{1}{12}$	$\frac{1}{12}$	$\frac{1}{12}$	$\frac{1}{12}$	$\frac{1}{12}$	$\frac{1}{12}$	$\frac{1}{12}$	$\frac{1}{12}$	$\frac{1}{12}$	$\frac{1}{12}$	$\frac{1}{12}$	$\frac{1}{12}$

$\frac{1}{16}$	$\frac{1}{16}$	$\frac{1}{16}$	$\frac{1}{16}$	$\frac{1}{16}$	$\frac{1}{16}$	$\frac{1}{16}$	$\frac{1}{16}$	$\frac{1}{16}$	$\frac{1}{16}$	$\frac{1}{16}$	$\frac{1}{16}$	$\frac{1}{16}$	$\frac{1}{16}$	$\frac{1}{16}$	$\frac{1}{16}$

$\frac{1}{24}$	$\frac{1}{24}$	$\frac{1}{24}$	$\frac{1}{24}$	$\frac{1}{24}$	$\frac{1}{24}$	$\frac{1}{24}$	$\frac{1}{24}$	$\frac{1}{24}$	$\frac{1}{24}$	$\frac{1}{24}$	$\frac{1}{24}$	$\frac{1}{24}$	$\frac{1}{24}$	$\frac{1}{24}$	$\frac{1}{24}$	$\frac{1}{24}$	$\frac{1}{24}$	$\frac{1}{24}$	$\frac{1}{24}$	$\frac{1}{24}$	$\frac{1}{24}$	$\frac{1}{24}$	$\frac{1}{24}$

Mayberry and Bath, Student Resource Manual to accompany Mathematics for Elementary
Teachers: An Interactive Approach by Sonnabend.

Activity Card 6.4b *Fraction Cubes*

Remove the pattern. Fold on
all heavy black lines. Put flap A
on top of flap B. Tuck flap C
inside the cube behind flap B.
Tuck in flap D. Tape if necessary.

A

1/2

| C | 1/16 | 1/2 | 1/4 | 1/16 | D |

1/8

B

A

1/2

| C | 1/16 | 1/3 | 1/4 | 2/3 | D |

1/8

B

Mayberry and Bath, Student Resource Manual to accompany Mathematics for Elementary
Teachers: An Interactive Approach by Sonnabend.

Activity Card 6.7 *Fraction Circles*

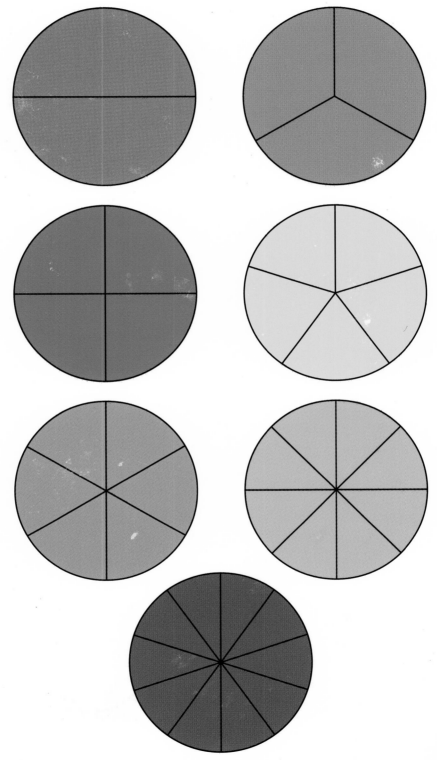

Mayberry and Bath, Student Resource Manual to accompany Mathematics for Elementary
Teachers: An Interactive Approach by Sonnabend.

Activity Card 7.1 *Decimal Pieces*

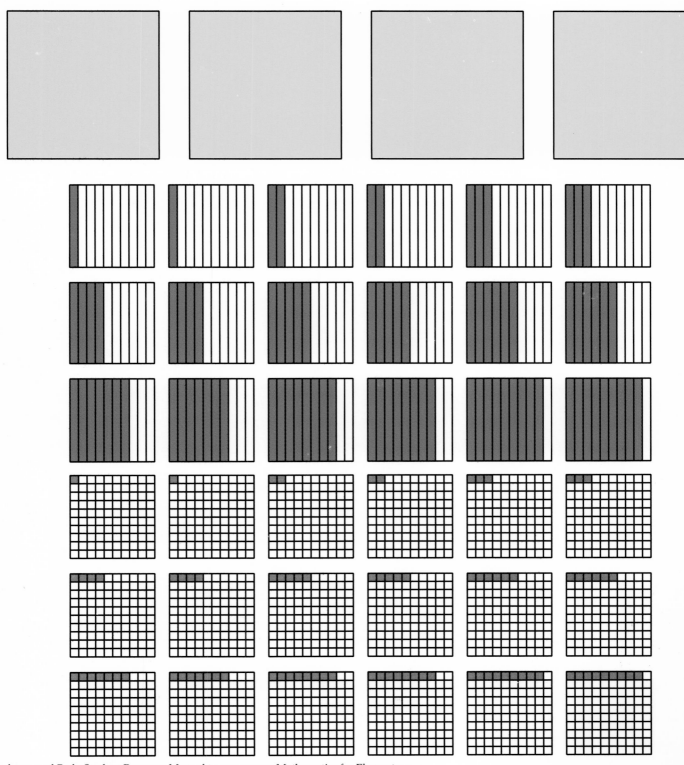

Mayberry and Bath, Student Resource Manual to accompany Mathematics for Elementary
Teachers: An Interactive Approach by Sonnabend.

Activity Card 8.1 *Pattern Pieces*

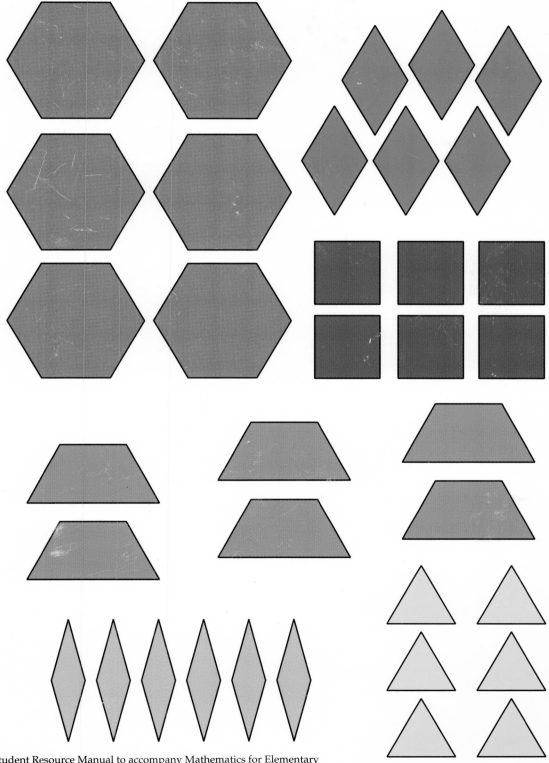